UGC NET Paper I Unlocked

Volume IV

Mathematical Reasoning And Data Interpretation

www.nerdschool.online

K.P VIJAYAKUMAR

ANKIT SHARMA

A Complete Guide for UGC NET

TO THE POINT NOTES BASED ON PREVIOUS YEARS
QUESTION PAPERS

Foreword

It is with great satisfaction and academic pride that I present to you UGC NET Paper I Unlocked Volume IV: Mathematical Reasoning and Aptitude & Data Interpretation. This book is the result of dedicated teamwork, years of classroom insight, and a shared vision to create a comprehensive, student-friendly resource that guides aspirants from the very basics to the advanced levels of Mathematical Reasoning and Data Interpretation — two crucial components of the UGC NET Paper I syllabus.

What sets this volume apart is its structured clarity. Each concept is introduced with simplicity, gradually leading to more complex applications. From number series and syllogisms to data charts and percentage-based interpretations, the explanations are thorough and learner-centric. Every topic is backed by **Previous Year Questions (PYQs)**, each provided with **step-by-step solutions** to ensure conceptual clarity and exam readiness.

The book includes a special **Concept Check Practice** at the end of every topic to encourage self-assessment and reinforce learning. The **Data Interpretation** section, often seen as a challenge by many students, has been explained in a logical, easy-to-grasp manner, helping students not just to solve questions but to develop a sharp analytical eye.

This volume is deeply enriched by the contributions of **K.P. Vijayakumar**, a retired mathematics teacher whose decades of experience and pedagogical brilliance shine through every page. His explanations are crisp, clear, and tailored for learners at all levels. It has been an honour to work alongside him in shaping this book into the valuable guide you now hold in your hands.

As the co-author, I have carefully curated, designed, and double-checked each section to ensure accuracy, consistency, and usability. We ensured a rigorous review process where every step, solution, and explanation was cross-checked for precision. Our goal was not just to prepare a book, but to build a resource that feels like a personal mentor for every UGC NET aspirant.

I hope this book serves as a dependable companion in your preparation journey. Whether you are revising core concepts or encountering them for the first time, UGC NET Paper I Unlocked Volume IV is here to make your learning journey more confident, strategic, and successful.

With best wishes,
Ankit Sharma
Educator and UGC NET Mentor
Author of 20+ Books on UGC NET Preparation

UNIT V

Mathematical Reasoning and Aptitude

- ❖ Types of reasoning.
- ❖ Number series, Letter series, Codes, and Relationships.
- ❖ Mathematical Aptitude (Fraction, Time & Distance, Ratio, Proportion and Percentage, Profit and Loss, Interest and Discounting, Averages etc.).

Table of Contents

CHAPTER 1

Number System, Arithmetic Progression (AP), Equations: Single & Multiple Variable Equations and Exponents

Introduction to Numbers

What is a Number?

A **number** is a mathematical symbol used for counting, measuring, and performing calculations. Numbers help us to represent **quantities**, compare values, and express mathematical relationships.

Numbers can be **whole or fractional**, **positive or negative**, and they follow specific properties that allow us to perform **arithmetic operations** such as addition, subtraction, multiplication, and division.

Example:

- ➢ Counting objects: **1 apple, 2 pens, 3 books**
- ➢ Measuring weight: **5 kg of rice**
- ➢ Identifying order: **Roll number 21 in class**
- ➢ Financial transactions: **₹500 in a bank account**

Importance of Numbers in Daily Life and Competitive Exams

Numbers are an **integral part of everyday life**, from simple counting to complex problem-solving in fields like **science, engineering, business, and economics**. Their importance extends to competitive exams, where strong numerical skills can significantly improve performance.

Importance in Daily Life:

- ➢ **Financial Transactions** – Managing money, calculating expenses, and understanding discounts.
- ➢ **Time Management** – Reading the clock, calculating time intervals, and scheduling.
- ➢ **Measurements** – Understanding weight, height, distance, and temperature.
- ➢ **Shopping & Budgeting** – Comparing prices, calculating total bills, and applying discounts.

Importance in Competitive Exams (UGC NET & Others):

In exams like **UGC NET Paper I**, mathematical aptitude is tested through numerical reasoning. Understanding numbers is crucial for solving questions on:

- ➢ **Basic Arithmetic** – Addition, subtraction, multiplication, division.
- ➢ **Data Interpretation (DI)** – Analysing tables, graphs, and charts.
- ➢ **LCM & HCF** – Solving problems related to divisibility and multiples.
- ➢ **Algebraic Equations** – Understanding number properties and solving equations.
- ➢ **Logical Reasoning** – Applying number sequences, series, and patterns.

Example UGC NET Question:

1. Which of the following is an irrational number?

(A) ⅖

(B) 0.75

(C) $\sqrt{2}$

(D) 1.2

Answer: (C) $\sqrt{2}$ (It cannot be expressed as a fraction).

Types of Numbers

Numbers are classified into different types based on their properties. Below is the **logical order** in which numbers are categorized, from the most basic to the most complex.

Natural Numbers (N)

- ➤ **Definition:**
    - ○ The numbers used for **counting**.
    - ○ They **start from 1** and go on infinitely.
    - ○ **Example: 1, 2, 3, 4, 5, …**
    - ○ **Zero (0) is NOT a natural number.**

Whole Numbers (W)

- ➤ **Definition:**
    - ○ Whole numbers include **all natural numbers and zero**.
    - ○ They do **not include negative numbers or fractions**.
    - ○ **Example: 0, 1, 2, 3, 4, …**
    - ○ **Negative numbers and decimals are NOT whole numbers.**

Even and Odd Numbers *(Subset of Natural & Whole Numbers)*

Even Numbers:

- ➤ Numbers that are **divisible by 2**.
- ➤ Their last digit is **0, 2, 4, 6, or 8**.
- ➤ **Example: 2, 4, 6, 8, 10, 12, …**

Odd Numbers:

- ➤ Numbers that are **NOT divisible by 2**.
- ➤ Their last digit is **1, 3, 5, 7, or 9**.
- ➤ **Example: 1, 3, 5, 7, 9, 11, …**

Positive Numbers

- ➢ **Greater than zero** (e.g., 1, 2, 3, …).
- ➢ **Used for counting and measurements.**
- ➢ **Represent profit, growth, and temperature rise.**
- ➢ **Placed right of zero on number line.**
- ➢ **Sum of two positives is always positive.**

Negative Numbers

- ➢ **Less than zero** (e.g., -1, -2, -3, …).
- ➢ **Used for debts, temperature drop, altitude.**
- ➢ **Represent loss, deficit, or below baseline.**
- ➢ **Placed left of zero on number line.**
- ➢ **Multiplying two negatives gives positive.**

Integers (Z)

- ➢ **Definition:**
  - ○ **All whole numbers** plus their **negative counterparts.**
  - ○ Still no fractions or decimals.
  - ○ **Example: … -3, -2, -1, 0, 1, 2, 3, …**

Non-Integers

- ➢ Numbers with fractional or decimal parts.
- ➢ Not whole numbers or integers.
- ➢ Can be positive or negative values.
- ➢ Include fractions, decimals, and irrational numbers.
- ➢ Examples: **3.14, -0.5, $\sqrt{2}$, 1/2.**
- ➢ Cannot be expressed as exact integers.
- ➢ Used for precise measurements in math.

Decimal Number

- ➢ Numbers expressed in base 10 system.
- ➢ Contains a decimal point for precision.
- ➢ Represents whole and fractional parts together.
- ➢ Examples: **3.14, 0.5, -2.75, 10.0.**
- ➢ Used for accurate measurements and calculations.
- ➢ Can be terminating or non-terminating (repeating).
- ➢ Essential in scientific and financial computations.

Rational Numbers (Q)

- ➢ **Definition:**
  - ○ Any number that can be written in the form **p/q**, where **p and q are integers and q ≠ 0.**
  - ○ Includes **fractions, terminating decimals, and repeating decimals.**
  - ○ **Example: 1/2, -3/4, 0.75, 5 (5/1), 0.333… (1/3)**
  - ○ **Irrational numbers are NOT rational numbers.**

Irrational Numbers (Q')

- ➢ **Definition:**
  - ○ Numbers that **cannot** be written as a fraction **p/q**.
  - ○ Their decimal expansion is **non-terminating and non-repeating.**
  - ○ **Example: $\sqrt{2}$, $\sqrt{3}$, π (Pi = 3.14159265…), e (Euler's Number = 2.71828…)**
  - ○ **Rational numbers are NOT irrational numbers.**

Real Numbers (R)

- ➢ **Definition:**
  - ○ **Combination of all rational and irrational numbers.**
  - ○ Includes **natural, whole, integers, fractions, terminating/repeating decimals, and irrational numbers.**
  - ○ **Example: -3, 0, 4.5, 1/3, $\sqrt{2}$, π**
  - ○ **Imaginary numbers are NOT real numbers.**

Complex Numbers (C)

- ➢ **Definition:**
  - ○ Numbers that include an **imaginary unit (i)**, where $i^2 = -1$.
  - ○ Used in advanced mathematics and engineering.
  - ○ **Example: 3 + 2i, -5i, 4 - 7i**
  - ○ **Real numbers do NOT include imaginary numbers.**

Prime and Composite Numbers *(Subset of Natural Numbers)*

Prime Numbers:

> ➢ Numbers **greater than 1** that have **only two factors: 1 and itself**.
> ➢ **Example: 2, 3, 5, 7, 11, 13, 17…**

Composite Numbers:

> ➢ Numbers **greater than 1** that have **more than two factors**.
> ➢ **Example: 4, 6, 8, 9, 10, 12, …**
> ➢ **1 is neither prime nor composite.**

Summary Table of Number Types

Number Type	Definition	Examples
Natural Numbers (N)	Counting numbers starting from 1	1, 2, 3, 4, …
Whole Numbers (W)	Natural numbers + zero	0, 1, 2, 3, …
Even Numbers	Divisible by 2	2, 4, 6, 8, 10
Odd Numbers	Not divisible by 2	1, 3, 5, 7, 9
Integers (Z)	Whole numbers + negative numbers	… -2, -1, 0, 1, 2 …
Rational Numbers (Q)	Numbers that can be written as p/q	1/2, 0.75, -3/4, 5
Irrational Numbers (Q')	Non-repeating, non-terminating decimals	$\sqrt{2}$, π, e
Real Numbers (R)	All rational and irrational numbers	-3, 0, 1.5, 2/3, π
Complex Numbers (C)	Numbers with an imaginary part	3 + 2i, -4i
Prime Numbers	Numbers with only two factors	2, 3, 5, 7, 11
Composite Numbers	Numbers with more than two factors	4, 6, 8, 9, 10

Fundamentals of Mathematics (For Absolute Beginners)

Mathematical Aptitude is a crucial component of **UGC NET Paper I**, testing a candidate's ability to solve numerical problems efficiently. One of the foundational topics in this section is the **Number System**, which forms the basis for understanding all mathematical calculations.

Many aspirants, especially those from non-mathematical backgrounds, may find this section challenging. However, mastering the **Number System** is essential because it serves as the **building block** for more advanced topics such as **fractions, percentages, algebra, data interpretation, and logical reasoning**.

Why is the Number System Important?

- ➤ **Foundation of all calculations** – Understanding different types of numbers helps in solving arithmetic problems quickly.
- ➤ **Essential for real-life applications** – Concepts like divisibility, LCM, and HCF are widely used in exams and everyday scenarios.
- ➤ **Key to other UGC NET topics** – Many mathematical aptitude questions are based on number properties.

In UGC NET, questions on the **Number System** can be direct (like classification of numbers) or applied (like problems on factors, multiples, and operations). Therefore, aspirants must develop a **clear understanding** of how numbers function.

Concept Check 1: Identify the Type of Number

1. **5** → ______________
2. **-8** → ______________
3. **0.25** → ______________
4. **$\sqrt{3}$** → ______________
5. **7 + 4i** → ______________
6. **12** → ______________
7. **1/7** → ______________
8. **13** → ______________

9. π (Pi) → _______________

Try to classify each number based on the types we covered!

What Will You Learn in This Chapter?

- **Different Types of Numbers**
    - Natural, Whole, Integers, Rational, and Irrational Numbers
    - Even, Odd, Prime, and Composite Numbers
- **Basic Operations on Numbers**
    - Addition, Subtraction, Multiplication, and Division
    - Order of Operations (BODMAS Rule)
- **Factors, Multiples, LCM, and HCF**
    - Finding the **Least Common Multiple (LCM)** and **Highest Common Factor (HCF)**
    - Applications in problem-solving
- **Negative Numbers and Their Operations**
    - How negative numbers behave under different operations

At the end of this chapter, you will be able to:

✓ **Identify different types of numbers**
✓ **Perform basic operations with confidence**
✓ **Solve LCM and HCF problems quickly**
✓ **Understand negative numbers and their properties**

Questions on Number System

Question

Which of the following numbers are non-prime?

A. 11
B. 13
C. 19
D. 21
E. 15

1. AE

2. BC
3. CE
4. DE

Explanations

Answer: 4. DE

> **Prime Numbers: A prime number has only two factors (1 and itself).**
> **Check each number for primality:**

Number	Prime?	Reason
11	Prime	Divisors: {1, 11}
13	Prime	Divisors: {1, 13}
19	Prime	Divisors: {1, 19}
21	**Not Prime**	**Divisors: {1, 3, 7, 21}**
15	**Not Prime**	**Divisors: {1, 3, 5, 15}**

Identifying Non-Prime Numbers

> **21** and **15** are non-prime.

Question

Match the column:

List I (Types of Number)	List II (Properties)
A. Natural numbers	I. (..-3,-2,-1,0,1,2)
B. Whole numbers	II. (1,2,3,4,...)
C. Integers	III. (0,1,2,3,..)
D. Prime numbers	IV. (2,3,5,7,11,13,...)

1. A-III B-I C-IV D-II
2. A-II B-III C-I D-IV
3. A-I B-II C-IV D-III
4. A-III B-II C-I D-IV

Explanations

Answer: (2) A-II, B-III, C-I, D-IV

Correct Matching

A → II (Natural numbers: {1,2,3,4,...})
B → III (Whole numbers: {0,1,2,3,...})
C → I (Integers: {...,-2,-1,0,1,2,...})
D → IV (Prime numbers: {2,3,5,7,11,13,...})

Question

The sum of 7 consecutive natural numbers is 1617. Find how many of these are prime numbers?

1. 2
2. 3
3. 1
4. 4

Explanations
Answer: 1. 2

➢ The **sum of 7 consecutive natural numbers = 1617**
➢ We need to find how many of these numbers are **prime**.

Step 1: Define the Consecutive Numbers
➢ Let the **first number** be x. The numbers will be:
$$x, x + 1, x + 2, x + 3, x + 4, x + 5, x + 6$$
➢ Their sum:
$$x + (x + 1) + (x + 2) + (x + 3) + (x + 4) + (x + 5) + (x + 6) = 1617$$

Step 2: Solve for x
$$7x + (1 + 2 + 3 + 4 + 5 + 6) = 1617$$
$$7x + 21 = 1617$$
$$7x = 1596$$
$$x = 228$$

Thus, the **seven consecutive numbers** are:
$$228, 229, 230, 231, 232, 233, 234$$

Step 3: Identify Prime Numbers
Now, let's check which numbers are **prime**:

Number	Prime?	Reason
228	✗	Divisible by 2
229	✓	**Prime**
230	✗	Divisible by 2
231	✗	Divisible by 3
232	✗	Divisible by 2
233	✓	**Prime**
234	✗	Divisible by 2

Prime numbers: 229, 233
Total prime numbers: 2

Question

The unit digit of the product of first 22 natural number is

1. 0
2. 2
3. 4
4. 6

Explanations
Answer: 1. 0

We need to find the **unit digit** of the **product of the first 22 natural numbers**:

$$1 \times 2 \times 3 \times \cdots \times 22$$

Step 1: Identify Factors That Affect the Unit Digit

The **unit digit of a product** depends on the **unit digits of the numbers being multiplied**.

Since **10 is included** in the sequence (**1 to 22**), it contributes a factor of **0**:

$$10 = 2 \times 5$$

Since any number multiplied by **0** gives a unit digit of **0**, the entire product has a **unit digit of 0**.

Unit digit = 0

Question

A two-digit number is 7 times the sum of its two digits. Another number, that is formed by reversing its digits, is 18 less than the original number. Find the original number.

1. 36
2. 63
3. 24
4. 42

Explanations
Answer: 4. 42

Step 1: Define the Two-Digit Number
 ➢ Let the **two-digit number** be represented as: $10x + y$

where:

 ➢ x = Tens digit
 ➢ y = Units digit

Step 2: Form the Equations

 ➢ **Condition 1:** The number is **7 times** the sum of its digits:

$$10x + y = 7(x + y)$$

Expanding:
$$10x + y = 7x + 7y$$

Rearrange:
$$10x - 7x = 7y - y$$
$$3x = 6y$$
$$x = 2y$$

 ➢ **Condition 2:** The reversed number is **18 less** than the original:
$$10y + x = (10x + y) - 18$$

Expanding:
$$10y + x + 18 = 10x + y$$

Rearrange:

$$10y - y + x - 10x = -18$$
$$9y - 9x = -18$$
$$Divide\ 9\ on\ both\ side$$
$$y - x = -2$$

Step 3: Solve for x and y

$$Using\ x = 2y\ in\ y - x = -2$$
$$y - 2y = -2$$
$$-y = -2$$
$$y = 2$$

Substituting **y=2** into **x=2y**:

$$x = 2 \times 2 = 4$$

Thus, the original number:

$$10 \times 4 + 2 = 42 \ldots Ans.$$

Final Answer: 42

Question

Which of the following statements are correct?

- A. The sum of three consecutive multiples of 3 is 72. The largest number is 27.
- B. A number when multiplied by 13 is increased by 180. The number is 13.
- C. The average of first 20 multiples of 7 is 73.5.

1. A and B only
2. B and C only
3. A and C only
4. A only

Explanations
Answer: 3. A and C only

Statement A: Sum of three consecutive multiples of 3 is 72
Let the three consecutive multiples of 3 be:

$$x, x + 3, x + 6$$

Their sum:

$$x + (x + 3) + (x + 6) = 72$$
$$3x + 9 = 72$$

$$3x = 63$$
$$x = 21$$

The numbers are **21, 24, 27**, and the **largest is 27. (Correct)**

Statement B: A number when multiplied by 13 is increased by 180
Let the number be **y**:

$$13y = y + 180$$
$$13y - y = 180$$
$$12y = 180$$
$$y = 15$$

The number is 15, not 13, so this statement is incorrect.

Statement C: Average of the first 20 multiples of 7 is 73.5
Formula for the average of the first **n** multiples of **k.**

$$\frac{k \times (n + 1)}{2}$$

Substituting k=7, n=20

$$\frac{7 \times (20 + 1)}{2} = \frac{7 \times 21}{2} = \frac{147}{2} = 73.5$$

This statement is correct.

A.   **Statement A is correct**
B.   **Statement B is incorrect**
Statement C is correct

Basic Operations and BODMAS Rule

Introduction for UGC NET Aspirants

Mathematical aptitude in **UGC NET Paper I** includes fundamental operations like **addition, subtraction, multiplication, and division,** which form the basis for problem-solving. These operations, when applied systematically using the **BODMAS rule**, help aspirants solve **complex numerical problems accurately and efficiently.**

Many students from **non-mathematical backgrounds** struggle with calculations due to a lack of clarity on **basic operations and their properties**. This chapter ensures a **step-by-step** approach to understanding **how numbers interact** through arithmetic operations and how **BODMAS** determines the correct sequence of calculations.

Why is Learning Basic Operations Important?

> - **Essential for numerical problem-solving** – Forms the base for **data interpretation, ratio-proportion, and percentages**.
> - **Helps in logical reasoning and quantitative aptitude** – Many competitive exams, including **UGC NET**, include basic arithmetic-based questions.
> - **Reduces calculation errors** – Knowing how to apply **BODMAS and arithmetic properties** ensures quick and accurate results.

Example:
What will be the result of 24 ÷ 6 + 3 × 4 - 2?

(A) 26

(B) 14

(C) 16

(D) 12

Answer: (C) 16 (Using BODMAS: 24 ÷ 6 + (3 × 4) - 2 = 4 + 12 - 2 = 14...Ans.)

What Will You Learn in This Chapter?

Basic Arithmetic Operations

> - **Addition and Subtraction**
>   - Properties of Addition (Commutative, Associative, Identity Element)
>   - Concept of **Carrying & Borrowing** in large numbers
> - **Multiplication and Division**
>   - Properties of Multiplication

- o   Quick Multiplication & Long Division methods

BODMAS Rule (Order of Operations)

- ➢ **Brackets → Order (Exponents) → Division → Multiplication → Addition → Subtraction**
- ➢ Why **BODMAS is necessary** for solving numerical expressions correctly

Factors, Multiples, LCM, and HCF

- ➢ Understanding **Factors and Multiples**
- ➢ **Finding LCM & HCF** using shortcut and prime factorization methods

At the end of this chapter, you will be able to:

- ➢ Perform arithmetic operations quickly and correctly
- ➢ Understand how to apply the BODMAS rule in complex calculations
- ➢ Find factors, multiples, LCM, and HCF efficiently

Basic Rules of Addition and Subtraction

Addition and subtraction are the **fundamental arithmetic operations** used in daily life and competitive exams. Understanding these operations is crucial for solving complex numerical problems.

Rules for Addition:

- ➢ **Adding positive numbers** increases the value.
  - o   Example: **5 + 3 = 8**
- ➢ **Adding negative numbers** decreases the value.
  - o   Example: **(-5) + (-3) = -8**
- ➢ **Adding a positive and a negative number:**
  - o   The larger absolute value decides the sign.
  - o   Example: **(-5) + 8 = 3, 7 + (-10) = -3**

Rules for Subtraction:

- ➤ Subtracting a **smaller number from a larger number** gives a positive result.
  - ○ Example: **9 - 3 = 6**
- ➤ Subtracting a **larger number from a smaller number** gives a negative result.
  - ○ Example: **3 - 9 = -6**
- ➤ **Subtracting a negative number is the same as addition.**
  - ○ Example: **6 - (-3) = 6 + 3 = 9**

Properties of Addition

1. **Commutative Property** *(Order does not change the sum)*
   - ○ **a + b = b + a**
   - ○ Example: **3 + 5 = 5 + 3 = 8**
2. **Associative Property** *(Grouping does not change the sum)*
   - ○ **(a + b) + c = a + (b + c)**
   - ○ Example: **(2 + 3) + 4 = 2 + (3 + 4) = 9**
3. **Additive Identity** *(Adding zero does not change a number)*
   - ○ **a + 0 = a**
   - ○ Example: **7 + 0 = 7**

Concept of Carrying & Borrowing (for Large Numbers)

1. **Carrying in Addition:**
   - ○ When adding two numbers, if the sum in a column is greater than 9, carry over the extra value.
   - ○ **Example**: 124+376=500
2. Borrowing in Subtraction:
   - ○ If the top digit is smaller than the bottom digit, borrow from the next left column.
   - ○ **Example**: 892-459=433

Multiplication and Division

Properties of Multiplication

1. **Commutative Property: a × b = b × a**

- o   Example: **3 × 4 = 4 × 3 = 12**
2. **Associative Property: (a × b) × c = a × (b × c)**
   - o   Example: **(2 × 3) × 4 = 2 × (3 × 4) = 24**
3. **Distributive Property: a × (b + c) = (a × b) + (a × c)**
   - o   Example: **3 × (4 + 2) = (3 × 4) + (3 × 2) = 18**

Multiplication by 10, 100, 1000 (Shortcuts)

- ➢ **Multiply by 10** → Add one **zero** (23 × 10 = 230)
- ➢ **Multiply by 100** → Add two **zeros** (15 × 100 = 1500)
- ➢ **Multiply by 1000** → Add three **zeros** (7 × 1000 = 7000)

Long Division Method

1. **Step 1:** Divide the first digit from the left.
2. **Step 2:** Multiply the quotient with the divisor.
3. **Step 3:** Subtract and bring down the next digit.
4. **Repeat** until no digits remain.

BODMAS Rule (Order of Operations)

What is BODMAS?

The order in which mathematical operations must be performed:

1. **B** → Brackets ( ) [ ] { }
2. **O** → Orders (Exponents, Powers, Square Roots)
3. **D** → Division (÷)
4. **M** → Multiplication (×)
5. **A** → Addition (+)
6. **S** → Subtraction (-)

Example: Solve

12 + 8 × 2 - (6 ÷ 3)

- ➢ **Without BODMAS:** (12 + 8) × 2 - 6 ÷ 3 = 40 - 2 = 38 (Wrong)
- ➢ **With BODMAS:** 12 + (8 × 2) - (6 ÷ 3) = 12 + 16 - 2 = 26 (Correct)
- ➢ **Quick Concept Check:** Solve 48 ÷ 6 + (5 × 3) - 4=_____?

Solve:
$$48 \div \{6 \times (4 + 2)\} + 5 \times [3 + (8 \div 2)]$$

Solution:

Step 1: Solve inside the **parentheses and brackets**
$$= 48 \div \{6 \times 6\} + 5 \times [3 + 4]$$

Step 2: Solve inside the **curly brackets**
$$= 48 \div 36 + 5 \times 7$$

Step 3: Perform **division and multiplication**
$$= 1.33 + 35$$

Step 4: Perform **addition**
$$= 36.33$$

Final Answer: 36.33

Solve:
$$(200 \div 5) \times \{4 + 6\} - [50 \div (2 \times 5)]$$

Solution:

Step 1: Solve inside the **parentheses and brackets**
$$= (200 \div 5) \times \{10\} - [50 \div 10]$$

Step 2: Solve **division inside the brackets**
$$= (200 \div 5) \times 10 - 5$$

Step 3: Solve **division and multiplication**
$$= 40 \times 10 - 5$$

Step 4: Perform **subtraction**
$$= 400 - 5$$

Final Answer: 395

Question

Solve:
$$\{[144 \div (12 \div 2)] + (7 \times 3)\} \div 4 + (18 - 6)$$

Solution:

Step 1: Solve inside the **parentheses**
$= \{[144 \div 6] + 21\} \div 4 + 12$

Step 2: Solve **division inside the brackets**
$= \{[24] + 21\} \div 4 + 12$

Step 3: Solve **addition inside brackets**
$= 45 \div 4 + 12$

Step 4: Perform **division**
$= 11.25 + 12$

Step 5: Perform **addition**
$= 23.25$

Final Answer: 23.25

Question

A store is offering a 20% discount on a laptop priced at ₹50,000. After the discount, a 5% tax is applied. What is the final price?

$$Final\ Price = \left(50000 - \frac{20}{100} \times 50000\right) + \frac{5}{100} \times \left(50000 - \frac{20}{100} \times 50000\right)$$

$$\frac{20}{100} \times 50000 = 10000$$

$$50000 - 10000 = 40000$$

$$(40000) + \frac{5}{100} \times (40000)$$

$$\frac{5}{100} \times 40000 = 2000$$

$$40000 + 2000 = 42000 \dots Ans.$$

Question

A car covers 180 km in 3 hours. In the next 2 hours, it covers 120 km. What is the average speed for the entire journey?

$$Average\ Speed = \frac{Total\ Distance}{Total\ Time} = \frac{180 + 120}{3 + 2} = \frac{400}{5} = 80 km \dots Ans.$$

Factors, Multiples, LCM, and HCF

Factors and Multiples

Factor: A factor of a number is any number that divides it exactly, leaving no remainder.

Multiple: A multiple of a number is obtained by multiplying it by an integer.
Example:

- ➢ **Factors of 12** → 1, 2, 3, 4, 6, 12
- ➢ **Multiples of 5** → 5, 10, 15, 20, 25, ...

Quick Tip:
- ➢ **Factors are limited** (they do not exceed the given number).
- ➢ **Multiples are infinite** (they continue indefinitely).

Least Common Multiple (LCM)

Definition: The **smallest number** that is a multiple of two or more given numbers.

Example:
- **LCM of 4 and 6**
  - Multiples of 4: **4, 8, 12, 16, 20, …**
  - Multiples of 6: **6, 12, 18, 24, 30, …**
  - **Smallest common multiple = 12**
- **Shortcut Method: Prime Factorization**
  Find the **prime factorization** of each number:
  - $4 = 2 \times 2$
  - $6 = 2 \times 3$
- Take **each prime factor with the highest power**:
  - $LCM = 2^2 \times 3 = 4 \times 3 = 12$
- **Final Answer: LCM (4, 6) = 12**

Highest Common Factor (HCF)

Definition: The **largest number** that can divide two or more given numbers exactly.

Example:
- **HCF of 8 and 12**
  - Factors of 8: **1, 2, 4, 8**
  - Factors of 12: **1, 2, 3, 4, 6, 12**
  - **Greatest common factor = 4**
- **Method: Find Common Prime Factors**
  Prime factorization:
  - $8 = 2 \times 2 \times 2$
  - $12 = 2 \times 2 \times 3$
- **Common prime factor: $2^2 = 4$**
  - **Final Answer: HCF (8, 12) = 4**

Concept Check : Find LCM and HCF of 18 and 24

Step 1: Prime Factorization
- $18 = 2 \times 3 \times 3 = 2 \times 3^2$
- $24 = 2 \times 2 \times 2 \times 3 = 2^3 \times 3$

Step 2: Find LCM

- ➤ LCM is obtained by **taking the highest power of each prime factor**.
- ➤ LCM $(18, 24) = 2^3 \times 3^2 = 8 \times 9 = 72$
- ➤ **LCM (18, 24) = 72**

Step 3: Find HCF

- ➤ HCF is obtained by **taking the lowest power of each common prime factor**.
- ➤ Common prime factors: **2 and 3**
- ➤ HCF $(18, 24) = 2^1 \times 3^1 = 2 \times 3 = 6$

HCF (18, 24) = 6

Equations: Single Variable & Multiple Variable Equations

What is an Equation?

An **equation** is a **mathematical statement** that shows the equality of two expressions. It contains **variables, constants, and operations** like addition, subtraction, multiplication, and division.

Example of an Equation:

$$5x + 3 = 18$$

This means that when **5x is added to 3**, the result is **18**.

Key Components of an Equation:

1. **Variable:** A symbol (like x, y, z) representing an unknown value.
2. **Constant:** A fixed number (like 3, 18, etc.).
3. **Operator:** Mathematical operations (+, -, ×, ÷).
4. **Equal Sign (=):** Indicates balance between two sides.

Types of Equations

1. Single-Variable Equations (Linear Equations in One Variable)

- An equation with **only one variable** (x, y, etc.).
- The highest power of the variable is **1** (linear).
- **General Form:** $ax + b = c$
- **Example:** $5x + 3 = 18$

2. Multiple-Variable Equations (Linear Equations in Two or More Variables)

- An equation with **two or more variables** (x, y, z, etc.).
- The highest power of any variable is **1**
- **General Form (Two Variables):** $ax + by = c$
- **Example (Two Variables):** $2x + 3y = 12$

Type of Equation	General Form	Example	Solution Method
Single-Variable Equation	$ax + b = c$	5x+3=18	Isolate the variable
Two-Variable Equation	ax+by=c	2x+3y=12	Solve using substitution/elimination
Three-Variable Equation	ax+by+cz=d	3x+2y−z=7	Solve using matrix or elimination

Single Variable Equations Questions

Question

A man divides Rs 8,60,000 (8.6 lakhs) among his 5 sons, 4 daughters and 2 nephews. If each daughter receives four times as much as each nephew and each son receives 5 times as much as each nephew, then how much does each daughter receive?

1. Rs 80,000
2. Rs 50,000
3. Rs 1,00,000

4. Rs 60,000

Explanations
Answer: 1. Rs 80,000

Given Information
- Total amount to be divided = **Rs 8,60,000**
- Number of **sons** = **5**
- Number of **daughters** = **4**
- Number of **nephews** = **2**
- **Each daughter receives 4 times as much as each nephew.**
- **Each son receives 5 times as much as each nephew.**
- We need to find **how much each daughter receives.**

Step 1: Define Variables
Let the amount received by **each nephew** be **x**.
- **Each daughter receives 4x.**
- **Each son receives 5x.**

Step 2: Express Total Distribution in Terms of x
- Total amount distributed:

$$(5\ sons) \times (5x) + (4\ daughters) \times (4x) + (2\ nephews) \times (x) = 8,60,000$$
$$(5 \times 5x) + (4 \times 4x) + (2 \times x) = 8,60,000$$
$$25x + 16x + 2x = 8,60,000$$
$$43x = 8,60,000$$

Multiplication (×) becomes Division (÷) when moved across the = sign.

$$x = \frac{8,60,000}{43}$$

Step 3: Solve for x

$$x = \frac{8,60,000}{43}$$
$$x = 20,000 \dots Ans$$

Step 4: Find the Amount Each Daughter Receives
- Since each daughter receives **4x**, we calculate:

$$4 \times 20,000 = 80,000$$

Each daughter receives Rs 80,000

Step 5: Verification
- Amount received by **each son**:
$$5x = 5 \times 20{,}000 = 1{,}00{,}000$$
- Amount received by **each daughter**: $4x = 80{,}000$
- Amount received by **each nephew**:$x = 20{,}000$
- **Total distributed amount check:**
$$= (5 \times 1{,}00{,}000) + (4 \times 80{,}000) + (2 \times 20{,}000)$$
$$= 5{,}00{,}000 + 3{,}20{,}000 + 40{,}000$$
$$= 8{,}60{,}000$$
- **The total matches Rs 8,60,000, confirming our answer is correct.**

Question

The total value of the collection of coins of denominations of Rs 20, Rs 10, Rs 5, Rs 2 and Rs 1 is 570. If the number of coins of each denomination is equal. So, what is the number of 1-rupee coins?

1. 10
2. 12
3. 15
4. 18

Explanations
Answer: 3. 15

Given Information
- The total value of coins = **Rs 570**
- Denominations: **Rs 20, Rs 10, Rs 5, Rs 2, Rs 1**
- The **number of coins of each denomination is equal**
- We need to find the **number of 1-rupee coins.**

Step 1: Define the Variable

Let the **number of coins** of each denomination be **x**.
Thus, the total value from each denomination is:

- **Rs 20 coins** → 20x
- **Rs 10 coins** → 10x
- **Rs 5 coins** → 5x

- o **Rs 2 coins** → 2x
- o **Rs 1 coins** → 1x

Step 2: Form the Equation

The total value of all the coins is **Rs 570**, so:

$$20x + 10x + 5x + 2x + 1x = 570$$
$$(20 + 10 + 5 + 2 + 1)x = 570$$
$$38x = 570$$

Multiplication (×) becomes Division (÷) when moved across the = sign

$$x = \frac{570}{38}$$

Step 3: Solve for x

$$x = \frac{570}{38}$$
$$x = 15 \dots Ans.$$

Step 4: Find the Number of 1-Rupee Coins

Since there are **x** coins of **each** denomination, the number of **1-rupee coins** is also **15**.

Question (Put in Power Type Question)

The population of a bacteria culture doubles every 2 minutes. How many minutes will it take for the population to grow from 1 to 1024?

1. 10
2. 14
3. 18
4. 20

Explanations
Answer: 4. 20

Given Information
- o The **bacteria population doubles** every **2 minutes**.
- o The **initial population = 1**.

- o The **final population = 1024**.
- o We need to find **how many minutes it takes** for the population to grow from **1 to 1024**.

Step 1: Identify the Growth Pattern

Since the bacteria **doubles** every **2 minutes**, the population follows **exponential growth**:

$$Population\ after\ n\ doublings = 1 \times 2^n$$

We need to find n such that:
$$2^n = 1024$$

Step 2: Solve for n

We check the powers of **2**:
$$1024 = 2^{10}$$

So,

$$2^n = 2^{10}$$
$$n - 10$$

Since **each doubling takes 2 minutes**, the total time required:

$$Total\ Time = n \times 2$$
$$= 10 \times 2 = 20\ minutes \ldots Ans.$$

Question

When a sum of money was distributed to 12 boys instead of 16 boys, each boy got Rs 40 more. What was the sum?

1. 1290
2. 1920
3. 480
4. 840

Explanations
Answer: 2. 1920

Given Information
- A sum of money was supposed to be distributed among **16 boys**.

- Instead, it was given to **12 boys**.
- Each boy received **Rs 40 more** than they would have received if shared among 16 boys.
- We need to find the **total sum of money**.

Step 1: Define the Variable

Let the **total sum of money** be **Rs** x

- o If **16 boys** were to receive it, each boy would get:
$$\frac{x}{16}$$

- o If **12 boys** were to receive it, each boy would get:
$$\frac{x}{12}$$

- o Since each boy **receives Rs 40 more** when distributed among **12 boys**, we can set up the equation:
$$\frac{x}{12} - \frac{x}{16} = 40$$

Step 2: Solve for x

Find the **LCM of 12 and 16**:

Step 1: Find the **Prime Factorization** of each number.
$$12 = 2 \times 2 \times 3 = 2^2 \times 3$$
$$16 = 2 \times 2 \times 2 \times 2 = 2^4$$
Step 2: Take the **highest power of each prime number**.
- **Highest power of 2 $= 2^4$**
- **Highest power of 3 $= 3^1$**
Step 3: Multiply these together:
$$LCM(12,16) = 2^4 \times 3^1$$
$$= 16 \times 3$$
$$= 48$$

$$LCM(12,16) = 48$$

Convert fractions:

$$\frac{x}{12} = \frac{4x}{48}, \frac{x}{16} = \frac{3x}{48}$$

Step 2: Convert $\frac{x}{12}$ and $\frac{x}{16}$ into *Equivalent Fractions*

We express $\frac{x}{12}$ *with denominator* 48:
$$\frac{x}{12} = \frac{4x}{48}$$

> (Since **12 × 4 = 48**, we multiply both numerator and denominator by 4.)
> Similarly, express $\frac{x}{16}$ *with denominator* 48:
> $$\frac{x}{16} = \frac{3x}{48}$$
> (Since **16 × 3 = 48**, we multiply both numerator and denominator by 3.)

So, the equation becomes:

$$\frac{4x}{48} - \frac{3x}{48} = 40$$

Now that both fractions have the **same denominator**, we subtract the numerators:

$$\frac{4x - 3x}{48} = 40$$

$$\frac{x}{48} = 40$$

Division (÷) becomes Multiplication (×) when moved across the = sign.

$$x = 40 \times 48$$

$$x = 1920 \dots Ans.$$

Two or Multi Variable Equations Type Questions

Question (Average)

The average of the ages of three persons A, B and C is 45 years, and the average age of A, C and D is 51 years. If the age of D is 56 years, what is the age of B?

1. 35 years
2. 38 years
3. 36 years
4. 36.5 years

Explanations
Answer: 2. 38 years

Given Information
- The **average age of A, B, and C = 45 years**
- The **average age of A, C, and D = 51 years**
- The **age of D = 56 years**

o   We need to find the **age of B**.

Step 1: Express in Equation Form

Equation 1: Average of A, B, and C

$$\frac{A + B + C}{3} = 45$$
$$A + B + C = 45 \times 3$$
$$A + B + C = 135 \ldots \ldots (1)$$

Equation 2: Average of A, C, and D

$$\frac{A + C + D}{3} = 51$$
$$A + C + D = 51 \times 3$$
$$A + C + D = 153 \ldots \ldots (2)$$

Step 2: Substitute the Value of D

Since **D = 56**, substitute it into Equation 2:

$$A + C + 56 = 153$$
$$\mathbf{A + C = 153 - 56}$$
$$A + C = 97$$

Step 3: Find the Value of B
From **Equation 1**:

$$A + B + C = 135$$

Substituting **A + C = 97**:

Note: Commutative Property (Order does not change the sum) For
Example: A+B+C = A+C+B.

$$97 + B = 135$$
$$B = 135 - 97$$
$$B = 38 \ldots Ans.$$

Question (Set Theory & Venn Diagram)

**In a school survey of 400 students 100 were taking apple juice, 150
orange juice and 75 were taking both apple and orange juice. How
many students were taking neither apple nor orange juice?**

1. 275

2. 250
3. 175
4. 225

Explanations
Answer: 4. 225

Given Information:

- Total students surveyed = 400
- Students taking Apple juice (A) = 100
- Students taking Orange juice (O) = 150
- Students taking both Apple and Orange juice (A ∩ O) = 75
- We need to find the number of students taking **neither Apple nor Orange juice**.

Step 1: Use the Formula for Union of Two Sets
Using the **principle of set inclusion-exclusion**:
Students taking either Apple or Orange juice:
$$= (Apple\ only + Orange\ only + Both)$$
The formula:

$$Total\ taking\ juice = |A \cup O| = |A| + |O| - |A \cap O|$$

Substituting the given values:
$$|A \cup O| = 100 + 150 - 75$$
$$|A \cup O| = 175$$

Step 2: Find the Students Taking Neither Juice:

Students taking neither $= Total\ students - |A \cup O|$
$$= 400 - 175$$
$$= 225 \ldots Ans.$$

Question

The age of the father is twice that of the elder son. Ten years hence the age of the father will be three times the age of the younger son. If the difference of ages of the two sons is 15 years, what is the age of the father?

1. 50 yrs
2. 45yrs
3. 43 yrs
4. 40 yrs

Explanations

Answer: 1. 50 yrs

Given Information

- The father's age is **twice** the age of the **elder son.**
- **10 years later**, the father's age will be **three times** the age of the **younger son**.
- The **age difference** between the **elder and younger son** is **15 years**.
- We need to find the **father's current age**.

Step 1: Define the Variables

Let:

- The **elder son's age** = **x**
- The **younger son's age** = **y**
- The **father's age** = **2x**(since it is twice the elder son's age)

The **difference of ages of the two sons is 15 years**: i.e. $x - y = 15$

Step 2: Set Up the Future Age Equation

After **10 years**:

- The father's age will be: **2x+10**
- The younger son's age will be: **y+10**
- According to the question, at that time: $2x + 10 = 3(y + 10)$

Step 3: Solve for x **and** y

Equation 1: x−y=15

Equation 2: 2x+10=3(y+10)

Expanding Equation 2: 2x+10=3y+30

Rearrange:

2x−3y=30-10

$$2x-3y=20$$

Step 4: Solve the System of Equations

We now solve:

$$x - y = 15$$
$$2x - 3y = 20$$

Express x in terms of y From

$$x - y = 15$$
$$x = y + 15$$

Substitute into the Second Equation

$$2(y + 15) - 3y = 20$$
$$2y + 30 - 3y = 20$$
$$-y + 30 = 20$$
$$-y = -10$$
$$y = 10$$

Step 5: Find the Values of x and the Father's Age Using **x=y+15**:

$$x = 10 + 15$$
$$x = 25$$

The father's age:

$$2x = 2 \times 25 = 50 \; years \ldots Ans.$$

Question

If the price of 3 kg potatoes and 4 kg tomatoes is Rs. 100 and the price of 4 kg potatoes and 3 kg tomatoes is Rs. 110, then what is the price of tomatoes per kg?

(1) 10
(2) 20
(3) 25
(4) 15

Explanations

Answer: (1) 10

Let:

- The price of **1 kg of potatoes** = x Rs
- The price of **1 kg of tomatoes** = y Rs

The given conditions:

1. **3 kg potatoes + 4 kg tomatoes = Rs 100**

$$3x + 4y = 100$$

2. **4 kg potatoes + 3 kg tomatoes = Rs 110**

$$4x + 3y = 110$$

We need to find the price of **1 kg of tomatoes** (y).

Solve the Two Equations

We have:

$$3x + 4y = 100 \ldots\ldots (1)$$
$$4x + 3y = 110 \ldots\ldots (2)$$

Multiply the first equation by 3 and the second equation by 4 to align the coefficients of x:

$$(3x + 4y) \times 3 = 100 \times 3$$
$$9x + 12y = 300$$
$$(4x + 3y) \times 4 = 110 \times 4$$
$$16x + 12y = 440$$

Step 2: Subtract the Two Equations:

$$(16x + 12y) - (9x + 12y) = 440 - 300$$
$$16x + 12y - 9x - 12y = 140$$
$$16x - 9x = 140$$
$$7x = 140$$
$$x = 20$$

Thus, **the price of 1 kg of potatoes is Rs 20**.

Step 3: Find the Price of Tomatoes

Substituting **x=20** into the first equation:

$$3(20) + 4y = 100$$
$$60 + 4y = 100$$
$$4y = 40$$
$$y = 10 \ldots Ans.$$

Thus, **the price of 1 kg of tomatoes is Rs 10**.

Question

In an examination, a student scores 4 marks for each correct answer and loses 1 mark for each wrong answer. A student attempted all 200 questions and scored 400 marks. The number of questions attempted correctly by him is.

1. 60
2. 100
3. 120
4. 150

Explanations

Answer: 3. 120

Define Variables:
   o   Let x be the number of correct answers.
   o   Let y be the number of wrong answers.

Set Up the Equations:
   o   The student attempted all 200 questions:

$$x + y = 200 \text{ equation (1)}$$

   o   The student scores 4 marks for each correct answer and loses 1 mark for each wrong answer, totalling 400 marks:

$$4x - y = 400 \text{ equation (2)}$$

   o   Solve the Equations:
   o   From equation (1), express y in terms of x:
$$y = 200 - x$$
   o   Substitute y into equation (2)
$$4x - (200 - x) = 400$$
$$4x - 200 + x = 400$$
$$5x - 200 = 400$$
$$5x = 600$$
$$x = 120 \dots Ans.$$

The student answered 120 questions correctly.

Question

There are some Cows and Ducks in a park. The total number of heads of Cows and Ducks together is 60. However, the total number legs of the cows and ducks together is 180. Find the number of cows and ducks in the park, respectively.

1. 30,30

2. 32,28
3. 28,32
4. 24,36

Explanations

Answer: 1. 30,30

To determine the number of cows and ducks in the park, let's analyze the problem step by step.

Define Variables:

- Let C be the number of cows.
- Let D be the number of ducks.

Set Up the Equations:

- Each cow and duck has one head. The total number of heads is 60:

$$C + D = 60 \quad Equation\ (1)$$

- Cows have 4 legs and ducks have 2 legs. The total number of legs is 180:

$$4C + 2D = 180 \quad Equation\ (2)$$

Simplify the Equations:

- From equation (1), express D in terms of C:

$$D = 60 - C$$

- Substitute D into equation (2):

$$4C + 2(60 - C) = 180$$
$$4C + 120 - 2C = 180$$
$$2C + 120 = 180$$
$$2C = 60$$
$$C = \frac{60}{2}$$
$$C = 30$$

- Substitute C=30 back into equation (1) to find D:

$$30 + D = 60$$
$$D = 30$$

There are **30 cows** and **30 ducks** in the park.

Question (Put this in Fraction)

The numerator of a fraction is 4 less than its denominator. If the numerator is decreased by 2 and denominator is increased by 1, then the denominator becomes 8 times the numerator, find the fraction.

1. $\frac{3}{7}$
2. 3.9
3. $\frac{3}{8}$
4. $\frac{2}{7}$

Explanations

Answer: 1. $\frac{3}{7}$

Define Variables:

- Let the denominator of the fraction be D.
- The numerator is 4 less than the denominator, so the numerator is $D-4$.
- The original fraction is:

$$\frac{D-4}{D}$$

Modify the Fraction:

- The numerator is decreased by 2:

$$New\ numerator = (D-4) - 2 = D - 6$$

- The denominator is increased by 1:

$$New\ denominator = D + 1$$

- The new fraction is:

$$\frac{D-6}{D+1}$$

Set Up the Equation:

- o According to the problem, the new denominator becomes 8 times the new numerator:

$$D + 1 = 8(D - 6)$$

Solve the Equation:

$$D + 1 = 8(D - 6)$$
$$D + 1 = 8D - 48$$
$$1 + 48 = 8D - D$$
$$49 = 7D$$
$$D = \frac{49}{7}$$
$$D = 7$$

Find the Numerator:

- o The numerator is $D-4$:

$$Numerator = 7 - 4 = 3$$

The original fraction is: $\frac{3}{7}$

Question

In a forest there are some Tigers and Peacocks. The total number of heads is 90 and the total number of legs is 240. Find the total no. of Tigers and total number of Peacocks in the forest i.e. (Tigers, Peacocks)

1. (35,55)
2. (45,45)
3. (40, 50)
4. (30, 60)

Explanations
Answer: 4. (30, 60)
Let:

- **T** be the number of Tigers.
- **P** be the number of Peacocks.

Step 1: Forming Equations

1. Each animal has **one head**, so the total number of heads equation is:

$$T + P = 90 \ldots\ldots (1)$$

2. Tigers have **4 legs**, and Peacocks have **2 legs**, so the total number of legs equation is:

$$4T + 2P = 240 \ldots\ldots (2)$$

Step 2: Solving the Equations

From Equation (1):

$$P = 90 - T$$

Substituting this into Equation (2):

$$4T + 2(90 - T) = 240$$
$$4T + 180 - 2T = 2404$$
$$2T + 180 = 240$$
$$2T = 60$$
$$T = \frac{60}{2}$$
$$T = 30 \ldots Ans.$$

Finding P:

$$P = 90 - 30 = 60 \ldots Ans.$$

The number of **Tigers = 30** and the number of **Peacocks = 60**.

Question

Karan was born 3 years after his parent's marriage. His father is 6 years older than his mother but 26 years older than Karan who is 12 years of age as on today. At what age did his mother get married?

1. 20 years
2. 19 years
3. 17 years
4. 18 years

Explanations

Answer: 3. 17 years

Define Variables:

- Let M be the current age of Karan's mother.
- Let F be the current age of Karan's father.
- Let K be the current age of Karan.
- Let A be the age of Karan's mother at the time of marriage.

Given Information:

- o Karan is currently 12 years old:
$$K = 12$$
- o Karan was born 3 years after his parents' marriage:
$$\text{Time since marriage} = K + 3 = 12 + 3 = 15\ years$$
- o Karan's father is 6 years older than his mother:
$$F = M + 6$$
- o Karan's father is 26 years older than Karan:
$$F = K + 26 = 12 + 26 = 38\ years$$

Find Mother's Current Age:

- o From the equation:
$$F = M + 6\ and\ F = 38$$
$$38 = M + 6$$
$$M = 38 - 6 = 32\ years$$

Determine Mother's Age at Marriage:

- o The mother's current age is 32 years.
- o The marriage occurred 15 years ago:
$$A = M - 15 = 32 - 15 = 17\ years$$

Conclusion: Karan's mother was 17 years old when she got married.

Question

Kavita's age is eight years more than thrice the sum of the ages of her two grandsons who are twins. Nine years later, Kavita's age will be one year more than two times the sum of the ages of her two grandsons.
What was the age of Kavita when her grandsons were born"?

1. 58 years
2. 68 years
3. 65 years
4. 28 years

Explanations
Answer: 1. 58 years

Define Variables:
- Let K be Kavita's current age.
- Let T be the current age of each twin grandson (since they are twins, their ages are the same).

Set Up the Equations:
- Kavita's age is eight years more than thrice the sum of the ages of her two grandsons:
$$K = 3(2T) + 8 = 6T + 8 \; Equation \; (1)$$
- Nine years later, Kavita's age will be one year more than two times the sum of the ages of her two grandsons:
$$K + 9 = 2\big(2(T + 9)\big) + 1 = 4(T + 9) + 1 (2)$$

Simplify the Equations:

From equation (1):
$$K = 6T + 8$$
Substitute KK into equation (2):
$$6T + 8 + 9 = 4(T + 9) + 1$$
$$6T + 17 = 4T + 36 + 1$$
$$6T + 17 = 4T + 37$$
$$6T - 4T = 37 - 17$$
$$2T = 20$$
$$T = 10$$

Find Kavita's Current Age:

- Substitute $T=10$ into equation (1):
$$K = 6(10) + 8 = 60 + 8 = 68 \; years$$

Determine Kavita's Age When Her Grandsons Were Born:
- The grandsons are currently 10 years old.
- Therefore, Kavita's age when her grandsons were born is:
$$K - T = 68 - 10 = 58 \; years$$

Conclusion: Kavita was **58 years old** when her grandsons were born.

Question

X is as much younger to Y as he is older to Z. If the sum of the ages of Y and Z is 36 years. What is the age of X?

1. 16 Years
2. 15 Years
3. 18 Years
4. 20 Years

Explanations

Answer: 3. 18 Years

Define Variables:
- Let X be the age of X.
- Let Y be the age of Y.
- Let Z be the age of Z.

Set Up the Equations:
- X is as much younger to Y as he is older to Z. This means the difference in age between Y and X is the same as the difference in age between X and Z:
$$Y - X = X - Z \; Equation \; (1)$$
- The sum of the ages of Y and Z is 36 years:
$$Y + Z = 36 \; Equation \; (2)$$

Simplify the Equations:
- From equation (1):
$$Y - X = X - Z$$
$$Y + Z = 2X$$
- From equation (2), we know
$$Y + Z = 36$$
$$36 = 2X$$
$$X = 18$$

Conclusion: The age of X is 18 years.

Question

A total of 324 coins of 20 paise and 25 paise make a sum of Rs 71. The number of 20 paise coins is

1. 144
2. 124
3. 200
4. 125

Explanations
Answer: 3. 200

Define Variables:
- o   Let x be the number of 20 paise coins.
- o   Let y be the number of 25 paise coins.

Set Up the Equations:
- o   The total number of coins is 324:

$$x + y = 324 \; Equation \; (1)$$

- o   The total sum of the coins is Rs 71. Since 1 rupee = 100 paise, Rs 71 = 7100 paise:

$$20x + 25y = 7100 \; Equation \; (2)$$

Simplify the Equations:
- o   From equation (1), express y in terms of x:

$$y = 324 - x$$

- o   Substitute y into equation (2):

$$20x + 25(324 - x) = 7100$$
$$20x + 8100 - 25x = 7100$$
$$-5x + 8100 = 7100$$
$$-5x = 7100 - 8100$$
$$-5x = -1000$$
$$x = 200$$

Conclusion: The number of 20 paise coins is 200.

Question

How tall is a tree that is 6 meters shorter than a wall that is seven times higher than the tree?

1.   7 meters
2.   2 meters
3.   1.25 meters
4.   1 meter

Explanations

Answer: 4. 1 meter

Define Variables:
- o   Let T be the height of the tree.
- o   Let W be the height of the wall.

Set Up the Equations:
- o   The tree is 6 meters shorter than the wall:

$$T = W - 6 \; Equation \; (1)$$

- o   The wall is seven times higher than the tree:

$$W = 7T \; Equation \; (2)$$

Substitute and Solve:
- o   Substitute equation (2) into equation (1):

$$T = 7T - 6$$

- o   Rearrange to solve for T:

$$T - 7T = -6$$
$$-6T = -6$$
$$T = 1$$

Conclusion: The height of the tree is 1 meter.

Question

Aman is 30 years older than his son. Five years ago, his age was 6 times the age of his son. Find the age of the son?

1.   10 years
2.   11 years
3.   12 years
4.   15 years

Explanations
Answer: 2. 11 years

Define Variables:
- o   Let S be the current age of the son.
- o   Let A be the current age of Aman.

Set Up the Equations:
- o   Aman is 30 years older than his son:

$$A = S + 30 \ \textit{Equation (1)}$$

- o Five years ago, Aman's age was 6 times the age of his son:

$$A - 5 = 6(S - 5) \ \textit{Equation (2)}$$

Substitute and Solve:
- o Substitute equation (1) into equation (2):

$$(S + 30) - 5 = 6(S - 5)$$
$$S + 25 = 6S - 30$$

- o Rearrange to solve for S:

$$25 + 30 = 6S - S$$
$$55 = 5S$$
$$S = 11$$

Conclusion: The current age of the son is 11 years.

Question

The difference between the ages of two men is 10 years. 15 years ago, the elder one was twice as old as the younger one. The present age of the elder man is

1. 25 years
2. 35 years
3. 45 years
4. 40 years

Explanations
Answer: 2. 35 years

Define Variables:
- o Let E be the present age of the elder man.
- o Let Y be the present age of the younger man.

Set Up the Equations:
- o The difference between their ages is 10 years:

$$E - Y = 10 \ \textit{Equatiion (1)}$$

- o 15 years ago, the elder man was twice as old as the younger man:

$$E - 15 = 2(Y - 15) \ \textit{Equation (2)}$$

Substitute and Solve:
- o From equation (1), express E in terms of Y:

$$E = Y + 10$$

- o Substitute E into equation (2):

$$(Y + 10) - 15 = 2(Y - 15)$$
$$Y - 5 = 2Y - 30$$

- o   Rearrange to solve for Y:

$$-5 + 30 = 2Y - Y$$
$$25 = Y$$

- o   Substitute Y=25 back into equation (1) to find E:

$$E = 25 + 10 = 35$$

Conclusion: The present age of the elder man is 35 years.

Question

The present age of the father is twice that of the elder son. Ten years hence the age of the father will be three times that of the younger son. If the difference in ages of the two sons is as 15 years, the present age of the father is:

1.   110 years
2.   70 years
3.   60 years
4.   50 years

Explanations
Answer: 4. 50 years
Define Variables:

- o   Let F be the present age of the father.
- o   Let E be the present age of the elder son.
- o   Let Y be the present age of the younger son.

Set Up the Equations:

- o   The present age of the father is twice that of the elder son:

$$F = 2E \quad Equation \ (1)$$

- o   Ten years hence, the age of the father will be three times that of the younger son:

$$F + 10 = 3(Y + 10) \quad Equation \ (2)$$

- o   The difference in ages of the two sons is 15 years:

$$E - Y = 15 \quad Equation \ (3)$$

Express Variables in Terms of E:

- o   From equation (1):

- o *Substitute $F = 2E$ and $Y = E - 15$ into equation (2):*

$$2E + 10 = 3\big((E - 15) + 10\big)$$
$$2E + 10 = 3(E - 5)$$
$$2E + 10 = 3E - 15$$

- o Rearrange to solve for E:

$$10 + 15 = 3E - 2E$$
$$25 = E$$

Find the Father's Age:
- o Substitute E=25 into equation (1):

$$F = 2 \times 25 = 50$$

Conclusion: The present age of the father is **50 years**.

Understanding LHS and RHS in Equations

What is LHS and RHS?

In any equation, the **equal sign (=)** divides the equation into two parts:

1. **LHS (Left-Hand Side)** – The part of the equation **before** the equal sign.
2. **RHS (Right-Hand Side)** – The part of the equation **after** the equal sign.

Example 1:

$$5x + 3 = 18$$

Here:
- **LHS** = 5x + 3 = 18
- **RHS** = 18

The equation is **balanced** because both sides represent the same value when **x is correctly solved**.

Why is LHS = RHS Important?

- ➢ To **check if an equation is correct**, the LHS must be **equal** to the RHS.
- ➢ When solving an equation, we perform **operations on both sides** to keep them balanced.

Basic Rule:

- ➤ **Addition (+) becomes Subtraction (-)** when moved across the = sign.
- ➤ **Subtraction (-) becomes Addition (+)** when moved across the = sign.
- ➤ **Multiplication (×) becomes Division (÷)** when moved across the = sign.
- ➤ **Division (÷) becomes Multiplication (×)** when moved across the = sign.

Solving an Equation by Keeping LHS = RHS

Example 2:

Solve: 3x+4=19

Start with the given equation:

$$3x+4=19$$

- ➤ LHS = 3x+4
- ➤ RHS = 19

$$3x + 4 = 19$$

Addition (+) becomes Subtraction (-) when moved across the = sign.

$$3x = 19 - 4$$

$$3x = 15$$

Multiplication (×) becomes Division (÷) when moved across the = sign.

$$x = \frac{15}{3}$$

$$x = 5 \ldots Ans.$$

Example 2:

Solve: $5x - 6 = 24$

$$5x - 6 = 24$$

Subtraction (-) becomes Addition (+) when moved across the = sign

$$5x = 24 + 6$$

$$5x = 30$$

Multiplication (×) becomes Division (÷) when moved across the = sign.

$$x = \frac{30}{5}$$

$$x = 6 \dots Ans.$$

Steps to Find the Equation from a Word Problem

To convert a **real-life word problem** into a **mathematical equation**, follow these structured steps:

Step 1: Identify the Unknown (Define the Variable)
- ➢ Read the question carefully and determine **what is being asked**.
- ➢ Assign a **variable** (usually x) to the unknown quantity.

Example:
"A father is three times as old as his son. After 10 years, the father will be twice as old as the son. What is the son's current age?"

- ➢ Let **son's age = x**.
- ➢ Then, **father's age = 3x**.

Step 2: Identify Relationships in the Problem
- ➢ Convert words into **mathematical relationships**.
- ➢ Look for **keywords** like *sum, difference, product, quotient, times, more than, less than.*

Example:
"After 10 years, the father will be twice as old as the son."
- ➢ **Son's age after 10 years** = x+10
- ➢ **Father's age after 10 years** = 3x+10
- ➢ The problem states that *father's age will be twice the son's age*:

$$3x + 10 = 2(x + 10)$$

Step 3: Set Up the Equation
- ➢ Arrange all known quantities and **form an equation** based on the problem statement.

Example:
We already formed the equation:

$$3x + 10 = 2(x + 10)$$

Step 4: Solve for the Variable
- ➢ Apply **basic algebraic operations** (addition, subtraction, multiplication, division).
- ➢ Keep the **LHS (Left-Hand Side) = RHS (Right-Hand Side)** balanced.

Solving our example equation:

$$3x + 10 = 2x + 20$$
$$3x - 2x = 20 - 10$$
$$x = 10 \dots Ans.$$

Arithmetic Progression (AP)

An **Arithmetic Progression (AP)** is a sequence of numbers in which the **difference between consecutive terms is constant**. This difference is called the **common difference** (d).

Definition of Arithmetic Progression
A sequence is called an **Arithmetic Progression (AP)** if:

$$a, a + d, a + 2d, a + 3d, \dots$$

where:
- ○ a_n = nth term
- ○ a = **First term**
- ○ d = **Common difference** (constant difference between consecutive terms)
- ○ n = **Number of terms**

General Formula for the nth Term

The **nth term** of an arithmetic progression is given by:

$$a_n = a + (n - 1)d$$

Example: Find the 10th term of the AP 3, 7, 11, 15, ...

Step 1: Identify Values

$$First\ term\ a = 3$$
$$Common\ difference\ d = 7 - 3 = 4$$
$$Number\ of\ terms\ n = 10$$

Step 2: Use Formula: $a_n = a + (n - 1)d$

$$a_{10} = 3 + (10 - 1) \times 4$$
$$= 3 + 9 \times 4$$
$$= 3 + 36 = 39$$

10th term = 39

Sum of First n Terms of an AP

The sum of the first **n terms** of an AP is:

$$Sn = \frac{n}{2} \times [2a + (n - 1)d]$$

Or

$$Sn = \frac{n}{2} \times (a + l)$$

Where

$$Sn = \textbf{Sum of first n terms}$$
$$l = \textbf{Last term of the sequence}$$

Example: Find the sum of the first 10 terms of the AP 3, 7, 11, 15, ...

Step 1: Identify Values

- a=3
- d=4
- n=10

Step 2: Use Formula

$$S_{10} = \frac{10}{2} \times [2 \times 3 + (10 - 1)4]$$

$$= 5 \times [6 + 36]$$
$$= 5 \times 42 = 210$$

Finding Common Difference

The **common difference d** is found by:

$$d = a_2 - a_1$$

Example: Find the common difference for AP 5, 9, 13, 17, ...

$$d = 9 - 5 = 4$$

Common Difference d=4

Properties of Arithmetic Progression

- If a constant is added to each term, the new sequence remains an AP.
- If all terms are multiplied by a constant, the sequence remains an AP.
- If three terms are in AP, the middle term is the average of the first and last terms:

$$b = \frac{a + c}{2}$$

Questions on Number System and Arithmetic Progression

Find the value of the expression given below, correct up to 2 decimal places.

$$\frac{[(0.96)^3 - (0.1)^3]}{[(0.96)^2 + 0.096 + (0.1)^2]}$$

1. 0.84
2. 0.81
3. 0.86
4. 0.82

Explanations
Answer: 3. 0.86

Given Expression

$$\frac{[(0.96)^3 - (0.1)^3]}{[(0.96)^2 + 0.096 + (0.1)^2]}$$

Step 1: Calculate the Numerator

$$(0.96)3 - (0.1)3$$
$$(0.96)3 = 0.884736$$
$$(0.1)3 = 0.001$$
$$0.884736 - 0.001 = 0.883736$$

Step 2: Calculate the Denominator

$$(0.96)2 + 0.096 + (0.1)2$$
$$(0.96)2 = 0.9216$$
$$(0.1)2 = 0.01$$
$$0.9216 + 0.096 + 0.01 = 1.0276$$

Step 3: Compute the Final Value

$$\frac{0.883736}{1.0276}$$
$$= 0.86$$

Question

The first term in an arithmetic series of 100 terms is 7. If the last term is 205, what is the 71th term of the series?

1. 157
2. 151
3. 147
4. 161

Explanations
Answer: 3. 147
Given Information:

- o **First term** (a) = **7**
- o **Last term** (l) = **205**

- o **Total number of terms (n) = 100**
- o **We need to find the 71st term (a_{71})**

Find the Common Difference (d)
- o Using the formula for the last term in an arithmetic progression:
$$l = a + (n-1)d$$
- o Substituting the values:

$$205 = 7 + (100 - 1)d$$
$$205 = 7 + 99d$$
$$99d = 198$$
$$d = \frac{198}{99} = 2$$

Step 2: Find the 71st Term
- o The formula for the **nth term** of an AP:
$$a_n = a + (n-1)d$$
- o Substituting $n = 71, a = 7$ and $d = 2$
$$a_{71} = 7 + (71 - 1) \times 2$$
$$= 7 + 70 \times 2$$
$$= 7 + 140$$
$$= 147 \dots Ans.$$

Question

In an arithmetic series having 50 terms, the first and last terms are 3 and 199, respectively. What is the sum of the series

(1) 4950
(2) 5050
(3) 5150
(4) 4850

Explanations
Answer: 2. 5050

Given Information
- o **First term (a) = 3**
- o **Last term (l) = 199**
- o **Total number of terms (n) = 50**
- o We need to find the **sum of the series (Sn).**

Step 1: To find the sum of the arithmetic series, we can use the formula for the sum of an arithmetic series:

$$Sn = \frac{n}{2} \times (a + l)$$

where:

- Sn = sum of the series
- n = number of terms
- a = first term
- l = last term

Step 2: Substitute Given Values:

$$S_{50} = \frac{50}{2} \times (3 + 199)$$
$$S_{50} = 25 \times 202$$
$$S_{50} = 5050 \dots Ans.$$

Question

Sum of 3 consecutive odd numbers and 3 consecutive even numbers together is 231. Also, the smallest, odd number is 11 less than the smallest even number. What is the sum of the largest, odd number and the largest even number?

1. 81
2. 73
3. 70
4. 79

Explanations
Answer: 1. 81

Step-by-Step Solution

- **Let the smallest even number be x.**
- **The smallest odd number is x−11.**
- Three consecutive even numbers: $x, x + 2, x + 4$
- Three consecutive odd numbers: $(x - 11), (x - 9), (x - 7)$
- Given sum equation:

  $(x - 11) + (x - 9) + (x - 7) + x + (x + 2) + (x + 4) = 231$
- Simplify:

$$(x - 11) + (x - 9) + (x - 7) + x + (x + 2) + (x + 4) = 231$$
$$6x - 21 = 231$$
$$6x = 252$$
$$x = 42$$

- **Largest Odd Number:** $x - 7 = 42 - 7 = 35$.
- **Largest Even Number:** $x + 4 = 42 + 4 = 46$.
- **Sum:** $35 + 46 = 81$ ... Ans.

Question

If 5th term of an Arithmetic progression (AP) series is 16 and 9th term is 22, then find the seventh (7th) term of the series.

1. 25
2. 22
3. 19
4. 205

Explanations
Answer: 3. 19

Given Information:

- 5th term $(a_5) = 16$
- 9th term $(a_9) = 22$
- Find the 7th term (a_7)

Step 1: Use the nth Term Formula:
$$a_n = a + (n - 1)d$$

- For the **5th term**: $a + 4d = 16$
- For the **9th term**: $a + 8d = 22$

Step 2: Solve for a and d
$$(a + 8d) - (a + 4d) = 22 - 16$$
$$4d = 6$$
$$d = \frac{6}{4} = 1.5$$
$$Substituting\ d = 1.5\ into\ a + 4d = 16$$
$$a + 4(1.5) = 16$$
$$a + 6 = 16$$

$$a = 10$$

Step 3: Find the 7th Term Using:

$$a_7 = a + (7 - 1)d$$
$$a_7 = 10 + 6(1.5)$$
$$a_7 = 10 + 9$$
$$a_7 = 19 \dots Ans.$$

Question

The sum of all even natural numbers between 1 and 81 is

(1) 3280
(2) 3321
(3) 1646
(4) 1640

Explanations
Answer: (4) 1640

Step 1: Identify the Even Numbers
The **even natural numbers** between **1 and 81** are:

$$2,4,6, \dots ,80$$

This forms an **Arithmetic Progression (AP)** with:
- **First term** (a) = 2
- **Last term** (l) = 80
- **Common difference** (d) = 2

Step 2: Find the Number of Terms (n)
Using the nth term formula of an AP:

$$l = a + (n - 1)d$$
$$80 = 2 + (n - 1) \times 2$$
$$80 - 2 = (n - 1) \times 2$$
$$78 = 2(n - 1)$$
$$n - 1 = \frac{78}{2} = 39$$
$$n = 40$$

Step 3: Use the Sum Formula
The sum of an AP is given by:

$$Sn = \frac{n}{2} \times (a + l)$$

Substituting the values:

$$S40 = \frac{40}{2} \times (2 + 80)$$
$$= 20 \times 82$$
$$= 1640 \dots Ans.$$

Exponents

An **exponent** tells us how many times a number (called the **base**) is multiplied by itself. It is written as:

$$a^n$$

where:

- o   **a** = **Base** (the number being multiplied)
- o   **n** = **Exponent** or **Power** (how many times to multiply)

Example: $2^3 = 2 \times 2 \times 2 = 8$

Understanding Exponent Notation:

Expression	Expanded Form	Value
3^2	3×3	9
5^3	5×5×5	125
7^1	7	7
4^0	1 (Any number to the power of 0 is 1)	1

Important Exponent Rules

Rule 1: Multiplication Rule

$$a^m \times a^n = a^{m+n}$$

Example: $2^3 \times 2^4 = 2^{3+4} = 2^7 = 128$

Rule 2: Division Rule

$$\frac{a^m}{a^n} = a^{m-n}$$

Example: $\frac{5^6}{5^2} = 5^{6-2} = 5^4 = 625$

Rule 3: Power of a Power Rule

$$(a^m)^n = a^{m \times n}$$

Example: $(3^2)^4 = 3^{2 \times 4} = 3^8 = 6561$

Rule 4: Zero Exponent Rule

$$a^0 = 1$$

Example: $7^0 = 1$ *And* $100^0 = 1$

Rule 5: Negative Exponent Rule

$$a^{-n} = \frac{1}{a^n}n$$

Example: $5^{-2} = \frac{1}{5^2} = \frac{1}{25}$

Rule 6: Fractional Exponents Rule:

$$a^{\frac{1}{n}} = \sqrt[n]{a}$$

Example:

$$16^{\frac{1}{2}} = \sqrt{16} = 4$$
$$a^{\frac{1}{2}} = \sqrt{a}$$

Special Cases

- o Any number raised to power 1 is the number itself: $a^1 = a$
- o Any number raised to power 0 is always **1**: $a^0 = 1$
- o Negative exponents represent reciprocals: $3^{-2} = \frac{1}{3^2} = \frac{1}{9}$

Quick Concept Check 2: Exponents

1. **Simplify:** $4^3 =?$

2. **Evaluate:** $\frac{9^5}{9^3}=?$

3. **What is** $10^0?$

4. **Find the value:** $(2^3)^2=?$

5. **Convert to fraction:** $5^{-3}=?$

CHAPTER 2

Fraction, Ratio and Average

Fraction:

A fraction is a part of a whole unit or quantity. It consists of two parts:

- o **Numerator:** The top half of a fraction represents the number of parts you have. $\frac{3}{5}$ here, 3 is the Numerator.
- o **Denominator:** The bottom of a fraction represents the number into which the whole object is divided. $\frac{3}{5}$ here, 5 is the Denominator.

Important keys to remember:

- o A fraction represents one or more equal parts of a whole.
- o The number above the line in a fraction is called the Numerator.
- o The number below the line is called the Denominator of the fraction.
- o When a fraction's Numerator and Denominator are equal, the fraction equals 1.
- o Fractions that have the same Denominator are said to have a Common Denominator.

Example: $\frac{5}{10}$, where 5 is the Numerator, and 10 is the Denominator.

Question: Kavita has decided to buy a new Dress. The Brand she chose costs around INR 450 but is due to go on sale at two-thirds (2/3) of the price. If Kavita waits for the sale, how much will she save?

Solution: To determine the sale price, we must first calculate $\frac{2}{3}$ of 450. For that we need to multiply the whole number by the Numerator, and then we must divide the result by the Denominator:

$$\frac{2}{3}450 = \frac{900}{3} = 300$$

The sale price would be INR 300, so we can subtract that from the original cost to calculate the savings:

$$450 - 300 = 150$$

Therefore, Kavita would save INR 150.

Question: Mohan had 120 teddy bears in his retail store. He sold $\frac{2}{3}$ of them at Rs 12 each. How much did he receive?

Solution: Find the number of teddy bears sold.

$$\frac{2}{3}120 = \frac{240}{3} = 80$$

He sold 80 teddy bears.
Find how much money he received.

$$80 \times 12 = 960$$

He received Rs 960.

Types of Fractions:

Fractions are classified into the following types:

I. Proper Fractions:

- When **Numerator is smaller than the Denominator, it** is called a proper fraction.
- **Example:** $\frac{3}{5}$

II. Improper Fraction:

- When the Numerator is larger than the Denominator, it is called an improper fraction.
- **Example:** $\frac{5}{3}$

III. Mixed Fractions:

- o A fraction comprising a natural number and a proper fraction is called a mixed fraction.
- o **Example:** $2\frac{2}{5}$

IV. Equivalent Fractions:

- o Fractions equal to the same value are called equivalent fractions upon simplification.
- o **Example:** $\frac{1}{2}$ and $\frac{50}{100}$ are equal to 0.5. Hence, these are equivalent fractions.

V. Like Fractions

- o The fractions with the same denominators are called like fractions.
- o **Example:** $\frac{1}{5}, \frac{2}{5}, \frac{3}{5}$, and $\frac{4}{5}$ are like fractions.
- o Now, let's simplify them if we are adding the fractions

$$\frac{1}{5} + \frac{2}{5} + \frac{3}{5} + \frac{4}{5} = \frac{1+2+3+4}{5} = \frac{10}{5} = 2$$

VI. Unlike Fractions

- o The fractions which have different denominators are called unlike fractions.
- o **Example:** $\frac{2}{3}$ and $\frac{1}{4}$ are unlike fractions.
- o The simplification of unlike fractions is not as straightforward as that of like fractions.
- o To add the two unlike fractions, we need to follow a few steps:
    - o To calculate the LCM of the two denominators 3 and 4.
    - o LCM of 3 & 4 = 12.
    - o This LCM will be the Denominator of both fractions.
    - o Calculate the equivalent value of the first fraction $\left(\frac{2}{3}\right)$.
        - To do this, divide the LCM calculated in the previous step (12) by the Denominator of the first fraction (3).
        - So, 12 ÷ 3 = 4. Now, multiply 4 by the Numerator (2), which gives 8.

- Therefore, the first fraction becomes $\frac{8}{12}$.
  - Likewise, calculate the equivalent value of the second fraction $\frac{1}{4}$.
    - To do this, divide the LCM calculated in the first step (12) by the second fraction's Denominator (4).
    - So, $12 \div 4 = 3$. Now, multiply the Numerator and the denominator by 3.
    - Therefore, the second fraction becomes 3/12. Now, both the fractions have the same Numerator, i.e. 12.
  - Add the two like fractions, as shown in the previous section.

So,

$$\left(\frac{8}{12}\right) + \left(\frac{3}{12}\right) = \frac{8 + 3}{12} = \frac{11}{12}.$$
$$So, \left(\frac{2}{3}\right) + \left(\frac{1}{4}\right) = \frac{11}{12}.$$

When we solve the problem of fractions, we encounter questions like adding, subtracting, multiplying and dividing. Let's solve them one by one. But first let's learn how to convert these fractions.

Converting Fractions

Converting Improper Fractions to Mixed Fractions

- **Divide** the numerator by the denominator.
- **Write the quotient** as the whole number.
- **Write the remainder** as the new numerator over the denominator.

Example:

$$\frac{9}{4} = 2\frac{1}{4}$$

(Divide 9 by 4: **Quotient = 2, Remainder = 1**)

Converting Mixed Fractions to Improper Fractions

- **Multiply** the whole number by the denominator.
- **Add** the numerator.
- **Write the sum** over the original denominator.

Example:

$$3\frac{2}{5} = \frac{(3 \times 5) + 2}{5} = \frac{15 + 2}{5} = \frac{17}{5}$$

Concept Check 3: Converting Fractions

1. Identify the type of fraction: $\frac{5}{7}, \frac{11}{6}, 3\frac{4}{9}$
2. Convert $\frac{13}{5}$ into a mixed fraction.
3. Convert $4\frac{2}{7}$ into an improper fraction.
4. If you eat $\frac{4}{9}$ of a cake, how much is left?

Fundamental Operations on Fractions

Simplifying Fractions

A fraction is **simplified** when the numerator and denominator have no common factors except **1**.

Steps to Simplify a Fraction:
1. Find the **Greatest Common Divisor (GCD)** of the numerator and the denominator.
2. Divide **both** by their **GCD**.

Example:

$$\frac{12}{18} = \frac{12 \div 6}{18 \div 6} = \frac{2}{3}$$

(GCD of 12 and 18 is 6)

Addition & Subtraction of Fractions

I. Adding Fraction:

Case 1: Fractions with the Same Denominator:

$$\frac{a}{c} + \frac{b}{c} = \frac{a + b}{c}$$

Example:

$$\frac{3}{8} + \frac{5}{8} = \frac{3+5}{8} = \frac{8}{8} = 1$$

Case 2: Fractions with Different Denominators
- o Find the Least Common Multiple (LCM) of the denominators.
- o Convert the fractions to have the same denominator.
- o Add or subtract the numerators.

How to Find LCM (Least Common Multiple)

The **Least Common Multiple (LCM)** of two or more numbers is the **smallest number that is divisible by all the given numbers.**

Methods to Find LCM
There are **three main methods** to find the LCM of numbers:
1. **Listing Multiples Method** (For small numbers)
2. **Prime Factorization Method** (For medium-sized numbers)
3. **Division Method** (For large numbers)

---

1. Listing Multiples Method
This method works best for **small numbers**.

Steps:
1. Write the **multiples** of each number.
2. Find the **smallest common multiple**.

Example: Find LCM (4, 6)
- o Multiples of 4: 4, 8, 12, 16, 20, 24, ...
- o Multiples of 6: 6, 12, 18, 24, 30, ...

Smallest common multiple = 12
LCM (4, 6) = 12

---

2. Prime Factorization Method
This method works well for **medium-sized numbers**.

Steps:
1. Find the **prime factors** of each number.
2. Take the **highest power** of each prime factor.
3. Multiply them to get the **LCM**.

Example: Find LCM (12, 18)
1. **Prime factors:**
   - o $12 = 2^2 \times 3^1$
   - o $18 = 2^1 \times 3^2$

2. **Take the highest power of each prime:**
   - Highest power of $2 = 2^2$
   - Highest power of $3 = 3^2$
3. **Multiply them together:**
$$LCM = 2^2 \times 3^2 = 4 \times 9 = 36$$

LCM (12, 18) = 36

3. Division Method (Ladder Method)

This method works best for **large numbers**.
Steps:

1. Write the numbers in a **row**.
2. Divide by **smallest prime numbers (2,3,5,7,...)** until all become **1.**
3. Multiply the **divisors** to get the **LCM**.

Example: Find LCM (24, 36, 48)

Prime Number	24	36	48
2	12	18	24
2	6	9	12
2	3	9	6
3	1	3	2
2	1	1	1

Multiply the divisors:
$$2\times2\times2\times3\times2=144$$

LCM (24, 36, 48) = 144

Example:
$$\frac{1}{4}+\frac{1}{6}$$

LCM of 4 and 6 = 12
Convert fractions:
$$\frac{1}{4}=\frac{3}{12}, \frac{1}{6}=\frac{2}{12}$$

Now add
$$\frac{3}{12}+\frac{2}{12}=\frac{5}{12}$$

Question: $\frac{2}{3} + \frac{3}{4}$ **(Adding two fractions with two different Denominators)**

Solution:

- o Multiply Denominators: $3 \times 4 = 12$
- o Cross Multiplication. $(2 \times 4) + (3 \times 3) = 8 + 9$
- o Sum of fractions is $\dfrac{8+9}{12} = \dfrac{17}{12}$
- o Therefore, our final fraction after adding is $\dfrac{17}{12}$.

Question: $\frac{1}{2} + \frac{2}{3} + \frac{3}{4}$ **(Adding three fractions with different Denominators)**

Solution:

- o **Step 1:** Find the LCM of denominators.
  - It is 12 here.
- o **Step 2:** Divide the LCM by the Denominator of each number to be added, which is are:

  - $\dfrac{12}{2} = 6$ is quotient 1

  - $\dfrac{12}{3} = 4$ is quotient 2

  - $\dfrac{12}{4} = 3$ is quotient 3

- o **Step 3:** Multiply the Numerator with the quotient (found in the above step). Which numerators are 1, 2, and 3, so multiply these with respective quotients.
  - $1\times6 = 6$
  - $2\times4 = 8$
  - $3\times3 = 9$
- o **Step 4:** Add the numerators we get after multiplying with quotients like simple addition.
  - $6 + 8 + 9 = 23$ which is the numerator.
- o **Step 5:** The Denominator will be the LCM.
  - Answer is 23/12

II. Subtracting Fraction:

Case 1: Fractions with the Same Denominator

$$\frac{a}{c} - \frac{b}{c} = \frac{a-b}{c}$$

Question: $\frac{9}{12} - \frac{7}{12}$.

Solution: Here, the denominator values are the same and keep the value as it is.

$$\frac{9}{12} - \frac{7}{12} = \frac{9-7}{12} = \frac{2}{12}$$

Simplify the fraction, and we get

$$\frac{2}{12} = \frac{1}{6} \dots Ans.$$

Case 2: Fractions with Different Denominators

Question:

$$\frac{3}{5} - \frac{2}{3}.$$

Solution:
- o   The LCM of 5 and 3 is 15.
- o   To make the denominators equal, convert the denominators to the LCM value.
- o   Thus,

$$\left(\frac{3}{5}\right) - \left(\frac{2}{3}\right) = \left(\frac{9}{15}\right) - \left(\frac{10}{15}\right)$$
$$\frac{(9-10)}{15} = \frac{1}{15} \dots Ans.$$

III. Multiplying Fractions:

There are three simple steps to multiply fractions

$$\frac{a}{b} \times \frac{c}{d} = \frac{a \times c}{b \times d}$$

1. Multiply the top numbers (the *numerators*).
2. Multiply the bottom numbers (the *denominators*).
3. Simplify the fraction if needed.

Example:

$$\frac{2}{5} \times \frac{3}{4} = \frac{2 \times 3}{5 \times 4} = \frac{6}{20} = \frac{3}{10} \ \ldots \text{Ans.}$$

Question:

$$\frac{1}{2} \times \frac{2}{5}$$

Solution:

Multiply the numerators:

Multiply the denominators:

$$\frac{1}{2} \times \frac{2}{5} = \frac{1 \times 2}{2 \times 5} = \frac{2}{10}$$

Simplify the fraction:

$$\frac{2}{10} = \frac{1}{5}$$

Question:

$$\frac{1}{4} \times \frac{2}{5} \times \frac{1}{8}.$$

Solution:

- In this, first multiply all the numerators: $1 \times 2 \times 1 = 2$
- Similarly, multiply all the denominators: $4 \times 5 \times 8 = 160$
- Now, the product of the three fractions will be $\frac{2}{160}$.
- Simplifying the fraction, we get $\frac{1}{80}$

IV. Division of Fractions:

$$\frac{a}{b} \div \frac{c}{d} = \frac{a}{b} \times \frac{d}{c}$$

For dividing by a fraction, multiply by its reciprocal.

There are 3 Simple Steps to Divide Fractions:

- o Turn the second fraction *(the one you want to divide by)* upside down (this is now the reciprocal).
- o Multiply the first fraction by that reciprocal.
- o Simplify the fraction (if needed)

Example

$$\frac{1}{2} \div \frac{1}{6}$$

Solution:

- o Turn the second fraction upside down (it becomes the **reciprocal**):
  - $\frac{1}{6}$ becomes $\frac{6}{1}$
- o Multiply the first fraction by that **reciprocal**:

$$\frac{1}{2} \times \frac{6}{1} = \frac{1 \times 6}{2 \times 1} = \frac{6}{2}$$

  - Simplifying the fraction:

$$\frac{6}{2} = 3$$

Question:

$$\frac{3}{5} \div \frac{2}{7} = \frac{3}{5} \times \frac{7}{2} = \frac{3 \times 7}{5 \times 2} = \frac{21}{10}$$

Concept Check 4: Operation on Fractions

1. Simplify: $\frac{16}{24}$

2. Solve: $\frac{5}{8} + \frac{3}{4}$

3. Multiply: $\frac{3}{5} \times \frac{4}{7}$

4. Divide: $\frac{7}{9} \div \frac{2}{3}$

5. Subtract: $\frac{9}{10} - \frac{3}{5}$

Advanced Concepts of Fractions

Complex Fractions

A **complex fraction** is a fraction in which the numerator, the denominator, or both contain another fraction.

How to Simplify a Complex Fraction:

1. To divide a fraction by another fraction.
2. **Multiply by the reciprocal** of the denominator. Then
3. **Simplify the resulting fraction**.

$$\frac{\frac{a}{b}}{\frac{c}{d}} = \frac{a}{b} \times \frac{d}{c}$$

Example:

$$\frac{\left(\frac{3}{4}\right)}{\left(\frac{5}{6}\right)}$$

Step 1: Convert to multiplication by reciprocal:

$$\frac{3}{4} \times \frac{6}{5} = \frac{18}{20} = \frac{9}{10}$$

Final Answer: $\frac{9}{10}$

Fractions & Decimals

Fractions can be converted into **decimals** and vice versa.

For Converting Fractions to Decimals:
1. Divide the numerator by the denominator.
2. If necessary, round to the required decimal places.

Example:

$$\frac{3}{4} = 3 \div 4 = 0.75$$

Converting Decimals to Fractions:
1. Identify the **place value** of the decimal.
2. Write the number as a fraction over **10, 100, 1000,** etc.

3. **Simplify the fraction**.

Example:

$$0.125 = \frac{125}{1000} = \frac{1}{8}$$

Comparing & Ordering Fractions:

To compare fractions:
1. Convert to **common denominators** using LCM.
2. Convert into **decimals** and compare.

Example:
Arrange in Ascending Order:

$$\frac{2}{5}, \frac{3}{7}, \frac{4}{9}$$

By making fractions with same denominators:

$$\frac{2}{5} = \frac{2 \times 63}{5 \times 63} = \frac{126}{315}$$
$$\frac{3}{7} = \frac{3 \times 45}{7 \times 45} = \frac{135}{315}$$
$$\frac{4}{9} = \frac{4 \times 35}{9 \times 35} = \frac{140}{315}$$
$$\frac{126}{315} < \frac{135}{315} < \frac{140}{315}$$

Answer:

$$\frac{2}{5} < \frac{3}{7} < \frac{4}{9}$$

Percentage, Ratio & Fractions:

Fractions are closely related to **percentages** and **ratios**.

Converting Fractions to Percentages:

$$Percentage = \left(\frac{Fraction}{Denominator}\right) \times 100$$

Example:

$$\frac{3}{4} \times 100 = 75\%, \qquad \frac{1}{2} \times 100 = 50\%$$

Ratios & Fractions:
1. A **ratio** represents a relationship between two numbers.
2. Ratios can be **expressed as fractions**.

Example: Convert 3:5 into a fraction

$$\frac{3}{5}$$

Concept Check 5: Advance Concepts of Fractions

- **Simplify the complex fraction:**

$$\frac{\frac{5}{6}}{\frac{2}{3}}$$

- **Convert to decimal:**

$$\frac{7}{8}$$

- **Convert to fraction:** 0.375.

- **Arrange in ascending order:**

$$\frac{5}{9}, \frac{2}{3}, \frac{7}{12}$$

- **Find the percentage:**

$$\frac{4}{5}$$

- **Convert to a fraction:** Ratio 7:9.

Word Problems & Real-Life Applications of Fractions:

Word Problems on Fractions

Fractions are commonly used in real-life scenarios such as **sharing, distances, money, and measurements**.

Common Steps to Solve Fraction Word Problems
1. **Identify the fraction given** in the problem.

2. **Determine the operation** (addition, subtraction, multiplication, or division).
3. **Convert to a common denominator** if necessary.
4. **Solve step by step and simplify** to get the final answer.

Example 1: Sharing a Cake

A cake is divided into **8 equal parts**. If **Sarah eats $\frac{3}{8}$ of the cake,** how much is left?

Solution:

$$Remaining\ Cake = 1 - \frac{3}{8} = \frac{8}{8} - \frac{3}{8} = \frac{8-3}{8} = \frac{5}{8}$$

Final Answer:

$$\frac{5}{8}\ of\ the\ cake\ is\ left$$

Example 2: Distance Covered by a Car:

A car travels $\frac{3}{5}$ of a journey in the morning and $\frac{1}{5}$ in the afternoon. What fraction of the journey is still left?

Solution:

$$\textbf{Total Distence Coverd} = \frac{3}{5} + \frac{1}{5} = \frac{4}{5}$$

$$Remaining\ Distance = 1 - \frac{4}{5} = \frac{1}{5}$$

$$Final\ Answer\ \frac{1}{5}\ of\ the\ journey\ is\ left.$$

Real-Life Applications of Fractions

Fractions are used in various real-world scenarios, including:

1. Cooking Measurements

- Recipes often require fractions, such as $\frac{1}{2}$ cup of sugar or $\frac{3}{4}$ teaspoon of salt.
- Doubling a recipe requires multiplying fractions.

Example:

If a recipe calls for $\frac{2}{3}$ **cup of flour,** how much is needed for **double the recipe**?

Solution:

$$\frac{2}{3} \times 2 = \frac{4}{3} = 1\frac{1}{3}$$

$$Final\ Answer: 1\frac{1}{3}$$

2. Time Calculations

- o   A day is divided into **fractions of 24 hours**.
- o   Half an hour $= \frac{1}{2}$ hour, Quarter-hour $= \frac{1}{4}$ hour.

Example:

A TV show is $\frac{3}{4}$ of an hour long. If it starts at **6:30 PM**, when will it end?

Solution:

$$\frac{3}{4} of\ an\ hour = \frac{3}{4} \times 60 = \frac{180}{4} = 44\ minutes$$

$$6:30 + \frac{3}{4} hour = 6:30 + 45 = 7:15\ PM$$

3. Finance & Discounts

- o   Discounts and tax calculations involve fractions.
- o   **Example:** A store offers $\frac{1}{4}$ **(25%)** **discount** on a Rs. 400 item.

Solution:

$$\frac{1}{4} \times 400 = 100$$

Final Answer: The discount is **Rs. 100**, so the final price is **Rs. 300**.

4. Fractions in Sports & Statistics

- o   A cricket player scoring $\frac{3}{5}$ **of the team's runs.**
- o   A basketball player making $\frac{7}{10}$ of free throws.

Example: A basketball player makes $\frac{4}{5}$ of her free throws. If she attempts **20** shots, how many does she make?

Solution:

$$\frac{4}{5} \times 20 = 16$$

Final Answer: The player makes **16 free throws.**

Concept Check 6: Word Problem

1.   A store gives a $\frac{2}{5}$ discount on a Rs. 500 item. Find the discount amount.

2. A train travels $\frac{2}{3}$ of a 300 km journey. How much distance is left?

3. A bottle holds $\frac{3}{4}$ of a liter of juice. How many liters are in 4 bottles?

4. If a student completes $\frac{5}{8}$ of an exam in 40 minutes, how long will the full exam take?

5. A movie is $\frac{5}{6}$ of 2 hours long. Find the duration in minutes.

Advanced Problem-Solving Techniques in Fractions

Solving Fractional Equations

Fractional equations involve **fractions** with variables, requiring techniques such as **cross multiplication, LCM, and clearing fractions**.

Steps to Solve a Fractional Equation
1. **Identify the denominators** and find the **LCM**.
2. **Multiply both sides by the LCM** to eliminate fractions.
3. **Solve for the variable** using basic algebra.

Example 1: Solve

$$\frac{x}{3} + 5 = \frac{7}{2}$$

Solution:
1. Find **LCM of 3 and 2**, which is **6**.
2. Multiply both sides by **6**

$$6 \times \left(\frac{x}{3} + 5\right) = 6 \times \frac{7}{2}$$

3. Distribute

$$2x + 30 = 21$$
$$2x = 21 - 30$$
$$2x = -9$$
$$x = \frac{-9}{2}$$

$$\textit{Final Answer } x = -\frac{9}{2}$$

Fractions in Algebra

Fractions appear in algebraic expressions and equations. The key techniques include **factoring, simplifying, and rationalizing denominators.**

Example 2: Simplify

$$\frac{x + 2}{x - 1} + \frac{x - 3}{x + 1}$$

Solution:

1. Find **LCM of denominators**: (x–1) (x+1).
2. Convert fractions to a common denominator

$$\frac{(x + 2)(x + 1) + (x - 3)(x - 1)}{(x - 1)(x + 1)}$$

$$\frac{x^2 + x + 2x + 2 + x^2 - x - 3x + 3}{(x - 1)(x + 1)}$$

$$\frac{x^2 + 3x + 2 + x^2 - 4x + 3}{(x - 1)(x + 1)}$$

$$\frac{2x^2 - x + 5}{(x - 1)(x + 1)}$$

Data Interpretation with Fractions

Fractions are often used in **data interpretation**, such as **pie charts, bar graphs, and percentage-based problems.**

Example 3: A survey of **500 people** shows that $\frac{2}{5}$ prefer tea, and $\frac{3}{10}$ prefer coffee. How many people prefer neither?

Solution:

1. **Find tea drinkers**

$$\frac{2}{5} \times 500 = 200$$

2. **Find coffee drinkers**:

$$\frac{3}{10} \times 500 = 150$$

3. Find those who prefer neither:

$$500 - (200 + 150) = 150$$

Final Answer: 150 people prefer neither

Concept Check 7: Problem Solving Techniques

1. Solve:

$$\frac{3x}{5} - 2 = \frac{x}{2}$$

2. Simplify:

$$\frac{x^2 - 4}{x + 2}$$

3. Interpret:

$$if \; \frac{3}{8} \; of \; a \; pie \; is \; eaten, what \; fraction \; remains?$$

4. Solve:

$$x: \frac{x + 1}{(x - 2)} = \frac{5}{3}$$

5. Find the total:

$$if \; \frac{1}{4} \; of \; a \; class \; prefers \; basketball \; and \; \frac{1}{3} \; prefers \; football.$$
$$What \; fraction \; prefers \; neither$$

Tips to Form Equations from Word Problems

Forming equations from word problems requires **understanding the relationship between quantities and translating them into mathematical expressions**. Follow these structured steps to form equations easily.

Step 1: Identify the Unknown (Define the Variable)
- o   Determine **what you are trying to find**.
- o   Assign a **variable** (usually x, y, or another letter) to the unknown quantity.

Example:
"A number increased by 7 equals 25. Find the number."
- o   Let the number be **x**.
- o   The equation is: x+7=25
- o $\therefore x = 25 - 7 = 18 \ldots Ans.$

Step 2: Identify Keywords and Mathematical Operations

Word/Phrase	Mathematical Operation
Sum, increased by, more than, added to	Addition (+)
Difference, decreased by, less than, minus	Subtraction (-)
Product, times, of, multiplied by	Multiplication (×)
Quotient, divided by, per, ratio of	Division (÷)
Is, equals, results in, gives	Equal sign (=)

Example:
"The sum of twice a number and 5 is 19."

- o   Let the number be **x**.
- o   **"Twice a number"** → 2x.
- o   **"Sum of twice a number and 5"** → 2x+5.
- o   **"Is 19"** → Equals 19.

$$2x + 5 = 19$$

Step 3: Convert Word Statements into Equations

Example 1: Age Problem
"A father is 3 times as old as his son. After 5 years, the sum of their ages will be 50. Find the son's current age."

1. **Let the son's age be x.**
2. **Father's current age** = 3x.
3. **After 5 years**, the son's age $x + 5$, $father's\ age = 3x + 5$
4. **Sum of their ages in 5 years** = 50

$$(x + 5) + (3x + 5) = 50$$
$$x + 5 + 3x + 5 = 50$$
$$4x + 10 = 50$$
$$4x = 40$$
$$x = \frac{40}{4} = 10 \dots Ans.$$

Son's current age =10.

Example 2: Money Problem
"A shopkeeper sold 3 pens and 4 pencils for Rs. 100. He also sold 4 pens and 3 pencils for Rs. 110. Find the price of each pen and pencil."

1. **Let the price of a pen be x, and a pencil be y**.
2. First equation (for 3 pens, 4 pencils): 3x+4y=100
3. Second equation (for 4 pens, 3 pencils): 4x+3y=110

We have the system of equations:

$$3x + 4y = 100 - (Equation\ 1)$$
$$4x + 3y = 110 - (Equation\ 2)$$

Multiply Equation (1) by 4 and Equation (2) by 3 to align coefficients:

$$(3x + 4y) \times 4 = 400$$

$$(4x + 3y) \times 3 = 330$$
$$12x + 16y = 400$$
$$12x + 9y = 330$$

Subtract the second equation from the first:
$$(12x + 16y) - (12x + 9y) = 400 - 330$$
$$7y = 70$$
$$y = 10$$

Step 4: Substitute y=10y = 10y=10 into Equation (1):
$$3x + 4(10) = 100$$
$$3x + 40 = 100$$
$$3x = 60$$
$$x = 20$$

Price of one pen = Rs. 20
Price of one pencil = Rs. 10

Example 3: Work/Time Problem
"A worker completes a task in 6 hours. Another worker does the same task in 8 hours. How long will they take together?"

1. **Work done by the first worker per hour** $= \frac{1}{6}$

2. **Work done by the second worker per hour** $= \frac{1}{8}$.

3. **Total work done together in x hours:**
$$\frac{x}{6} + \frac{x}{8} = 1$$

Step 4: Solve the Equation
- **Isolate the variable** (using addition, subtraction, multiplication, or division).
- **Use LCM** if there are fractions.
- **Check your answer** by substituting it back into the problem.

Example:
Solve:
$$2x + 5 = 19$$
$$2x = 19 - 5$$
$$2x = 14$$
$$x = \frac{14}{2}$$
$$x = 7$$

Concept Check 8: Equations

1. A number is tripled and then reduced by 7 to give 20. Find the number.
2. The sum of two numbers is 45, and their difference is 15. Find the numbers.
3. A father's age is twice his son's age. After 5 years, their total age will be 80. Find the son's age.
4. A shopkeeper sells 5 apples and 3 bananas for Rs. 120. He also sells 3 apples and 5 bananas for Rs. 100. Find the price of an apple and a banana.
5. Two pipes fill a tank in 4 hours and 6 hours respectively. How long will they take to fill the tank together?

UGC NET PYQ Questions and Explanations on Fraction

Question

Two-fifth of the students at a school go to school by bus, One-fourth by car and the remaining walk down to school. One-third of those who walk to school are not accompanied by anyone, the rest are escorted by their parents. If 224 students walk to school on their own, what is the total number of students in the school?

1. 640
2. 970
3. 1290
4. 1920

Explanations
Answer: 4. 1920

Step 1: Define Variables
Let the total number of students be x.

- Students who go by bus $= \frac{2}{5} \times x$
- Students who go by car $= \frac{1}{4} \times x$
- Remaining students walk =

$$x - \left(\frac{2}{5} \times x + \frac{1}{4} \times x\right)$$

Step 2: Find the Students Who Walk

Find the LCM of 5 and 4, which is 20, then express fractions:

$$\frac{2}{5} = \frac{8}{20}, \quad \frac{1}{4} = \frac{5}{20}$$

$$\frac{8}{20}x + \frac{5}{20}x = \frac{13}{20}x$$

$$Students\ who\ walk = x - \frac{13}{20}x = \frac{7}{20}x$$

Step 3: Find Students Who Walk Alone

- **One-third of the walkers walk alone:**

$$\frac{1}{3} \times \frac{7}{20}x = \frac{7}{60}x$$

- We are given that 224 students walk alone:

$$\frac{7}{60}x = 224$$

Step 4: Solve for x

Multiply both sides by $\frac{60}{7}$:

$$x = \frac{224 \times 60}{7}$$

$$x = \frac{13440}{7} = 1920$$

Final Answer: 1920 students.

Question

Which of the following expressions has the value equal to 1 (one)?

1. $\dfrac{(0.011)^2 \cdot}{(1.1)^2 \times (0.01)^2}$

2. $\dfrac{(0.11)^2}{(1.1)^2 \times 0.1}$

3. $\dfrac{(1.1)^2}{(11)^2 \times (0.01)^2}$

4. $\dfrac{(0.11)^2}{(11)^2 \times (0.01)^2}$

Explanations

Answer: 1. $\dfrac{(0.011)^2}{(1.1)^2 \times (0.01)^2}$

Compute Each Term:

$$(0.011)^2 = 0.000121$$
$$(1.1)^2 = 1.21$$
$$(0.01)^2 = 0.0001$$
$$(1.1)^2 \times (0.01)^2$$
$$1.21 \times 0.0001 = 0.000121$$

Compute the Final Value:

$$\frac{0.000121}{0.000121} = 1$$

Question

Arrange the following fraction in decreasing order:

A. $\dfrac{12}{19}$

B. $\dfrac{7}{12}$

C. $\dfrac{11}{17}$

D. $\dfrac{17}{28}$

1. ABCD
2. CADB
3. BCDA
4. DABC

Explanations

Answer: CADB

$$A. \frac{12}{19} = 0.6316$$

$$B. \frac{7}{12} = 0.5833$$

$$C. \frac{11}{17} = 0.6471$$

$$D. \frac{17}{28} = 0.6071$$

Now, sorting them in **decreasing order**:

$$\frac{11}{17}(C) > \frac{12}{19}(A) > \frac{17}{28}(D) > \frac{1}{12}(B)$$

Final Order: 2. CADB

Question

If a fraction is multiplied by itself and then divided by the reciprocal of the same fraction; the result obtained is $49\frac{8}{27}$ Find the fraction.

1. $3\frac{2}{3}$

2. $1\frac{1}{3}$

3. $2\frac{2}{3}$

4. $4\frac{1}{3}$

Explanations
Answer:
Let the fraction be x.
Step 1: Form the Equation

The given condition states:

$$\frac{x \times x}{\frac{1}{x}} = 49\frac{8}{27}$$

$$\text{Convert } 49\frac{8}{27} \text{ to an improper Fraction}$$

$$49\frac{8}{27} = \frac{(49 \times 27) + 8}{27} = \frac{1331}{27}$$

Thus, the equation becomes:

$$\frac{x^2}{\frac{1}{x}} = \frac{1331}{27}$$

Since **dividing by the reciprocal** is the same as **multiplying:**

$$x^2 \times x\frac{1331}{27}$$

$$x^3 = \frac{1331}{27}$$

Solve for x

$$x = \frac{\sqrt[3]{1331}}{\sqrt[3]{27}}$$

Since:

$$\sqrt[3]{1331} = 11$$
$$\sqrt[3]{27} = 3$$
$$x = \frac{11}{3}$$

$$Convert \; \frac{11}{3} \; to \; a \; mixed \; Fraction$$

$$\frac{11}{3} = 3 \times \frac{2}{3} = 3\frac{2}{3}$$

Final Answer: $3\frac{2}{3}$

Question

Arrange the following fractions in increasing order-

$$A.\frac{7}{11} \quad B.\frac{11}{17} \quad C.\frac{9}{13} \quad D.\frac{13}{21}$$

1. A, B, C, D
2. A, D, B, C
3. D, A, B, C
4. B, D, C, A

Explanations

Answer: (3) D, A, B, C

$$A.\frac{7}{11} = 0.6364$$
$$B.\frac{11}{17} = 0.6471$$
$$C.\frac{9}{13} = 0.6923$$
$$D.\frac{13}{21} = 0.6190$$

Now, sorting them in **increasing order**:

$$\frac{13}{21}(D) < \frac{7}{11}(A) < \frac{11}{17}(B) < \frac{9}{13}(C)$$

Correct Option: (3) D, A, B, C

Question

Rs 3080 is divided among A, B and C so that half of A's part, one third of B's part and one sixth of C's part are equal. Then B's part is

1. Rs 840
2. Rs 960
3. Rs 1080
4. Rs 720

Explanations

Answer: 1. Rs 840

We are given that:

$$\frac{1}{2}A = \frac{1}{3}B = \frac{1}{6}C = K$$

$$Where\ K\ is\ some\ constant$$
$$Express\ A, B, and\ C\ in\ terms\ of\ K$$
$$A = 2K, B = 3K, C = 6K$$
$$Use\ the\ given\ Total\ Amount = Rs\ 3080;$$
$$A + B + C = 3080$$
$$2K + 3K + 6K = 3080$$
$$11K = 3080$$
$$K = \frac{3080}{11} = 280$$
$$Find\ B's\ Share$$
$$B = 3K = 3 \times 280 = 840$$

Final Answer: Rs 840

Question

A student was asked to divide half of a number by 5 and the other half by 3 and then add the two quantities Instead of doing all this the student divides the given number by 4 which results into 5 short of the correct value.

What is the initial number?

1. 300
2. 400
3. 350
4. 450

Explanations

Answer: 1. 300

Define the Variable

Let the initial number be x.

- Half of the number $= \frac{x}{2}$
- First half divided by 5 $= \frac{x}{10}$
- Second half divided by 3 $= \frac{x}{6}$
- sum $= \frac{x}{10} + \frac{x}{6}$

The student instead **divided the full number by 4**, which resulted in a value **5 less than the correct value**:

$$\frac{x}{10} + \frac{x}{6} - \frac{x}{4} = 5$$

Find the LCM of $10, 6,$ *and* $4,$ *which is* $60.$

Multiply the entire equation by 60 *to eliminate fractions:*

$$\left(\frac{x}{10} \times 60\right) + \left(\frac{x}{6} \times 60\right) - \left(\frac{x}{4} \times 60\right) = 5 \times 60$$

$$6x + 10x - 15x = 300$$

$$x = 300$$

Final Answer: 300

Question

If the numerator and denominator of a fraction are increased by 7, then fraction becomes $\frac{2}{3}$. Find the original fraction.

$$1.\frac{4}{5} \qquad 2.\frac{3}{5} \qquad 3.\frac{3}{8} \qquad 4.\frac{5}{3}$$

Explanations

Answer: 3. $\frac{3}{8}$

Let the original fraction be:

$$\frac{x}{y}$$

According to the problem, when **7 is added to both the numerator and denominator**, the fraction becomes:

$$\frac{x + 7}{y + 7} = \frac{2}{3}$$

Cross multiplying:

$$3(x + 7) = 2(y + 7)$$

$$3x + 21 = 2y + 14$$

$$3x - 2y = -7$$

Since the answer must be one of

$$\frac{4}{5}, \frac{3}{5}, \frac{3}{8}, \frac{5}{3}$$

$$x = 3, and\ y = 8\ satisfy\ the\ equation.$$

$$Final\ Answer: \frac{3}{8}$$

Question

What shall be the value when 0.07 is divided by 3507

1. 0.0002
2. 0.002
3. 0.02
4. 0.00002

Explanations

Answer: 4. 0.00002

$$0.07 \div 3507$$
$$0.07 \div 3507 = 0.00001996$$
$$Round\ to\ 5\ Decimal\ Places = 0.00002$$

Question

Which of the following fractions is the smallest?

$$1.\frac{65}{80} \qquad 2.\frac{11}{16} \qquad 3.\frac{5}{8} \qquad 4.\frac{29}{40}$$

Explanations

Answer: 3. $\frac{5}{8}$

$$1.\frac{65}{80} = 0.8125 \quad 2.\frac{11}{16} = 0.6875 \quad 3.\frac{5}{8} = 0.625 \quad 4.\frac{29}{40} = 0.725$$

$$Smallest\ Fraction\ is\ 3.\frac{5}{8} = 0.625$$

Question

Match the column:

Question	Answer:
A. The sum of first forty-five natural number is.	I. 19

B. The least prime number is.	II. 75
C. The total number of prime numbers less than 70 is.	III. 1035
D. On dividing 4150 by a certain number the quotient is 55 and the remainder is 25. The divisor is	IV. 2

1. A-II B-III C-I D-IV
2. A-III B-II C-IV D-I
3. A-III B-IV C-I D-II
4. A-II B-IV C-III D-I

Explanations

Answer: 3. A-III B-IV C-I D-II

A. The sum of the first 45 natural numbers

Using the formula:

$$Sn = \frac{n(n+1)}{2}$$

$$Substituting\ n = 45$$

$$45 = \frac{45(45+1)}{2} = \frac{45 \times 46}{2} = 1035$$

$$A \rightarrow III = 1035$$

B. The least prime number: The smallest prime number is **2 (B → IV.2)**

C. The total number of prime numbers less than 70: Using the prime number list below 70:

$$2,3,5,7,11,13,17,19,23,29,31,37,41,43,47,53,59,61,67$$

Total 19 prime numbers.

D. Find the divisor: Using the division formula:

$$Dividend = Divisor \times Quotient + Remainder$$

$$4150 = D \times 55 + 25$$

$$D = \frac{4150 - 25}{55} = \frac{4125}{55} = 75$$

$$D \rightarrow II.75$$

Question

A rational number has its denominator greater than its numerator by 6. If the numerator is increased by 4 and the denominator is decreased by 8, the number becomes $\frac{5}{3}$. What is the original rational number?

$$1.\frac{11}{17} \qquad 2.\frac{5}{11} \qquad 3.\frac{7}{13} \qquad 4.\frac{13}{19}$$

Explanations

Answer: 1. $\frac{11}{17}$

Define Variables

Let:

Numerator $= x$

Denominator $= x+6$

(Since the denominator is **6 more** than the numerator)

After changing the values:

$$New\ numerator = x + 4$$
$$New\ denominator = (x + 6) - 8 = x - 2$$
$$The\ fraction\ becomes\ \frac{5}{3}$$
$$Form\ the\ Equation: \frac{x + 4}{x - 2} = \frac{5}{3}$$
$$Cross\ multiplying:$$
$$3(x + 4) = 5(x - 2)$$
$$3x + 12 = 5x - 10$$
$$12 + 10 = 5x - 3x$$
$$22 = 2x$$
$$x = 11 \ldots Ans.$$

Find the Denominator:

$$Denominator = x + 6 = 11 + 6 = 17$$
$$Answer: \frac{11}{17}$$

Question

Rohan gave three-fifth of the amount he had, to Sahil. Rohan now has 2000 rupees. How much did he give to Sahil?

1. 1200 rupees
2. 2000 rupees
3. 3000 rupees
4. 5000 rupees

Explanations

Answer: 3. 3000 rupees
Define Variables:

- Let Rohan's total amount be x
- He gave $\frac{3}{5}$ of his total amount to Sahil.
- He now has 2000 rupees left.

$$Form\ the\ Equation: x - \frac{3}{5}x = 2000$$

$$Factor\ out\ x:$$

$$\left(1 - \frac{3}{5}\right)x = 2000$$

$$\frac{2}{5}x = 2000$$

$$x = 2000 \times \frac{5}{2}$$

$$x = 5000$$

So, **Rohan originally had 5000 rupees**.
Find the Amount Given to Sahil

$$\frac{3}{5} \times 5000 = 3000$$

Final Answer: 3000 rupees

Question

Before death a man left the following instructions for his fortune: half to his wife; $\frac{1}{7}$ of what was left to his son; $\frac{2}{3}$ of what was left to his daughter; the man's pet dog got the remaining Rs 20000. How much money did the man leave behind altogether?

1. 140000
2. 100000
3. 40000
4. 70000

Explanations
Answer: 1. 140000
We need to determine the **total money** the man left behind, given:

- $\frac{1}{2}$ *of the money goes to his* **wife**.
- $\frac{1}{7}$ *of the* **remaining** *goes to his* **son**.
- $\frac{2}{3}$ *of the* **remaining** *goes to his* **daughter**.
- *The* **dog** *gets the* **remaining ₹20000**.

Step 1: Let Total Money be ₹X

- o Wife gets $\frac{1}{2}$ of **X**, so the remaining money after giving to the wife:

$$\frac{X}{2}$$

Step 2: Son's Share ($\frac{1}{7}$ of Remaining)

- o Son gets $\frac{1}{7}$ **of the remaining**:

$$Son's\ Share = \frac{1}{7} \times \frac{X}{2} = \frac{X}{14}$$

- o Money left after son's share:

$$\frac{X}{2} - \frac{X}{14} = \frac{7X}{14} - \frac{X}{14} = \frac{6X}{14} = \frac{3X}{7}$$

Step 3: Daughter's Share (2/3 of Remaining)

- o Daughter gets $\frac{2}{3}$ **of the remaining**:

$$Daughter's\ Share = \frac{2}{3} \times \frac{3X}{7} = \frac{6X}{21} = \frac{2X}{7}$$

- o Money left after daughter's share:

$$\frac{3X}{7} - \frac{2X}{7} = \frac{X}{7}$$

Step 4: The Dog's Share

- o The dog gets the **remaining ₹20000**, so:

$$\frac{X}{7} = 20000$$

Step 5: Solve for X

$$X = 20000 \times 7 = \textbf{140000} \dots \textbf{\textit{Ans.}}$$

Ratio

Introduction to Ratios

What is a Ratio?

A **ratio** is a way to compare two or more quantities. It tells us **how much of one quantity is related to another**.

Example:
A school has **40 boys** and **60 girls**. The ratio of boys to girls is:
$$40:60$$
To simplify, divide both numbers by **their Greatest Common Divisor (GCD = 20)**:

To find the Greatest Common Divisor (GCD) of 40 and 60:
1. **Find the factors:**
   - Factors of 40: **1, 2, 4, 5, 8, 10, 20, 40**
   - Factors of 60: **1, 2, 3, 4, 5, 6, 10, 12, 15, 20, 30, 60**
2. **Identify the highest common factor:** The common factors are **1, 2, 4, 5, 10, 20.**
   - The largest is **20**, so **GCD = 20.**

$$40:60 = \frac{40}{20}:\frac{60}{20} = 2:3$$

Final Ratio: 2:3 (For every 2 boys, there are 3 girls)

How to Write a Ratio?

Ratios can be written in **three different ways**:
1. Using a **colon** → **5:7**
2. As a **fraction** → $\frac{5}{7}$
3. Using the word **"to"** → **5 to 7**

Example: If a fruit basket contains **8 apples and 12 oranges**, the ratio of apples to oranges is:

$$8:12 = \frac{8}{12} = \frac{2}{3}$$

Final Ratio: 2:3

Types of Ratios

Type	Definition	Example
Simple Ratio	Compares two quantities	5:3 (Boys:Girls)
Compound Ratio	Compares three or more quantities	5:3:2 (Boys:Girls:Teachers)
Duplicate Ratio	The square of a given ratio	If 3:4, then 9:16
Triplicate Ratio	The cube of a given ratio	If 3:4, then 27:64
Sub-duplicate Ratio	The square root of a ratio	If 9:16, then 3:4
Sub-triplicate Ratio	The cube root of a ratio	If 27:64, then 3:4

Ratios in Real Life

Ratios are widely used in **daily life, business, and science**.
Examples:

- ➢ **Cooking Recipes** → A recipe calls for **3 cups of flour and 2 cups of sugar** → Ratio **3:2**.
- ➢ **Speed & Time** → If a car travels **240 km in 4 hours**, its speed ratio is **240:4 = 60:1** (60 km per hour).
- ➢ **Financial Planning** → The ratio of **savings to expenses** in a budget.

Equivalent Ratios

Equivalent ratios are **ratios that represent the same relationship**.
Example: Find two equivalent ratios of **4:5**

- • Multiply by 2 → (4×2):(5×2) = 8:10
- • Multiply by 3 → (4×3):(5×3) = 12:15

Equivalent Ratios: 8:10 and 12:15

Concept Check 9: Ratio

1. Write 24:36 in the simplest form.
2. Find two equivalent ratios of 6:8.
3. A store sells pens and pencils in the ratio 3:5. If there are 75 pencils, how many pens are there?
4. A team has 12 boys and 8 girls. What is the ratio of boys to the total students?

5. If a car covers 300 km in 5 hours, find the ratio of distance to time.

Simplifying and Equivalent Ratios

How to Simplify Ratios

A ratio is simplified when its terms **no longer have a common factor except 1.**

Steps to Simplify a Ratio
1. **Find the Greatest Common Divisor (GCD)** of both terms.
2. **Divide both terms** by the GCD.

Example 1: Simplify 18:24
1. GCD of 18 and 24 = 6.
2. Divide both by 6

$$\frac{18}{6} : \frac{24}{6} = 3:4$$

Final Answer: $3:4$

Example 2: Simplify 75:100
1. GCD of 75 and 100 = 25.
2. Divide both by 25

$$\frac{75}{25} : \frac{100}{25} = 3:4$$

Final Answer: $3:4$

Finding Equivalent Ratios

Two ratios are **equivalent** if they have the **same value when simplified.**

How to Find Equivalent Ratios
1. **Multiply or divide** both terms by the **same number.**
2. The ratio remains **the same.**

Example 3: Find two equivalent ratios for 3:5
- Multiply by 2 → (3×2):(5×2) = 6:10
- Multiply by 3 → (3×3):(5×3) = 9:15
- **Equivalent Ratios: 6:10 and 9:15**

Example 4: Check if 4:6 and 6:9 are equivalent Convert both to their simplest form:

$$4:6 \rightarrow GCD = 2, so\ 4 \div 2:6 \div 2 = 2:3$$
$$6:9 \rightarrow GCD = 3, so\ 6 \div 3:9 \div 3 = 2:3$$

Since both simplify to **2:3**, they are **equivalent.**
Final Answer: 4:6 and 6:9 are equivalent

Comparing Ratios

To compare two ratios, convert them to the **same denominator** or **convert to decimals**.

Example 5: Compare 3:4 and 5:6

1. Convert to **decimal**:

$$3 \div 4 = 0.75$$
$$5 \div 6 = 0.8333$$

2. *Since* $\mathbf{0.75 < 0.8333, 3:4 < 5:6.}$

Final Answer: $3:4 < 5:6$

Concept Check 10: Simplifying Ratio

1. Simplify: 36:48
2. Find two equivalent ratios for 7:9.
3. Compare 5:8 and 3:4.
4. Are 10:15 and 20:30 equivalent?
5. If a school has 25 boys and 40 girls, simplify the ratio of boys to girls.

Ratio and Proportion

What is Proportion?

A proportion is an equation that shows that two ratios are equal.

Example:

$$If\ \frac{2}{3} = \frac{4}{6}, then:$$

$$2:3 :: 4:6$$

*which is read as "**2 is to 3 as 4 is to 6**".*

Properties of Proportion:

o **Cross Multiplication Rule**

$$a:b = c:d \Rightarrow a \times d = b \times c$$

Example:

$$If \frac{2}{5} = \frac{4}{10},$$
$$2 \times 10 = 5 \times 4 \rightarrow \textbf{\textit{True}}$$

- Mean and Extreme Terms
  - **Extreme terms**: First and last numbers (a, d)
  - **Mean terms**: Middle numbers (b, c)
  - **Product of means = Product of extremes**

Example: 2: 5: : 6: 15
- **Extremes:** 2 and 15
- **Means:** 5 and 6

Types of Proportion

Type	Definition	Example
Direct Proportion	If one quantity increases, the other increases	Distance & time at constant speed
Inverse Proportion	If one quantity increases, the other decreases	Speed and travel time

Example of Direct Proportion:
If **5 kg of rice costs Rs. 200**, then the cost of **10 kg of rice** is:
$$\frac{5}{200} = \frac{10}{x}$$
$$Cross\ Multiplying$$
$$5x = 200 \times 10$$
$$x = 400 \dots Ans.$$

Example of Inverse Proportion:
If **6 workers complete a task in 10 days**, how many days will **10 workers** take?
$$Workers \times Days = Constant$$
$$6 \times 10 = 10 \times x$$
$$x = \frac{60}{10} = 6 \dots Ans.$$

Continued Proportion

A proportion of the form $a: b = b: c$ is called a **continued proportion**.
Example: Find the third proportion of **4 and 8**.
$$Using\ a: b = b: c$$

$$\frac{4}{8} = \frac{8}{x}$$

$$Cross\ multiply$$
$$4x = 8 \times 8$$
$$x = 16 \dots Ans.$$

Mean Proportion

The **mean proportion** between two numbers *a and b* is given by:

$$x = \sqrt{a \times b}$$

Example: Find the mean proportion between **9 and 16**.

$$x = \sqrt{9 \times 16}$$
$$x = \sqrt{144}$$
$$x = 12 \dots Ans.$$

Concept Check 11: Ratio and Proportion

1. Find the missing number: $3:7::?:21$
2. If 8 notebooks cost Rs. 320, find the cost of 12 notebooks.
3. A tap fills a tank in 6 hours. Another tap fills it in 8 hours. How long will both take together?
4. Find the third proportion of 5 and 10.
5. Find the mean proportion between 25 and 49.

Applications of Ratios

Ratios in Daily Life

Ratios are commonly used in **everyday situations**, such as:

- **Cooking Recipes** → Ingredients need to be mixed in correct proportions.
- **Financial Planning** → The ratio of savings to expenses helps in budgeting.
- **Maps & Scale Drawings** → A map might show **1 cm = 10 km**.
- **Work Distribution** → In a company, the ratio of managers to workers is often used for planning.

Example 1: Cooking Ratio
A recipe requires **3 cups of flour and 2 cups of sugar**. The ratio is: $3:2$.

If we double the recipe, we multiply both by 2:
$(3 \times 2) : (2 \times 2) = 6 : 4$
Final Ratio: 6 : 4

Ratio in Business and Finance

Example 2: Profit Distribution
Three partners **A, B, and C** invest money in a business in the ratio **2:3:5**. If
the total profit is **Rs. 50,000**, how much does each get?

Solution:

$$Total\ parts = 2 + 3 + 5 = 10.$$
$$A's\ share = \frac{2}{10} \times 50000 = 10,000$$
$$B's\ share = \frac{3}{10} \times 50000 = 15,000$$
$$C's\ share = \frac{5}{10} \times 50000 = 25,000$$
$$Answer: A = Rs.\,10,000, B = Rs.\,15,000, C = Rs.\,25,000.$$

Ratio in Speed, Distance & Time

Ratios are used to compare **speed, distance, and time** in motion problems.
Example 3: Speed Ratio
A car covers 240 km in 4 hours, while another covers 360 km in 6 hours.
Find the ratio of their speeds.
Solution:

$$Speed = \frac{Distance}{Time}$$
$$1st\ car: \frac{240}{4} = 60\ kmph$$
$$2nd\ car: \frac{360}{6} = 60\ kmph$$
$$Since\ both\ cars\ have\ the\ same\ speed$$
$$Answer: 1 : 1\ (Same\ speed).$$

Ratio in Work and Wages

Example 4: Work Done in Ratio
Two workers **A and B** do a job in the ratio **3:2**. If A completes his part in **6
hours,** how long will B take?

Solution:

$$A's\ work\ rate\ = \frac{1}{6}\ per\ hour$$

$$Work\ done\ by\ B\ = \frac{2}{3} of\ A's\ work$$

$$Total\ time\ for\ B = 6 \times \frac{3}{2} = 9\ hours$$

$$Final\ Answer: B\ will\ take\ 9\ hours$$

Mixture and Alligation

This concept is used when mixing two different **ratios** or **solutions**.

Example 5: Mixing Milk and Water

A shopkeeper mixes **milk and water in the ratio of 3:2**. If the total mixture is **50 litres**, find the amount of **milk and water**.

Solution:

$$Total\ parts\ =\ 3 + 2\ =\ 5.$$

$$Milk = \frac{3}{5} \times 50 = 30\ liters$$

$$Water = \frac{2}{5} \times 50 = 20\ liters$$

$$Answer: 30\ liters\ of\ milk, 20\ liters\ of\ water.$$

Concept Check 12: Applications of Ratio

1. *A store sells apples and oranges in the ratio 3:5. If there are 75 oranges, how many apples are there?*
2. *Two cars travel at speeds of 50 km/h and 80 km/h. Find the ratio of their speeds.*
3. *A worker completes a task in 8 hours. Another takes 12 hours. If they work together, how long will they take?*
4. *A solution contains salt and water in the ratio 4:5. If there are 36 liters of solution, how much salt is in it?*
5. *Two people invest money in a business in a ratio of 5:7. If the total investment is Rs. 48,000, find their shares.*

Advanced Ratio Problems

Solving Word Problems Using Ratios

Ratios help to solve **complex word problems** involving **mixtures, speed, work, and finance**.

Example 1: Income Ratio

*The monthly incomes of A and B are in the ratio **5:3**. If A earns Rs. 45,000, how much does B earn?*

Solution:

$$\frac{A}{B} = 5:3$$

$$B = \frac{3}{5} \times 45000 = 27000$$

Answer: B earns Rs. 27,000.

Ratio in Work and Time

When multiple workers complete a task together, the ratio of their work speeds is used.

Example 2: Work Completion Ratio

*A can finish a job in **6 days**, and **B** can finish it in **9 days**. In how many days will they complete it together?*

Solution:

$$Work\ per\ day:$$

$$A's\ rate = \frac{1}{6}$$

$$B's\ rate = \frac{1}{9}$$

$$Total\ rate: \frac{1}{6} + \frac{1}{9}$$

Least Common Denominator (LCD) of 6 and 9 is 18

$$\frac{1}{6} + \frac{1}{9} = \frac{3}{18} + \frac{2}{18} = \frac{3+2}{18} = \frac{5}{18}$$

$$Total\ time: \frac{\frac{1}{5}}{18} = \frac{18}{5} = 3.6$$

Final Answer: 3.6 days

Ratio in Speed, Distance, and Time

Ratios are used in **motion problems** to compare speeds and distances.

Example 3: Speed Ratio
A train covers **360 km in 6 hours**, and a car covers **240 km in 4 hours**.
Find the ratio of their speeds.
Solution:

$$Speed = \frac{Distance}{Time}$$

$$Train\ speed: \frac{360}{6} = 60\ kmph$$

$$Car\ speed: \frac{240}{4} = 60\ kmph$$

Answer: 1:1 (Both have the same speed)

Ratio in Mixtures (Alligation Method)

This is used for **mixing two different substances** to form a new substance.

Example 4: Mixing Two Solutions
A milkman mixes **milk and water in the ratio of 4:3**. If the total mixture is
49 liters, find the quantity of milk and water.
Solution:

$$Total\ parts = 4 + 3 = 7$$

$$Milk = \frac{4}{7} \times 49 = 28\ liters$$

$$Water = \frac{3}{7} \times 49 = 21\ liters$$

***Answer*: 28 *liters of milk,* 21 *liters of water*.**

Ratio in Business and Profit Sharing

Example 5: Partnership Ratio
A, B, and C start a business, investing in the ratio **5:7:8**. If the total profit is
Rs. 1,20,000, how much does each person get?
Solution:

$$Total\ parts = 5 + 7 + 8 = 20.$$

$$A's\ share = \frac{5}{20} \times 120000 = 30,000.$$

$$B's\ share = \frac{7}{20} \times 120000 = 42,000.$$

$$C's\ share = \frac{8}{20} \times 120000 = 48,000.$$

Answer: A = Rs. 30,000, B = Rs. 42,000, C = Rs. 48,000

Concept Check 13: Advanced Ratio

1. *Two partners invest Rs. 40,000 and Rs. 60,000. Find the profit share if the total profit is Rs. 50,000.*
2. *A and B complete a work in the ratio of 2:3. If A takes 10 days, how long will B take?*
3. *A and B start a business in a 3:5 ratio. If A's share of profit is Rs. 24,000, find B's profit.*
4. *A mixture contains milk and water in the ratio 5:2. If there are 42 liters of solution, find the quantity of milk.*
5. *A car covers 500 km in 10 hours. A bike covers 200 km in 5 hours. Find the ratio of their speeds.*

UGC NET PYQ Questions and Explanations on Ratio:

Question

A sum of Rs 3800 is divided among three persons A, B. and C in the ratio
$$\frac{1}{2} : \frac{1}{3} : \frac{3}{4}.$$
What is the share of the person C?

1. Rs. 3360
2. Rs. 2240
3. Rs. 2150
4. Rs. 1800

Explanations
Answer: 4. Rs. 1800

Convert the ratio to a common denominator:

The given ratio is $\frac{1}{2} : \frac{1}{3} : \frac{3}{4}.$

The least common denominator (LCD) for 2, 3, and 4 is 12.
Convert each fraction to have the denominator 12:

$$\frac{1}{2} = \frac{6}{12}, \quad \frac{1}{3} = \frac{4}{12}, \quad \frac{3}{4} = \frac{9}{12}$$

The ratio becomes $6:4:9$

Calculate the total number of parts:

$$6 + 4 + 9 = 19 \ parts$$

Determine the value of one part:

$$Value \ of \ one \ part = \frac{3800}{19} = 200$$

Calculate the share of person C:

Person C corresponds to 9 parts

$$Share \ of \ C = 9 \times 200 = 1800$$

Answer: 1800

Question

If 7: x= 17.5: 22.5, find the value of x.

1. 9
2. 12
3. 15
4. 8

Explanations

Answer: 1. 9

Write the proportion: $7:x = 17.5:22.5$

Convert the proportion to an equation: $\dfrac{7}{x} = \dfrac{17.5}{22.5}$

Cross − multiply to solve for x: $7 \times 22.5 = 17.5 \times x$

Calculate the left side: $7 \times 22.5 = 157.5$

Set up the equation: $157.5 = 17.5x$

Solve x: $x = \dfrac{157.5}{17.5} = 9 \dots Ans.$

Question

When 20% of a number (x) is added to another number (y), the number (y) increases by 50%. What is the respective ratio between the two numbers x and y?

1. 2:3
2. 3:5
3. 5:2

4. 5:3

Explanations

Answer: 3. 5:2

To determine the respective ratio between the two numbers xx and yy, let's break down the problem step by step.

1. **Define the Problem:**
   - When 20% of x is added to y, y increases by 50%.
2. **Set Up the Equation:**
   - 20% of x is 0.2x.
   - Adding this to y gives $y + 0.2x$
   - This results in y increasing by 50%, so:
   $$y + 0.2x = y + 0.5y$$
   $$y + 0.2x = 1.5y$$
3. **Simplify the Equation:**
   - Subtract y from both sides: $0.2x = 0.5y$
   - Divide both sides by 0.1 to simplify: $2x = 5y$
4. Find the Ration $x: y$
   - Rearrange the equation to find the ratio:
   $$\frac{x}{y} = \frac{5}{2}$$
   - Therefore, the ratio $x: y$ is $5:2 ... Ans.$

Question

Find the fourth proportional to 4, 9, 12 and third proportional to 16 and 36.

1. 25, 77 respectively
2. 27, 81 respectively
3. 28, 81 respectively
4. 27, 77 respectively

Explanations

Answer: 2. 27, 81 respectively

To solve the problem, we need to find two things:

1. The fourth proportional to the numbers 4, 9, and 12.
2. The third proportional to the numbers 16 and 36.

Fourth Proportional to 4, 9, 12

- The fourth proportional to three numbers $a, b, and c$ is a number x such that:

$$\frac{a}{b} = \frac{c}{x}$$

Here, $a = 4$, $b = 9$, and $c = 12$. Substituting these values:

$$\frac{4}{9} = \frac{12}{x}$$

Cross $-$ multiply to solve for x

$$4x = 9 \times 12$$

$$4x = 108$$

$$x = \frac{108}{4} = 27$$

- So, the fourth proportional is **27**.

Third Proportional to 16 and 36

- The third proportional to two numbers a and b is a number x such that:

$$\frac{a}{b} = \frac{b}{x}$$

- Here, $a = 16$ and $b = 36$. Substituting these values:

$$\frac{16}{36} = \frac{36}{x}$$

- Simplify the fraction:

$$\frac{4}{9} = \frac{36}{x}$$

- Cross-multiply to solve for x:

$$4x = 9 \times 36$$

$$4x = 324$$

$$x = \frac{334}{4} = 81$$

- So, the third proportional is **81**.

Answer: The fourth proportional to 4, 9, 12 is 27, and the third proportional to 16 and 36 is 81.

Question

Two numbers are in the ratio 5: 6. If 8 is subtracted from each number, then the ratio becomes 4: 5. The two numbers are respectively:

1. 40, 48
2. 32, 40
3. 48, 40
4. 35, 42

Explanations

Answer: 1. 40, 48

Step 1: Define the Numbers

- Let the two numbers be in the ratio 5:6. Let:

$$First\ number = 5x$$
$$Second\ number = 6x$$
$$where\ x\ is\ a\ common\ multiplier.$$

Step 2: Subtract 8 from Each Number

- When 8 is subtracted from each number, the new numbers become:

$$First\ number\ after\ subtraction = 5x - 8$$
$$Second\ number\ after\ subtraction = 6x - 8$$

Step 3: Set Up the New Ratio

- The new ratio after subtraction is given as 4:5. Therefore:

$$\frac{5x - 8}{6x - 8} = \frac{4}{5}$$

Step 4: Solve for x

- Cross-multiply to solve for x:

$$5(5x - 8) = 4(6x - 8)$$
$$25x - 40 = 24x - 32$$
$$25x - 24x = -32 + 40$$
$$x = 8$$

Step 5: Find the Two Numbers

- Substitute $x = 8$ into the original numbers:

$$First\ number = 5x = 5 \times 8 = 40$$
$$Second\ number = 6x = 6 \times 8 = 48$$

Answer: The two numbers are 40 and 48 respectively.

Question (Profit)

Two persons X and Y invested 15,000 and 20,000, respectively. in a business. At the end of the year, they share the profit in the ratio of 3:1. If X has invested his money for the whole year, for how many months Y has invested his money?

1. 3
2. 6
3. 5
4. 4

Explanations

Answer: 1. 3

To determine the number of months Y invested his money, we need to analyse the profit-sharing ratio and the investments made by X and Y.

Step 1: Understand the Problem

- X invested **15,000** for **12 months** (whole year).
- Y invested **20,000** for t **months** (unknown).
- The profit-sharing ratio is **3:1**.

Step 2: Formula for Profit Sharing

- The profit-sharing ratio is based on the product of the investment amount and the time. Thus:

$$Profit - sharing\ ratio = \frac{Investment\ of\ X \times Time\ of\ X}{Investment\ of\ Y \times Time\ of\ Y}$$

- Substitute the given values:

$$\frac{15000 \times 12}{20000 \times t} = \frac{3}{1}$$

Step 3: Solve for t

- Simplify the equation:

$$\frac{15000 \times 12}{20000 \times t} = \frac{3}{1}$$

$$\frac{15000 \times 12}{20000 \times t} = 3$$

$$\frac{180000}{20000 \times t} = 3$$

$$\frac{180000}{20000} = 3t$$

$$9 = 3t$$

$$\frac{9}{3} = t = 3$$

Final Answer: Y invested his money for 3 months

Question

In a school. there were 1582 students, and the ratio of the number of the boys and girls was 4:3. After few days, 30 girls joined the school, but few boys left the school and as a result, the ratio of the boys and girls became 7:6.

The number of boys who left the school is.

1. 84
2. 74
3. 86
4. 78

Explanations

Answer: 4. 78

Step 1: Initial Setup

- Total number of students initially = **1582**.
- Ratio of boys to girls initially = **4:3**.

Let:

- Number of boys initially = $4x$.
- Number of girls initially = $3x$.
- The total number of students is:

$$4x + 3x = 1582$$
$$7x = 1582$$
$$x = \frac{1582}{7} = 226$$

Thus:

- Number of boys initially = $4x = 4(226) = 904$.
- Number of girls initially = $3x = 3(226) = 678$.

Step 2: After Changes

- **30 girls joined**, so the new number of girls is:

$$678 + 30 = 708$$

- Let y be the number of boys who left. The new number of boys is:

$$904 - y$$

- The new ratio of boys to girls is **7: 6**.

Step 3: Set Up the Ratio

- The new ratio is:

$$\frac{904 - y}{708} = \frac{7}{6}$$

- o   Cross-multiply to solve for y:

$$6(904 - y) = 7(708)$$
$$5424 - 6y = 4956$$
$$5424 - 4956 = 6y$$
$$468 = 6y$$
$$y = \frac{468}{6} = 78 \dots Ans.$$

Question

Three positive numbers are in the ratio 2:3:4. If the sum of their squares is 2349, then the numbers respectively are

1. 14, 21 and 28
2. 18, 27 and 36
3. 16, 24 and 32
4. 12, 18 and 24

Explanations
Answer: 2. 18, 27 and 36

To determine the three numbers in the ratio $2:3:4$ such that the sum of their squares is 2349, follow these steps:

Step 1: Define the Numbers

- o   Let the three numbers be: $2x, 3x, 4x$
- o   where x is a common multiplier.

Step 2: Sum of Squares

- o   The sum of their squares is given as 2349. Thus:

$$(2x)^2 + (3x)^2 + (4x)^2 = 2349$$
$$4x^2 + 9x^2 + 16x^2 = 2349$$
$$29x^2 = 2349$$

Step 3: Solve for x

$$x^2 = \frac{2349}{29} = 81$$
$$x = \sqrt{81} = 9$$

Step 4: Find the Numbers

- o   Substitute $x = 9$ into the numbers:

$$2x = 2(9) = 18$$
$$3x = 3(9) = 27$$
$$4x = 4(9) = 36$$

Step 5: Verify the Sum of Squares

$$18^2 + 27^2 + 36^2 = 324 + 729 + 1296 = 2349$$

- The sum of squares matches the given value.

Answer: The three numbers are 18, 27, and 36 respectively.

Question

A sum of 50 is divided among A, B, and C in such a way that A gets 5 less than B, and B gets 10 less than C. What is the ratio of their money share?

1. 1:2:3
2. 2:3:4
3. 1:2:4
4. 2:3:5

Explanations

Answer: 4. 2:3:5

To determine the ratio of the money shares among A, B, and C, let's break down the problem step by step.

Step 1: Define Variables

Let:

- C be the amount received by C.
- B be the amount received by B.
- A be the amount received by A.

Step 2: Express Relationships

From the problem:

1. B gets 10 less than C:

$$B = C - 10$$

2. A gets 5 less than B:

$$A = B - 5$$

Substitute $B = C - 10$ into the equation for A:

$$A = (C - 10) - 5 = C - 15$$

Step 3: Total Sum

The total sum is 50:

$$A + B + C = 50$$

Substitute $A = C - 15$ and $B = C - 10$ into the total sum:

$$(C - 15) + (C - 10) + C = 50$$
$$3C - 25 = 50$$

Step 4: Solve for C

$$3C = 50 + 25$$
$$3C = 75$$
$$C = \frac{75}{3} = 25$$

Step 5: Find B and A

$$B = C - 10 = 25 - 10 = 15$$
$$A = C - 15 = 25 - 15 = 10$$

Step 6: Determine the Ratio

The amounts received by A, B, and C are:

$$A = 10, B = 15, C = 25$$
$$The\ ratio\ A{:}B{:}C\ is{:}\ 10{:}15{:}25$$

Simplify the ratio by dividing each term by 5:

$$2{:}3{:}5$$

Answer: The ratio of their money share is **2:3:5**.

Question

Total monthly salary of a couple (husband and wife) is Rs 2.0 lakh. Their salaries are in the ratio of 5:3. If husband and wife spend 40 % and 20% of their salaries, respectively, what is the ratio of their savings?

> (1) 3:2
> (2) 5:3
> (3) 5:4
> (4) 3:1

Explanations
Answer: 3. 5:4

To determine the ratio of savings between the husband and wife, let's break down the problem step by step.

Step 1: Define Variables
- Let the husband's salary be $5x$.
- Let the wife's salary be $3x$.

Step 2: Total Salary
The total monthly salary is Rs 2.0 lakh:

$$5x + 3x = 2,00,000$$
$$8x = 2,00,000$$
$$x = \frac{2,00,000}{8} = 25,000$$

Thus:
- Husband's salary = $5x = 5 \times 25,000 = 1,25,000$.
- Wife's salary = $3x = 3 \times 25,000 = 75,000$.

Step 3: Calculate Expenditures
- Husband spends 40% of his salary:

$$Husband's\ expenditure = 40\% \times 1,25,000 = 0.4 \times 1,25,000 = 50,000$$

- Wife spends 20% of her salary:

$$Wife's\ expenditure = 20\% \times 75,000 = 0.2 \times 75,000 = 15,000$$

Step 4: Calculate Savings
- Husband's savings:

$$Husband's\ savings = 1,25,000 - 50,000 = 75,000$$

- Wife's savings:

$$Wife's\ savings = 75,000 - 15,000 = 60,000$$

Step 5: Determine the Ratio of Savings
- The savings of the husband and wife are:

$$75,000 : 60,000$$

Simplify the ratio by dividing both terms by 15,000:

$$5 : 4$$

Answer: The ratio of their savings is **5:4**.

Question

The present age of the father of a boy is twice the age of the boy. Six years later the ratio of their ages will be 11:6. Find the present age of the boy?

1. 30 years
2. 28 years
3. 25 years
4. 23 years

Explanations

Answer: 1. 30 years

To determine the present age of the boy, let's break down the problem step by step.

Step 1: Define Variables

- Let the present age of the boy be x.
- The present age of the father is twice the age of the boy, so:

$$Father's\ age = 2x$$

Step 2: Six Years Later

- Six years later, the boy's age will be:

$$x + 6$$

- Six years later, the father's age will be:

$$2x + 6$$

Step 3: Set Up the Ratio

The ratio of their ages six years later is given as $11:6$. Thus:

$$\frac{2x + 6}{x + 6} = \frac{11}{6}$$

Step 4: Solve for x

Cross-multiply to solve for xx:

$$6(2x + 6) = 11(x + 6)$$
$$12x + 36 = 11x + 66$$
$$12x - 11x = 66 - 36$$
$$x = 30$$

Step 5: Verify the Solution

- Present age of the boy $= x = 30\ years$.
- Present age of the father $= 2x = 60\ years$.
- Six years later:
    - Boy's age $= 30 + 6 = 36\ years$.
    - Father's age $= 60 + 6 = 66\ years$.
- The ratio of their ages six years later:

$$\frac{66}{36} = \frac{11}{6}$$

This matches the given ratio.

Answer: The present age of the boy is **30 years**.

Question

If a man invested 20,000 in some shares in the ratio 2:3:5 which pay dividends of 10%. 30% and 20%. respectively. on the investments in that year. Find the total dividend income of the man.

1. 4200
2. 4500
3. 4800
4. 5000

Explanations

Answer: 1. 4200

To determine the total dividend income of the man, let's break down the problem step by step.

Step 1: Define Variables

The total investment is Rs 20,000, and it is divided in the ratio $2:3:5$. Let:

- The first part of the investment be $2x$.
- The second part of the investment be $3x$.
- The third part of the investment be $5x$.

Step 2: Calculate the Value of x

The total investment is:

$$2x + 3x + 5x = 20,000$$
$$10x = 20,000$$
$$x = \frac{20,000}{10} = 2,000$$

Step 3: Calculate Each Part of the Investment

- o *First part (2x):*

$$2x = 2(2,000) = 4,000$$

- o *Second part (3x):*

$$3x = 3(2,000) = 6,000$$

- o *Third part (5x):*

$$5x = 5(2,000) = 10,000$$

Step 4: Calculate Dividend Income from Each Part

- o Dividend from the first part (10%):

$$10\% \times 4,000 = 0.10 \times 4,000 = 400$$

- o Dividend from the second part (30%):

$$30\% \times 6,000 = 0.30 \times 6,000 = 1,800$$

- o Dividend from the third part (20%):

$$20\% \times 10,000 = 0.20 \times 10,000 = 2,000$$

Step 5: Total Dividend Income

Add up the dividends from all three parts:

$$400 + 1,800 + 2,000 = 4,200$$

Answer:

The total dividend income of the man is **4,200**.

Question

The ages of two sisters A and B are in the ratio of 7:6. After 12 years, the ratio of their ages will be 9:8. Find the difference between their ages.

1. 5 years
2. 4 years
3. 6 years
4. 8 years

Explanations

Answer: 3. 6 Years

To determine the difference between the ages of the two sisters, let's break down the problem step by step.

Step 1: Define Variables

Let the present ages of sisters A and B be in the ratio 7: 6. Thus:

- o   Let the present age of sister A be $7x$.
- o   Let the present age of sister B be $6x$.

Step 2: After 12 Years

After 12 years:

- o   Sister A's age will be: $7x + 12$
- o   Sister B's age will be: $6x + 12$

Step 3: Set Up the Ratio After 12 Years

The ratio of their ages after 12 years is given as $9:8$ Thus:

$$\frac{7x + 12}{6x + 12} = \frac{9}{8}$$

Step 4: Solve for x

Cross-multiply to solve for x:

$$8(7x + 12) = 9(6x + 12)$$
$$56x + 96 = 54x + 108$$
$$56x - 54x = 108 - 96$$
$$2x = 12$$
$$x = 6$$

Step 5: Find Their Present Ages

- o   Sister A's present age: $7x = 7 \times 6 = 42\ years$
- o   Sister B's present age: $6x = 6 \times 6 = 36\ years$

Step 6: Calculate the Difference

The difference between their ages is:

$$42 - 36 = 6\ years \ldots Ans.$$

Answer: The difference between their ages is **6 years**.

Question (Profit and Loss)

The ratio between Sale price (S.P.) and Cost price (C.P) of an article is 5:3. Find the ratio between profit and the cost price of that article.

1. 2:3
2. 4:5
3. 2:5
4. 5:2

Explanations

Answer: 1. 2:3

To determine the ratio between profit and the cost price (C.P.) of the article, let's break down the problem step by step.

Step 1: Define Variables

Given:
- The ratio of Sale Price (S.P.) to Cost Price (C.P.) is $5:3$.
- Let the Sale Price (S.P.) be $5x$.
- Let the Cost Price (C.P.) be $3x$.

Step 2: Calculate Profit

Profit is the difference between Sale Price (S.P.) and Cost Price (C.P.):

$$Profit = S.P. - C.P. = 5x - 3x = 2x$$

Step 3: Find the Ratio of Profit to Cost Price

The ratio of profit to cost price is:

$$\frac{Profit}{C.P.} = \frac{2x}{3x} = \frac{2}{3}$$

Answer: The ratio of profit to cost price is **2:3**.

Question

Three numbers are in the ratio of 3:5:7 and the sum of these numbers is 975. Find the three numbers-

1. 195, 315, 465
2. 185, 335, 455
3. 175, 345, 455
4. 195, 325, 455

Explanations

Answer: 4. 195, 325, 455

To determine the three numbers in the ratio 3:5:7 such that their sum is 975, follow these steps:

Step 1: Define Variables

Let the three numbers be: $3x, 5x, 7x$

where x is a common multiplier.

Step 2: Sum of the Numbers

The sum of the three numbers is given as 975. Thus:

$$3x + 5x + 7x = 975$$
$$15x = 975$$

Step 3: Solve for x

$$x = \frac{975}{15} = 65$$

Step 4: Find the Three Numbers

Substitute $x = 65$ into the numbers:

$$3x = 3 \times 65 = 195$$
$$5x = 5 \times 65 = 325$$
$$7x = 7 \times 65 = 455$$

Step 5: Verify the Sum

$$195 + 325 + 455 = 975$$

The sum matches the given value.

Answer: The three numbers are **195, 325, and 455**.

Question

Two numbers are in the ratio of 7:8. If the difference between the numbers is 30. then find the numbers.

1. 215, 245
2. 205, 235
3. 220, 250
4. 210, 240

Explanations

Answer: 4. 210, 240

To determine the two numbers in the ratio $7:8$ such that their difference is 30, follow these steps:

Step 1: Define Variables

Let the two numbers be: $7x \ and \ 8x$
where x is a common multiplier.

Step 2: Difference Between the Numbers

The difference between the two numbers is given as 30. Thus:

$$8x - 7x = 30$$
$$x = 30$$

Step 3: Find the Two Numbers

Substitute $x = 30$ into the numbers:

$$7x = 7 \times 30 = 210$$
$$8x = 8 \times 30 = 240$$

Step 4: Verify the Difference

$$240 - 210 = 30$$

The difference matches the given value.

Answer: The two numbers are **210 and 240**.

Average

The average (or **mean**) is the sum of all values divided by the total number of values.

Formula for Average:

$$Average = \frac{Sum\ of\ all\ values}{Total\ number\ of\ Values}$$

Types of Averages:

1. **Simple Average:** When all values have equal importance.
2. **Weighted Average:** When some values have more importance than others.

Simple Average

Example 1:
Find the average of **5, 10, 15, 20, 25**.
Solution

$$Sum = 5 + 10 + 15 + 20 + 25 = 75$$
$$Total\ numbers = 5$$
$$Average = \frac{75}{5} = 15$$

Shortcut for Simple Average (Consecutive Numbers)

- If numbers are in arithmetic order, the average is:
$$Average = \frac{First\ Term + Last\ Term}{2}$$

For **5, 10, 15, 20, 25**

$$\frac{5 + 25}{2} = \frac{30}{2} = 15$$

Weighted Average

Used when different values have different weights.
Formula:

$$Weighted\ Average = \frac{\Sigma(Value \times Weight)}{\Sigma Weights}$$

Example 2:

A class has two sections. Section A has **40 students** with an average score of **60**, and Section B has **60 students** with an average score of **80**. Find the overall average score.

Solution:

$$Total\ sum\ of\ scores = (40 \times 60) + (60 \times 80)$$
$$= 2400 + 4800 = 7200$$
$$Total\ students = 40 + 60 = 100$$
$$Average = \frac{7200}{100} = 72$$

Finding a Missing Number Using Average

If the average of **5 numbers** is **25**, and the first four numbers are **20, 22, 26, and 30**, find the fifth number.

Solution:

$$Sum\ of\ 5\ numbers = 5 \times 25 = 125$$
$$Sum\ of\ first\ 4\ numbers = 20 + 22 + 26 + 30 = 98$$
$$Fifth\ number = 125 - 98 = 27$$

Average Speed Formula

If a vehicle covers a distance at different speeds, the average speed is:

$$Average\ Speed = \frac{2ab}{a + b}$$

where:

- a = Speed for first half
- b = Speed for second half

Example 3:

A car travels **120 km** at **60 km/h** and returns at **40 km/h**. Find the average speed.

Solution

$$Average\ Speed = \frac{2 \times 60 \times 40}{(60 + 40)} = \frac{4800}{100} = 48\ km/h$$

Grouped Data (Average)

For grouped data, use:

$$Average = \frac{\sum Midpoint \times Frequency}{\sum Frequency}$$

Key Tricks for Competitive Exams

1. **If each value increases by x, the average also increases by x.**
2. **If a new value is added to the list, use:**

$$New\ Average = \frac{Old\ Sum + New\ Value}{New\ Count}$$

3. Average of first n natural numbers:

$$\frac{n+1}{2}$$

4. Average of first n even numbers:

$$\frac{n+1}{2} \times 2$$

5. Average of first n odd numbers: n

UGC NET PYQ Questions and Explanations on Average:

Question

If the mean of x, y and z is K, then the mean of $\frac{x}{y}, 1, \frac{z}{y}$

1. K
2. $\frac{K}{y}$
3. $\frac{K}{x}$
4. $\frac{K}{z}$

Explanations

Answer: 2. $\frac{k}{y}$

Step 1: Given Information

$$The\ mean\ of\ x, y, z\ is\ K.\ Thus:$$
$$\frac{x+y+z}{3} = k$$
$$x + y + z = 3K$$

Step 2: Find the Mean of

$$The\ mean\ of\ \frac{x}{y}, 1, \frac{z}{y}\ is$$

$$Mean = \frac{\frac{x}{y} + 1 + \frac{z}{y}}{3}$$

$$Simplify\ the\ numerator:$$

$$\frac{x}{y} + 1 + \frac{z}{y} = \frac{x+y+z}{y}$$

From Step 1, we know $x + y + z = 3K$. *Substitute this into the equation:*

$$\frac{x + y + x}{y} = \frac{3k}{y}$$

$$Mean = \frac{\frac{3k}{y}}{3} = \frac{k}{y} \ \dots. Ans.$$

Question

A man gets annual pay of Rs 9.0 lakh. His expenditure and savings are in the ratio 5:1. What is his average savings per month?

1. Rs 15,000
2. Rs 12,500
3. Rs 16,000
4. Rs 18,000

Explanations

Answer: 2. Rs 12,500

Step 1: Define Variables

- Let the man's annual income be Rs 9.0 lakh.
- The ratio of expenditure to savings is 5:1.

Let:

- Expenditure = $5x$.
- Savings = x.

Step 2: Total Income

The total income is the sum of expenditure and savings:

$$5x + x = 9.0 \ lakh$$

$$6x = 9.0 \ lakh$$

$$x = \frac{9.0}{6} = 1.5 \ lakh$$

Thus:

- Annual savings $= x = 1.5 \ lakh$.

Step 3: Calculate Monthly Savings

To find the average savings per month:

$$Monthly \ savings = \frac{Annual \ savings}{12} = \frac{1.5 \ lakh}{12} = 12,500$$

Answer: The man's average savings per month is **Rs 12,500**.

Question

In an examination, average marks of six students is 50. However. during cross checking of the papers, it is found that the marks of one student has been misread as 48 instead of 84. Find the correct average marks of the students.

1. 52
2. 54
3. 56
4. 58

Explanations

Answer: 3. 56

To determine the correct average marks of the six students, let's break down the problem step by step.

Step 1: Calculate the Incorrect Total Marks

The average marks of six students is 50. Thus, the incorrect total marks is:

$$Incorrect\ total = Average \times Number\ of\ students = 50 \times 6 = 300$$

Step 2: Identify the Error

One student's marks were misread as 48 instead of 84. The difference between the correct and incorrect marks is:

$$84 - 48 = 36$$

Step 3: Calculate the Correct Total Marks

Add the difference to the incorrect total to get the correct total marks:

$$Correct\ total = Incorrect\ total + Difference = 300 + 36 = 336$$

Step 4: Calculate the Correct Average

Divide the correct total by the number of students to find the correct average:

$$Correct\ average = \frac{Correct\ total}{Number\ of\ students} = \frac{336}{6} = 56\ Ans.$$

Answer: The correct average marks of the students is **56**.

Question

There are three positive numbers. One third of the average of all the three numbers is 8 less than the value of the highest number. If the average of the lowest and the second lowest number is 8, then what is the highest number?

1. 9
2. 10
3. 11
4. 12

Explanations

Answer: 3. 11

To determine the highest number, let's break down the problem step by step.

Step 1: Define Variables

Let the three positive numbers be:

$$a \leq b \leq c$$

where:

- a is the lowest number,
- b is the second lowest number,
- c is the highest number.

Step 2: Given Information

1. The average of the lowest and second lowest numbers is 8:

$$\frac{a + b}{2} = 8$$

$$a + b = 16 \underline{\qquad}(1)$$

2. One-third of the average of all three numbers is 8 less than the highest number:

$$\frac{1}{3}\left(\frac{a + b + c}{3}\right) = c - 8$$

Simplify:

$$\frac{a + b + c}{9} = c - 8$$

$$a + b + c = 9(c - 8)\underline{\qquad}(2)$$

Step 3: Substitute $a + b$ from Equation (1) into Equation (2)

From equation (1), $a + b = 16$. Substitute this into equation (2):

$$16 + c = 9(c - 8)$$
$$16 + c = 9c - 72$$
$$16 + 72 = 9c - c$$
$$88 = 8c$$
$$c = \frac{88}{8} = 11 \dots Ans.$$

Answer: The highest number is **11**.

Question

The geometric mean of the number 9, 12 and 16 is:

1. 12:33
2. 11.66
3. 12
4. 12.66

Explanations

Answer: 3. 12

To find the geometric mean of the numbers 9,12, and 16, follow these steps:

Step 1: Formula for Geometric Mean

The geometric mean of n numbers is given by:
$$Geometric\ Mean = \sqrt[n]{x_1 \times x_2 \times \dots \times x_n}$$
For three numbers 9,12, and 16, the geometric mean is:
$$Geometric\ Mean = \sqrt[3]{9 \times 12 \times 16}$$

Step 2: Calculate the Product

First, compute the product of the numbers:
$$9 \times 12 = 108$$
$$108 \times 16 = 1728$$

Step 3: Compute the Cube Root

Now, find the cube root of 1728:
$$\sqrt[3]{1728} = 12.\ Ans.$$

Final Answer: The geometric mean of 9,12, and 16 is **12**.

Question

The average age of a labour force is 42 years. If 8 (eight) new workers with average age of 36 years join the group, then the average age of the group becomes 40 years.

Tell the number of workers initially present in the group.

1. 17
2. 16
3. 18
4. 20

Explanations

Answer: 2. 16

Step 1: Define Variables

- Let n be the initial number of workers.
- The average age of the initial group is 42 years. Thus, the total age of the initial group is:

$$\text{Total age of initial group} = 42n$$

Step 2: Add New Workers

- 8 new workers join the group, and their average age is 36 years. Thus,

$$\text{Total age of new workers} = 8 \times 36 = 288$$

Step 3: Combined Group

- After adding the new workers, the total number of workers becomes $n + 8$.

$$\text{Total age of combined group} = 42n + 288$$

- The new average age of the group is 40 years. Thus:

$$\frac{42n + 288}{n + 8} = 40$$

Step 4: Solve for n

Multiply both sides by $n + 8$:

$$42n+288=40(n+8)$$
$$42n+288=40n+320$$
$$42n-40n=320-288$$
$$2n=32$$
$$n=16\ldots\text{Ans.}$$

Answer: The initial number of workers in the group is **16.**

Question

Let L and M be the sum and average of four consecutive odd numbers (a, b, c and d) respectively and, P and Q be the sum and average of three consecutive even numbers (x, y and z) respectively. If M= Q-6 and P=L-16, then M=

1. 32
2. 34
3. 36
4. 30

Explanations

Answer: 2. 34

To determine the value of M, let's break down the problem step by step.

Step 1: Define the Numbers

1. **Four consecutive odd numbers:**
   Let the four consecutive odd numbers be:
   $$a, b = a + 2, c = a + 4, d = a + 6$$
2. **Three consecutive even numbers:**
   Let the three consecutive even numbers be:
   $$x, y = x + 2, z = x + 4$$

Step 2: Calculate Sums and Averages

1. **For the odd numbers:**
   - Sum L:
   $$L = a + b + c + d = a + (a + 2) + (a + 4) + (a + 6) = 4a + 12$$
   - Average M:
   $$M = \frac{L}{4} = \frac{4a + 12}{4} = a + 3$$
2. **For the even numbers:**
   - Sum P:
   $$P = x + y + z = x + (x + 2) + (x + 4) = 3x + 6$$
   - Average Q:
   $$Q = \frac{P}{3} = \frac{3x + 6}{3} = x + 2$$

Step 3: Use the Given Conditions

1. **Condition 1:** $M = Q - 6$
   $$a + 3 = (x + 2) - 6$$
   $$a + 3 = x - 4$$

$$a = x - 7 \dots\dots\dots Eqa.\,(1)$$

2. **Condition 2:** $P = L - 16$

$$3x + 6 = (4a + 12) - 16$$
$$3x + 6 = 4a - 4$$

Substitute $a = x - 7$ from equation (1):

$$3x + 6 = 4(x - 7) - 4$$
$$3x + 6 = 4x - 28 - 4$$
$$3x + 6 = 4x - 32$$
$$6 + 32 = 4x - 3x$$
$$x = 38$$

Step 4: Find M

From equation (1):

$$a = x - 7 = 38 - 7 = 31$$

Thus:

$$M = a + 3 = 31 + 3 = 34 \dots Ans.$$

Answer: The value of M is **34**.

Question

If the average of 10 numbers is 40 and the average of six of them is 28, then the average of the remaining four numbers is:

(1) 52
(2) 54
(3) 56
(4) 58

Explanations

Answer: 4. 58

Step 1: Calculate the Total Sum of 10 Numbers

The average of 10 numbers is 40. Thus, the total sum of these numbers is:

$$Total\ sum\ of\ 10\ numbers = 10 \times 40 = 400$$

Step 2: Calculate the Sum of Six Numbers

The average of six of these numbers is 28. Thus, the sum of these six numbers is:

$$Sum\ of\ six\ numbers = 6 \times 28 = 168$$

Step 3: Calculate the Sum of the Remaining Four Numbers

Subtract the sum of the six numbers from the total sum to find the sum of the remaining four numbers:

$$Sum\ of\ remaining\ four\ numbers = 400 - 168 = 232$$

Step 4: Calculate the Average of the Remaining Four Numbers

Divide the sum of the remaining four numbers by 4 to find their average:

$$Average\ of\ remaining\ four\ numbers = \frac{232}{4} = 58\ ...\ Ans.$$

Answer: The average of the remaining four numbers is **58**.

Question

In an organisation, there are a total of 40 employees consisting of 5 Executive officers, 15 Senior Staff and 20 Junior staff. The monthly salaries of an Executive officer, a Senior staff and a junior staff are Rs 2,50,000, Rs 80,000 and Rs 45,000 respectively.

What is the average salary of an employee of the organisation?

1. 1,20,000 Rs
2. 90,250 Rs
3. 82,750 Rs
4. 83750 Rs

Explanations

Answer: 4. 83750 Rs

Step 1: Calculate the Total Salary for Each Category

1. **Executive Officers:**
   - Number of Executive Officers = 5
   - Salary per Executive Officer = Rs 2,50,000
   - Total salary for Executive Officers:
     $$5 \times 2,50,000 = 12,50,000\ Rs$$
2. **Senior Staff:**
   - Number of Senior Staff = 15
   - Salary per Senior Staff = Rs 80,000
   - Total salary for Senior Staff:
     $$15 \times 80,000 = 12,00,000\ Rs$$
3. **Junior Staff:**
   - Number of Junior Staff = 20
   - Salary per Junior Staff = Rs 45,000

o   Total salary for Junior Staff:
$$20 \times 45{,}000 = 9{,}00{,}000 \ Rs$$

Step 2: Calculate the Total Salary for All Employees
Add the total salaries of all categories:
$$12{,}50{,}000 + 12{,}00{,}000 + 9{,}00{,}000 = 33{,}50{,}000 \ Rs$$

Step 3: Calculate the Average Salary
The total number of employees is 40. Thus, the average salary is:
$$Average\ salary = \frac{Total\ salary}{Number\ of\ employees} = \frac{33{,}50{,}000}{40} = 83{,}750 \ Rs$$

Answer: The average salary of an employee in the organization is **83,750 Rs**.

Question

In a factory, the average salary of the employees is Rs 7000. If the average salary of 12 officers is Rs 40000 and that of the remaining employees is Rs 6000, then the number of employees is:

(1) 402
(2) 404
(3) 406
(4) 408

Explanations
Answer: 4. 408
Step 1: Define Variables
- Let n be the total number of employees.
- Number of officers = 12.
- Number of remaining employees = $n-12$.

Step 2: Calculate Total Salaries
1. **Total salary of all employees:**
$$Total\ salary = Average\ salary \times Number\ of\ employees = 7000 \times n$$
2. **Total salary of officers:**
$$Total\ salary\ of\ officers = 40000 \times 12 = 480000$$
3. **Total salary of remaining employees:**
$$Total\ salary\ of\ remaining\ employees = 6000 \times (n - 12)$$

Step 3: Set Up the Equation

The total salary of all employees is the sum of the salaries of officers and remaining employees:

$$7000n = 480000 + 6000(n - 12)$$

Step 4: Solve for n

Expand and simplify the equation:

$$7000n = 480000 + 6000n - 72000$$
$$7000n = 6000n + 408000$$
$$7000n - 6000n = 408000$$
$$1000n = 408000$$
$$n = \frac{408000}{1000} = 408. \, Ans.$$

Answer: The total number of employees is **408**.

Question

The average of 5 consecutive odd numbers in descending order is 95. Find the fourth number in the descending

1. 95
2. 97
3. 99
4. 93

Explanations

Answer: 4. 93

Step 1: Define the Numbers

Let the five consecutive odd numbers in descending order be:

$$x, x - 2, x - 4, x - 6, x - 8x$$

where x is the largest number.

Step 2: Calculate the Average

The average of these five numbers is given as 95. Thus:

$$\frac{x + (x - 2) + (x - 4) + (x - 6) + (x - 8)}{5} = 95$$

Simplify the numerator:

$$x + x - 2 + x - 4 + x - 6 + x - 8 = 5x - 20$$

Thus:

$$\frac{5x - 20}{5} = 95$$
$$x - 4 = 95$$
$$x = 99$$

Step 3: Find the Fourth Number
The fourth number in descending order is:
$$x - 6 = 99 - 6 = 93 \dots Ans.$$

Answer: The fourth number in descending order is **93**.

Question

Five years ago, the average age of 4 persons A, B, C and D was 45 years. If another person E is included in the group, then the present average age of all the five persons becomes 49 years, what is the present age of E?

1. 45 years
2. 50 years
3. 43 years
4. 48 years

Explanations
Answer: 1. 45 years
Step 1: Calculate the Total Age Five Years Ago
Five years ago, the average age of persons A,B,C, and D was 45 years. Thus, the total age of A,B,C, and D five years ago was:
$$Total\ age\ five\ years\ ago = 4 \times 45 = 180$$

Step 2: Calculate the Present Total Age of A,B,C, and D
Since five years have passed, each of the four persons has aged by 5 years. Thus, the present total age of A,B,C, and D is:
$$Present\ total\ age\ of\ A, B, C, D = 180 + (4 \times 5) = 180 + 20 = 200$$

Step 3: Calculate the Total Age Including E
When person E is included, the average age of the five persons becomes 49 years. Thus, the total age of all five persons is:
$$Total\ age\ of\ five\ persons = 5 \times 49 = 245\ years$$

Step 4: Find the Age of E

Subtract the total age of A,B,C, and D from the total age of all five persons to find the age of E:

$$Age\ of\ E = 245 - 200 = 45\ years.... Ans.$$

Answer: The present age of E is **45 years**.

Question

The average weight of six members of a family is 30 kg. If the head of the family is not considered, the average weight of the rest of the family members is 5 kg less than the earlier average. Find the weight of the head of the family.

1. 55 kg
2. 53 kg
3. 60 kg
4. 57 kg

Explanations

Answer: 1. 55 kg

Step 1: Calculate the Total Weight of Six Members

The average weight of six family members is 30 kg. Thus, the total weight of the six members is:

$$Total\ weight\ of\ six\ members = 6 \times 30 = 180\ kg$$

Step 2: Calculate the New Average Without the Head

If the head of the family is not considered, the average weight of the remaining five members is 5 kg less than the earlier average. Thus:

$$New\ average = 30 - 5 = 25\ kg$$

Step 3: Calculate the Total Weight of the Remaining Five Members

The total weight of the five members (excluding the head) is:

$$Total\ weight\ of\ five\ members = 5 \times 25 = 125\ kg$$

Step 4: Find the Weight of the Head of the Family

Subtract the total weight of the five members from the total weight of the six members to find the weight of the head:

$$Weight\ of\ the\ head = 180 - 125 = 55\ kg\ ...\ Ans.$$

Answer: The weight of the head of the family is **55 kg**.

Question

The average of a group of 20 numbers is 30 and that of another group of 30 numbers is 50. What is the average of all the numbers in both the groups?

1. 435
2. 45
3. 40
4. 42

Explanations

Answer: 4. 42

Step 1: Calculate the Total Sum of Each Group

1. **First Group:**
   - Number of numbers = 20
   - Average = 30
   - Total sum = 20 × 30 = 600
2. **Second Group:**
   - Number of numbers = 30
   - Average = 50
   - Total sum = 30 × 50 = 1500

Step 2: Calculate the Combined Total Sum

Add the total sums of both groups:

$$Combined\ total\ sum = 600 + 1500 = 2100$$

Step 3: Calculate the Combined Total Count

Add the number of numbers in both groups:

$$Combined\ total\ count = 20 + 30 = 50$$

Step 4: Calculate the Combined Average

Divide the combined total sum by the combined total count:

$$Combined\ average = \frac{2100}{50} = 42 \ ... \ Ans.$$

Answer: The average of all the numbers in both groups is **42**.

Question

The average age of a family of six members is 30 years. The youngest members of the family are twins with age 10 years. Find the average age of the family just before the birth of the twins.

1. 28 years
2. 25 years
3. 30 years
4. 32 years

Explanations

Answer: 3. 30 years.

Step 1: Calculate the Total Age of the Family Now

The average age of the six family members is 30 years. Thus, the total age of the family is:

$$Total\ age = 6 \times 30 = 180\ years$$

Step 2: Subtract the Age of the Twins

The twins are each 10 years old. Thus, the total age of the twins is:

$$Total\ age\ of\ twins = 2 \times 10 = 20\ years$$

Subtract the age of the twins from the total age of the family to find the total age of the remaining four members:

$$Total\ age\ of\ remaining\ members = 180 - 20 = 160\ years$$

Step 3: Calculate the Total Age Before the Birth of the Twins

The twins were born 10 years ago. Thus, 10 years ago, each of the four members was 10 years younger. The total reduction in age for the four members is:

$$Total\ reduction = 4 \times 10 = 40\ years$$

Subtract this reduction from the total age of the remaining members to find the total age of the family just before the birth of the twins:

$$Total\ age\ before\ the\ birth\ of\ twins = 160 - 40 = 120\ years$$

Step 4: Calculate the Average Age Before the Birth of the Twins

Just before the birth of the twins, there were four members in the family. Thus, the average age is:

$$Average\ age\ before\ twins = \frac{120}{4} = 30\ years \ldots Ans.$$

Answer: The average age of the family just before the birth of the twins was **30 years**.

Question

A person pays 10% tax on his income up to 4.0 lakhs. For the amount between 4.0 lakhs to 8.0 lakhs he pays tax of 20% and for the amount above 8.0 lakhs, he pays 30% tax. If the total tax paid by the person is 1.8 lakh, then find his average percentage of tax paid on the whole income.

1. 15%
2. 18%
3. 20%
4. 25%

Explanations

Answer: 2. 18%

Step 1: Define Variables

Let the total income be x lakhs.

Step 2: Calculate Tax for Each Slab

1. **First Slab (Up to 4.0 lakhs):**
   - Tax rate = 10%
   - $Tax = 10\% \times 4.0 = 0.40$
2. **Second Slab (4.0 lakhs to 8.0 lakhs):**
   - $Tax\ rate = 20\%$
   - $Taxable\ amount = min\ (x, 8.0) - 4.0$
   - $Tax = 20\% \times (min\ (x, 8.0) - 4.0)$
3. **Third Slab (Above 8.0 lakhs):**
   - $Tax\ rate = 30\%$
   - $Taxable\ amount = x - 8.0\ (if\ x > 8.0)$
   - $Tax = 30\% \times (x - 8.0)$

Step 3: Total Tax Paid

The total tax paid is given as 1.8 lakhs. Thus:

$$0.40 + 0.20 \times (min(x, 8.0) - 4.0) + 0.30 \times max(x - 8.0, 0) = 1.8$$

Step 4: Solve for x

Assume $x > 8.0$ (since the tax paid is 1.8 lakhs, which is more than the tax for the first two slabs). Then:

$$0.40 + 0.20 \times (8.0 - 4.0) + 0.30 \times (x - 8.0) = 1.8$$
$$0.40 + 0.20 \times 4.0 + 0.30 \times (x - 8.0) = 1.8$$
$$0.40 + 0.80 + 0.30x - 2.40 = 1.8$$
$$0.30x - 1.20 = 1.8$$
$$0.30x = 3.0$$
$$x = 10.0 \; lakhs$$

Step 5: Calculate Average Tax Percentage

The total tax paid is 1.8 lakhs, and the total income is 10.0 lakhs. Thus, the average tax percentage is:

$$Average\ tax\ percentage = \left(\frac{1.8}{10.0}\right) \times 100 = 18\%. \; Ans.$$

Answer: The average percentage of tax paid on the whole income is **18%**.

Question

What is the average of the first 6 multiples of 11?

1. 27.5
2. 40.5
3. 38.5
4. 51.5

Explanations

Answer: 3. 38.5

Step 1: List the First 6 Multiples of 11

The first 6 multiples of 11 are:

$$11,22,33,44,55,66$$

Step 2: Calculate the Sum of These Multiples

Add the first 6 multiples of 11:

$$11 + 22 + 33 + 44 + 55 + 66$$

Calculate the sum:

$$11 + 22 = 33$$
$$33 + 33 = 66$$
$$66 + 44 = 110$$
$$110 + 55 = 165$$

$$165 + 66 = 231$$

*Thus, the total sum is **231**.*

Step 3: Calculate the Average

Divide the sum by the number of multiples (6):

$$Average = \frac{231}{6} = 38.5 \ldots Ans.$$

Answer: The average of the first 6 multiples of 11 is **38.5**.

Question

The average age of students in a class was 15 years. When 5 new boys whose average age was 12 years 6 months were admitted in the class, the average age was reduced by 6 months. How many students were there in the class originally?

1. 15
2. 20
3. 18
4. 16

Explanations

Answer: 2. 20

Step 1: Define Variables

- o   Let n be the original number of students in the class.
- o   The average age of the original students is 15 years. Thus, the total age of the original students is:

$$Total\ age\ of\ original\ students = 15n$$

Step 2: Add New Students

- o   5 new boys are admitted, and their average age is 12 years 6 months (12.5 years). Thus, the total age of the new students is:

$$Total\ age\ of\ new\ students = 5 \times 12.5 = 62.5\ years$$

Step 3: Combined Group

- o   After adding the new students, the total number of students becomes $n + 5$.
- o   The total age of the combined group is:

$$Total\ age\ of\ combined\ group = 15n + 62.5$$

- o The new average age is reduced by 6 months (0.5 years), so the new average age is:

$$New\ average\ age = 15 - 0.5 = 14.5\ years$$

Step 4: Set Up the Equation

The total age of the combined group is equal to the new average age multiplied by the total number of students:

$$15n + 62.5 = 14.5(n + 5)$$

Step 5: Solve for n

Expand and simplify the equation:

$$15n + 62.5 = 14.5n + 72.5$$
$$15n - 14.5n = 72.5 - 62.5$$
$$0.5n = 10$$
$$n = \frac{0.5}{10}$$
$$\therefore n = \frac{10}{0.5} = \frac{10 \times 10}{5} = \frac{100}{5} 20 \ldots Ans.$$

Answer: The original number of students in the class was **20**.

Question

Find the average of the squares of the consecutive odd numbers from 1 to 21.

1. 162
2. 159
3. 161
4. 160

Explanations

Answer: 3. 161

Step 1: List the Consecutive Odd Numbers

The consecutive odd numbers from 1 to 21 are:

$$1,3,5,7,9,11,13,15,17,19,21$$

Step 2: Calculate the Squares of These Numbers

Square each of the numbers:

$$1^2 = 1$$
$$3^2 = 9$$
$$5^2 = 25$$

$$7^2 = 49$$
$$9^2 = 81$$
$$11^2 = 121$$
$$13^2 = 169$$
$$15^2 = 225$$
$$17^2 = 289$$
$$19^2 = 361$$
$$21^2 = 441$$

Step 3: Calculate the Sum of the Squares

Add up all the squared numbers:

$$1 + 9 + 25 + 49 + 81 + 121 + 169 + 225 + 289 + 361 + 441$$

Calculate the sum step by step:

$$1 + 9 = 10$$
$$10 + 25 = 35$$
$$35 + 49 = 84$$
$$84 + 81 = 165$$
$$165 + 121 = 286$$
$$286 + 169 = 455$$
$$455 + 225 = 680$$
$$680 + 289 = 969$$
$$969 + 361 = 1330$$
$$1330 + 441 = 1771$$

Thus, the total sum of the squares is **1771**.

Step 4: Calculate the Average

There are 11 numbers in the list. Thus, the average of the squares is:

$$Average = \frac{1771}{11} = 161 \dots Ans.$$

Answer: The average of the squares of the consecutive odd numbers from 1 to 21 is **161**.

Question

Six persons went to a hotel for a dinner. Five of them spent Rs 150 each on their meals, while the sixth person spent Rs 80 more than the average expenditure of all the six persons. What is the total money spent by all the six persons?

1. 996
2. 999
3. 1000
4. 1001

Explanations

Answer: 1. 996

Step 1: Define Variables

Let the **average expenditure** of all six persons be **A**.

- o   **Five persons** spent **Rs 150 each**.
- o   The **sixth person** spent **Rs 80 more than the average expenditure.**

Thus, the expenditure of the sixth person = $A + 80$.

Step 2: Form the Equation

Total expenditure of all six persons:

$$5 \times 150 + (A + 80) = 750 + A + 80$$
$$= 830 + A$$

Using the average formula:

$$A = \frac{Total\ expenditure}{6}$$

Thus,

$$A = \frac{830 + A}{6}$$

Step 3: Solve for A

Multiply both sides by 6:

$$6A = 830 + A$$

Rearrange:

$$6A - A = 830$$
$$5A = 830$$
$$A = \frac{830}{5} = 166$$

Step 4: Find Total Expenditure

Total expenditure:

$$6A = 6 \times 166 = 996 \ldots Ans.$$

Thus, the correct answer is **996**.

CHAPTER 3

Percentage, Profit and Loss, Interest and Discounting

Percentage, Profit and Loss, Interest and Discounting

Percentage

Definition and Basic Formula

A **percentage** is a number expressed as a fraction of 100. It is represented using the symbol **%**.

$$Percentage = \frac{Value}{Total\ Value} \times 100$$

Example:

If a student scores **45 marks out of 60**, the percentage is:

$$\frac{45}{60} \times 100 = 75\%$$

Conversion Between Percentage, Fractions, and Decimals

Fraction	Decimal	Percentage
$\frac{1}{2}$	0.5	50%
$\frac{1}{3}$	0.333	33.33%
$\frac{1}{4}$	0.25	25%
$\frac{2}{5}$	0.4	40%
$\frac{3}{8}$	0.375	37.5%

Trick to Convert:

- o   **Fraction to Percentage:** Multiply by 100.

- Example:

$$\frac{3}{5} \times 100 = 60\%$$

  - **Decimal to Percentage:** Multiply by 100.
    - Example:

$$0.75 \times 100 = 75\%$$

  - **Percentage to Decimal:** Divide by 100.
    - Example:

$$25\% = \frac{25}{100} = 0.25$$

Percentage Increase and Decrease

Formula for Percentage Increase:

$$Pecentahe\ Increase = \left(\frac{(New\ Value) - (Old\ Value)}{(Old\ Value)}\right) \times 100$$

Formula for Percentage Decrease:

$$Pecentahe\ Decrease = \left(\frac{(Old\ Value) - (New\ Value)}{(Old\ Value)}\right) \times 100$$

Example:
The price of a mobile phone increases from ₹20,000 to ₹22,000. Find the percentage increase.

$$\frac{22000 - 20000}{20000} \times 100 = \frac{2000}{20000} \times 100 = 10\%$$

Successive Percentage Change
If there are two percentage changes, say $x\%$ *and* $y\%$, the net effect is:

$$Total\ Percentage\ Change = x + y + \frac{xy}{100}$$

Example:
The price of an item is increased by **10%** and then decreased by **20%**. Find the overall change.

$$Total\ Change = 10 - 20 + \frac{10 \times (-20)}{100}$$
$$= -10 - 2 = -12\%$$

Thus, the overall decrease is **12%**.

Finding the Original Value

If **x%** of a number is **y**, then the original number is:

$$Original\ Number = \frac{y \times 100}{x}$$

Example:

40% of a number is 80. Find the number.

$$Number = \frac{80 \times 100}{40} = 200$$

Population Growth and Depreciation

Formula for Population Increase:

$$Final\ Population = P \times \left(1 + \frac{r}{100}\right)^t$$

Formula for Population Decrease:

$$Final\ Population = P \times \left(1 - \frac{r}{100}\right)^t$$

Where:

- P = Initial population
- r = Growth/Decline rate per year
- t = Time in years

Example:

A town has **50,000** people. If the population increases by **5% annually**, find the population after **2 years**.

$$Final\ Population = 50000 \times \left(1 + \frac{5}{100}\right)^2$$
$$= 50000 \times (1.05)^2$$
$$= 50000 \times 1.1025 = 55{,}125$$

Application in Discounts

If an item is originally priced at ₹**2000** and a **20% discount** is given:

$$Discount = \left(\frac{20}{100} \times 2000\right) = 400$$
$$Selling\ Price = 2000 - 400 = 1600$$

For **successive discounts** of **x%** and **y%**, use:

$$Effective\ Discount = x + y - \frac{xy}{100}$$

Example:

A **20% discount** is followed by a **10% discount**.

$$Effective\ Discount = 20 + 10 - \frac{20 \times 10}{100} = 30 - 2 = 28\%$$

Shortcut Tricks for Percentage

1. **To Find x% *of y* Quickly:**
   - *Instead of $x \times \frac{y}{100}$ break it down:*
   Example: 12% *of* 250
     - **10% *of* 250 = 25**
     - **1% *of* 250 = 2.5, *so* 2% = 5**
     - ***Total* = 25 + 5 = 30**
2. **If a quantity increases by x% and then decreases by x%, the net effect is always a decrease:**
   - Example: A price increases by 20% and then decreases by 20%, the net change is:
   $$-\frac{20 \times 20}{100} = -4\%$$
   - So, the final price is **4% lower than the original.**

Commonly Used Percentage Values

Percentage	Fraction	Decimal
10%	1/10	0.1
20%	1/5	0.2
25%	1/4	0.25
33.33%	1/3	0.333
50%	1/2	0.5
75%	3/4	0.75
90%	9/10	0.9

Concept Check 14: Percentage

1. *A number is increased by 30% and then decreased by 20%. What is the overall percentage change?*
2. *The population of a town is 80,000. If it increases by 5% every year, what will be the population after 3 years?*
3. *If 40% of a number is 120, what is the number?*
4. *A shopkeeper gives two successive discounts of 15% and 10% on an item marked at ₹5000. What is the final price?*
5. *A person spends 30% of his salary on rent and 40% on food. If his salary is ₹50,000, how much does he save?*

UGC NET PYQ Questions and Explanations on Percentage:

Question

Suppose there is a fraction whose numerator and denominator are both positive integers. If the numerator is increased by 20% and the denominator is decreased by 20% then its value becomes $\frac{6}{9}$. **What is that fraction?**

$$1.\frac{1}{9} \qquad 2.\frac{2}{9} \qquad 3.\frac{1}{3} \qquad 4.\frac{4}{9}$$

Explanations

Answer: 4. $\frac{4}{9}$

Step 1: Apply the changes to the numerator and denominator

- The numerator is **increased by 20%**, so the new numerator becomes:

$$x + 0.2x = 1.2x$$

- The denominator is **decreased by 20%**, so the new denominator becomes:

$$y - 0.2y = 0.8y$$

Thus, the new fraction is:

$$\frac{1.2x}{0.8y}$$

Step 2: Simplify the new fraction

The new fraction is given as $\frac{6}{9}$. So:

$$\frac{1.2x}{0.8y} = \frac{6}{9}$$

Simplify the equation:

$$\frac{1.2x}{0.8y} = \frac{2}{3}$$

Cross-multiply:

$$1.2x \times 3 = 0.8y \times 2$$
$$3.6x = 1.6y$$

Step 3: Solve for x and y

Divide both sides by 0.4 to simplify:

$$\frac{3.6x}{0.4} = \frac{1.6y}{0.4}$$
$$9x = 4y$$

$$Solve\ for\ y:$$
$$y = 9x/4$$

Since x and y are positive integers, x must be a multiple of 4. Let x=4k, where k is a positive integer. Then:

$$y = \frac{9(4k)}{4} = 9k$$

Step 4: Find the original fraction

The original fraction is:

$$\frac{x}{y} = \frac{4k}{9k} = \frac{4}{9}.\ Ans.$$

Question

Choose the correct statements:

    A. $x\%\ of\ y$ is equal to $y\%\ of\ 100x$

    B.   If $40\%\ of\ 60\%\ of\ \left(\frac{3}{5}\right)$ of a number is $504,\ then\ 25\%\ of\ \left(\frac{2}{5}\right)$ of that number is equal to 350

    C.   If $A\ is$ 15% more than $B,\ then\ B\ is$ ~13.04% less than A.

    D. $10\%\ of\ 5\ and\ 5\%\ of\ 10\ add\ up\ to\ 0.1$

Choose the correct answer from the options given below:

    1.   A B

    2.   B C

    3.   C D

    4.   A D

Explanations

Answer: 2. B C

Statement 1:

"x% of y is equal to y% of 100x."

    ○   **x% of y** is calculated as:

$$\frac{x}{100} \times y = \frac{xy}{100}$$

    ○   **y% of 100x** is calculated as:

$$\frac{y}{100} \times 100x = yx$$

    ○ $Clearly, \frac{xy}{100} \neq yx.$ **This statement is false.**

Statement 2:

"If 40% of 60% of $\left(\frac{3}{5}\right)$ of a number is 504, then 25% of $\left(\frac{2}{5}\right)$ of that number is equal to 350."

Let the number be N.

1. Calculate **40% of 60% of (3/5) of N**:

$$0.40 \times 0.60 \times \frac{3}{5} \times N = 504$$

Simplify:

$$0.40 \times 0.60 \times 0.60 \times N = 504$$
$$0.144N = 504$$

Solve for N:

$$N = \frac{504}{0.144} = 3500$$

2. *Now, calculate* **25% of** $\left(\frac{2}{5}\right)$ **of N**:

$$0.25 \times \frac{2}{5} \times 3500 = 0.25 \times 1400 = 350.$$

This matches the given condition. **This statement is true.**

Statement 3:
"If A is 15% more than B, then B is ~13.04% less than A."

1. If A is 15% more than B, then:
$$A = B + 0.15B = 1.15B$$

2. To find how much B is less than A, use the formula:
$$Percentage\ less = \frac{A - B}{A} \times 100$$
$$Substitute\ A = 1.15B:$$
$$Percentage\ less = \frac{1.15B - B}{1.15B} \times 100 = \frac{0.15B}{1.15B} \times 100 = \frac{0.15}{1.15} \times 100$$
$$\approx 13.04\%$$

This statement is true.

Statement 4:
"10% of 5 and 5% of 10 add up to 0.1."

1. Calculate **10% of 5**:
$$0.10 \times 5 = 0.5$$

2. Calculate **5% of 10**:
$$0.05 \times 10 = 0.5$$

3. Add them together:
$$0.5 + 0.5 = 1.0$$

The sum is **1.0**, not **0.1**. **This statement is false.**

Question

The population of the village is 11000. If the number of children increases by 11% and the number of adults increases by 20%. The population becomes 12660.

Find the population of children and adults separately in the village.

1. 7000, 4000
2. 4500, 6500
3. 6000, 5000
4. 5500, 5500

Explanations

Answer: 3. 6000, 5000

Step 1: Define Variables

Let:

- C = initial population of children
- A = initial population of adults

Given:

- Total initial population = 11,000

$$C + A = 11{,}000 \quad \ldots\ldots (1)$$

Step 2: Apply Population Growth

- The number of children increases by **11%**, so the new population of children becomes:

$$C + 0.11C = 1.11C$$

- The number of adults increases by **20%**, so the new population of adults becomes:

$$A + 0.20A = 1.20A$$

- The total population after the increase is **12,660**:

$$1.11C + 1.20A = 12{,}660 \quad \ldots. (2)$$

Step 3: Solve the Equations

From equation (1), express A in terms of C:

$$A = 11{,}000 - C$$

Substitute A=11,000−C into equation (2):

$$1.11C + 1.20(11{,}000 - C) = 12{,}660$$

Expand and simplify:

$$1.11C + 13{,}200 - 1.20C = 12{,}660$$
$$-0.09C + 13{,}200 = 12{,}660$$

$$-0.09C = 12{,}660 - 13{,}200$$
$$-0.09C = -540$$
$$C = \frac{-540}{-0.09} = 6{,}000$$

Now, substitute C=6,000 into equation (1) to find A:

$$A = 11{,}000 - 6{,}000 = 5{,}000$$

Answer: The population of children and adults in the village is **6,000** and **5,000**, respectively.

Question

The monthly income of a person in the year 2020 was Rs 65,000 and his monthly expenditure was Rs 45.000. In the year 2021 his monthly income increased by 15% and his monthly expenditure by 7%. **What is the percentage increase in his savings?**

1. 33%
2. 31%
3. 35%
4. 28%

Explanations

Answer: 1. 33%

Step 1: Calculate Savings for 2020

- **Income in 2020** = Rs 65,000
- **Expenditure in 2020** = Rs 45,000
- **Savings in 2020** = Income - Expenditure
  $$Savings\ in\ 2020 = 65{,}000 - 45{,}000 = Rs20{,}000$$

Step 2: Calculate Income and Expenditure for 2021

- **Income in 2021** increases by **15%**:
  $$Income\ in\ 2021 = 65{,}000 + (0.15 \times 65{,}000)$$
  $$= 65{,}000 + 9{,}750 = Rs74{,}750$$
- **Expenditure in 2021** increases by **7%**:
  $$Expenditure\ in\ 2021 = 45{,}000 + (0.07 \times 45{,}000$$
  $$= 45{,}000 + 3{,}150 = Rs48{,}150$$

Step 3: Calculate Savings for 2021

- **Savings in 2021** = Income - Expenditure
  $$Savings\ in\ 2021 = 74{,}750 - 48{,}150 = Rs26{,}600$$

Step 4: Calculate Percentage Increase in Savings
- o **Increase in Savings** = Savings in 2021 - Savings in 2020

$$Increase\ in\ Savings = 26{,}600 - 20{,}000 = Rs6{,}600$$

- o **Percentage Increase in Savings**:

$$Percentage\ Increase = \left(\frac{Increase\ in\ Savings}{Savings\ in\ 2020}\right) \times 100$$

$$Percentage\ Increase = \left(\frac{6{,}600}{20{,}000}\right) \times 100 = 1.33\% \dots Ans.$$

Question

$\frac{5}{9}$ *of a number is equal to twenty five percent of a second number. Second number is equal to* $\frac{1}{4}$ *of a third number. The value of the third number is 2960.* **How much is the 30% of the first number?**

1. 9.99
2. 99.9
3. 89.9
4. 88.9

Explanations

Answer: 2. 99.9

Step 1: Define the Variables

Let:

- $N_1 = First\ number$
- $N_2 = Second\ number$
- $N_3 = Third\ number$

Step 2: Use the Given Information

1. **Third number (N_3) is given as 2960:**

$$N_3 = 2960$$

2. **Second number (N_2) is equal to** $\frac{1}{4}$ **of the third number:**

$$N_2 = \frac{1}{4} \times N_3 = \frac{1}{4} \times 2960 = 740$$

3. **Five-ninths of the first number (N_1) is equal to 25% of the second number (N_2):**

$$\frac{5}{9} \times N_1 = 0.25 \times N_2$$

$$Substitute\ N_2 = 740$$

$$\frac{5}{9} \times N_1 = 0.25 \times 740$$

$$\frac{5}{9} \times N_1 = 185$$

Step 3: Solve for N_1

Multiply both sides of the equation by $\frac{9}{5}$ to isolate N_1 :

$$N_1 = 185 \times \frac{9}{5}$$
$$N_1 = 185 \times 1.8$$
$$N_1 = 333$$

Step 4: Calculate 30% *of* N_1

$$30\% \ of \ N_1 = 0.30 \times 333 = 99.9.. Ans.$$

Question

In a competitive examination held in the year 2000, a total of 6,00,000 (6.0 lakh) students appeared and 40% passed the examination. Forty percent (40%) of the total students were females and the rest were males. The pass percentage among the males was 50%. **Find the pass percentage among the females.**

1. 25%
2. 30%
3. 35%
4. 40%

Explanations

Answer: 1. 25%

Step 1: Total Students and Pass Percentage
- o Total students = **6,00,000**
- o **40%** of the students passed the examination:
$$Total \ passed = 0.40 \times 6,00,000 = 2,40,000$$

Step 2: Number of Females and Males
- o **40%** of the students are females:
$$Number \ of \ females = 0.40 \times 6,00,000 = 2,40,000$$
- o The remaining **60%** are males:
$$Number \ of \ males = 0.60 \times 6,00,000 = 3,60,000$$

Step 3: Pass Percentage Among Males
- o The pass percentage among males is **50%**:
$$Number\ of\ males\ passed = 0.50 \times 3,60,000 = 1,80,000$$

Step 4: Number of Females Passed
- o Total passed students = **2,40,000**
- o Number of males passed = **1,80,000**
- o Number of females passed:
$$Number\ of\ females\ passed = 2,40,000 - 1,80,000 = 60,000$$

Step 5: Pass Percentage Among Females
- o Number of females = **2,40,000**
- o Number of females passed = **60,000**
- o Pass percentage among females:
$$Pass\ percentage\ among\ females = \left(\frac{60,000}{2,40,000}\right) \times 100 = 1.25\% \ldots Ans.$$

Question

"A person spends 20% of his money for clothes. 10% of the money is spent on books, 9% for purchasing gifts for family and friends and 7% on some other items. At the end he is left with Rs 5400." **How much money was there with the person initially?**

1. 8,000
2. 9,000
3. 12,000
4. 10,000

Explanations
Answer: 4. 10,000
Step 1: Define the Total Money
Let the total money the person initially has be x.

Step 2: Calculate the Amount Spent
The person spends money on the following:
1. **Clothes**: 20% *of x*
$$0.20x$$
2. **Books**: 10% *of x*

$$0.10x$$

3. **Gifts**: 9% *of x*

$$0.09x$$

4. **Other items**: 7% *of x*

$$0.07x$$

Step 3: Total Amount Spent
Add up all the amounts spent:
$$0.20x + 0.10x + 0.09x + 0.07x = 0.46x$$

Step 4: Calculate the Remaining Amount
The remaining amount is given as **Rs 5400**. This is equal to the total money minus the amount spent:
$$x - 0.46x = 0.54x$$
$$0.54x = 5400$$

Step 5: Solve for x
Divide both sides by 0.54 *to find x*:
$$x = \frac{5400}{0.54} = 10,000..Ans.$$

Question

Price of a mobile is first increased by 20% and later decreased by 25%. **What is the net percentage change in final price of the mobile?**

1. 10%
2. 18%
3. 20%
4. 12%

Explanations
Answer: 1. 10%
Step 1: Assume the Original Price
Let the original price of the mobile be **P**.

Step 2: First Change - Increase by 20%
The price is increased by **20%**. The new price becomes:
$$P + 0.20P = 1.20P$$

Step 3: Second Change - Decrease by 25%

The new price (1.20P) is decreased by **25%**. The final price becomes:

$$1.20P - 0.25 \times 1.20P = 1.20P \times (1 - 0.25) = 1.20P \times 0.75 = 0.90P$$

Step 4: Calculate the Net Percentage Change

The final price is **0.90P**, which means the price has decreased from the original price P. The net change is:

$$P - 0.90P = 0.10P$$

The net percentage change is:

$$\frac{0.10P}{P} \times 100 = 10\% \ldots Ans.$$

Question

If A is 20% of C and B is 25% of C, then what percent is A of B?

1. 60%
2. 80%
3. 70%
4. 50%

Explanations

Answer: 2. 80%

Step 1: *Express A and B in Terms of C*

Given:

- $A = 20\% \ of \ C$

$$A = 0.20C$$

- $B = 25\% \ of \ C$

$$B = 0.25C$$

Step 2: Find the Ratio of AA to BB

We need to find what percent A is of B. This is given by:

$$\frac{A}{B} \times 100$$

Substitute the values of A and B:

$$\frac{A}{B} \times 100 = \frac{0.20C}{0.25C} \times 100$$

Simplify:

$$\frac{0.20}{0.25} \times 100 = 0.80 \times 100 = 80\% .. Ans.$$

Question

In a test consisting of 150 questions carrying 1 mark each, Rishab answered 80% of the first 75 questions correctly. What percent of the other 75 questions does he need to answer correctly to score 60% overall?

1. 20
2. 40
3. 50
4. 60

Explanations

Answer: 2. 40

Step 1: Total Marks and Target Score

- o   Total questions = **150**
- o   Each question carries **1 mark**, so total marks = **150**
- o   Rishab wants to score **60% overall**:

$$Target\ score = 0.60 \times 150 = 90\ marks$$

Step 2: Marks Obtained from the First 75 Questions

- o   Rishab answered **80%** of the first 75 questions correctly:

$$Marks\ from\ first\ 75\ questions = 0.80 \times 75 = 60\ marks$$

Step 3: Marks Required from the Other 75 Questions

Let x be the percentage of the **other 75 questions** that Rishab needs to answer correctly. Then:

$$Marks\ from\ other\ 75\ questions = \frac{x}{100} \times 75$$

The total marks obtained will be:

$$60 + \frac{x}{100} \times 75 = 90$$

Step 4: Solve for x

Subtract 60 from both sides:

$$\frac{x}{100} \times 75 = 30$$

Multiply both sides by 100:

$$x \times 75 = 3000$$

Divide both sides by 75:

$$x = \frac{3000}{75} = 40 \ldots Ans.$$

Question

If A's income is 40% less than B's income, then how much percent is B's income more than A's income?

1. 65.66
2. 64.66
3. 66.66
4. 55.66

Explanations

Answer: 3. 66.66

Step 1: Define the Incomes

Let:

- o B's income = **100 units** (for simplicity)
- o A's income is **40% less** than B's income:

$$A = B - 0.40B = 0.60B$$

Substituting $B = 100$:

$$A = 0.60 \times 100 = 60 \, units$$

Step 2: Calculate the Difference

The difference between B's income and A's income is:

$$B - A = 100 - 60 = 40 \, units$$

Step 3: Calculate the Percentage Increase

To find how much percent B's income is more than A's income, use the formula:

$$Percentage \; increase = \left(\frac{B - A}{A}\right) \times 100$$

Substitute the values:

$$Percentage \; increase = \left(\frac{40}{60}\right) \times 100 = \frac{2}{3} \times 100 = 66.66\% \ldots Ans.$$

Question

A, Band C share a certain sum of money among themselves. A gets 35%, B gets Rs.1500 and C gets 1/20. How much is the original sum of money?

1. Rs. 1500
2. Rs. 2000
3. Rs. 1250
4. Rs. 2500

Explanations

Answer: 4. Rs. 2500

Step 1: Define the Total Sum

Let the total sum of money be x.

Step 2: Express the Shares

- **A** gets **35%** of x:

$$A = 0.35x$$

- **B** gets **Rs. 1500**:

$$B = 1500$$

- **C** gets $\left(\frac{1}{20}\right)$ of x:

$$C = \frac{1}{20}x = 0.05x$$

Step 3: Sum of All Shares

The sum of all shares equals the total sum xx:

$$A + B + C = x$$

Substitute the values:

$$0.35x + 1500 + 0.05x = x$$

Step 4: Solve for x

Combine like terms:

$$0.40x + 1500 = x$$

Subtract $0.40x$ from both sides:

$$1500 = x - 0.40x$$
$$1500 = 0.60x$$

Divide both sides by 0.60:

$$x = \frac{1500}{0.60} = 2500 \ldots Ans.$$

Question

A man weighs 75% of his own weight plus 39 lbs. How much does he weigh?

1. 165 lbs
2. 160 lbs
3. 156 lbs
4. 166 lbs

Explanations

Answer: 3. 156 lbs

Step 1: Define the Weight

Let the man's weight be *x lbs*.

Step 2: Translate the Problem into an Equation

The man weighs **75% of his own weight plus 39 lbs**. This can be written as:

$$x = 0.75x + 39$$

Step 3: Solve for *x*

$$Subtract\ 0.75x\ from\ both\ sides:$$
$$x - 0.75x = 39$$
$$0.25x = 39$$
$$Divide\ both\ sides\ by\ 0.25:$$
$$x = \frac{39}{0.25} = 156 \dots Ans.$$

Question

63% of employees in a company are female. If the number of male employees is 111, then the total number of employees is-

1. 270
2. 290
3. 300
4. 310

Explanations

Answer: 3. 300

Step 1: Define the Total Number of Employees

Let the total number of employees be *x.*

Step 2: Express the Number of Female and Male Employees

    o   **63%** of the employees are female:

$$Number\ of\ female\ employees = 0.63x$$

- o   The remaining employees are male. Since the total percentage is 100%, the percentage of male employees is:

$$100\% - 63\% = 37\%$$
$$Number\ of\ male\ employees = 0.37x$$

Step 3: Use the Given Information

The number of male employees is given as **111**:

$$0.37x = 111$$

Step 4: Solve for x

Divide both sides by 0.37:

$$x = \frac{111}{0.37} = 300 \dots Ans.$$

Question

In a class, there are 60% female students, and the remaining are male. 40% of the female students and 70% of the male students have opted for the research methodology course. If in all. 60 students have not opted for the research methodology course, which of the following is the total number of students in the class?

1. 120
2. 125
3. 130
4. 140

Explanations

Answer: 2. 125

Step 1: Define the Total Number of Students

Let the total number of students in the class be x.

Step 2: Calculate the Number of Female and Male Students

- o   **60%** of the students are female:

$$Number\ of\ female\ students = 0.60x$$

- o   The remaining **40%** are male:

$$Number\ of\ male\ students = 0.40x$$

Step 3: Calculate Students Who Opted for the Course

- **40%** of the female students opted for the research methodology course:

$$Female\ students\ who\ opted = 0.40 \times 0.60x = 0.24x$$

- **70%** of the male students opted for the research methodology course:

$$Male\ students\ who\ opted = 0.70 \times 0.40x = 0.28x$$

Step 4: Calculate Students Who Did Not Opt for the Course

- Total students who opted for the course:

$$0.24x + 0.28x = 0.52x$$

- Total students who did **not** opt for the course:

$$x - 0.52x = 0.48x$$

- It is given that **60 students did not opt** for the course:

$$0.48x = 60$$

Step 5: Solve for x

Divide both sides by 0.48:

$$x = \frac{60}{0.48} = 125 \dots Ans.$$

Question

A student obtains overall 78% marks in his examination consisting of Physics, Chemistry, Mathematics, Computer Science and General English. Marks obtained in each subject and the maximum marks are indicated in the following table:

Subject	Max Marks	Marks Obtained
Physics	200	155
Chemistry	100	80
Mathematics	200	165
Computer Science	200	140
General English	100	X

The marks (X) obtained by the student in General English would be?

1. 68
2. 74
3. 84
4. 90

Explanations

Answer: 3. 84

Step 1: Calculate Total Maximum Marks

The maximum marks for all subjects are:

- o   Physics: 200
- o   Chemistry: 100
- o   Mathematics: 200
- o   Computer Science: 200
- o   General English: 100

Total maximum marks:

$$200 + 100 + 200 + 200 + 100 = 800$$

Step 2: Calculate Total Marks Obtained

The marks obtained by the student in each subject are:

- o   Physics: 155
- o   Chemistry: 80
- o   Mathematics: 165
- o   Computer Science: 140
- o   General English: X

Total marks obtained:

$$155 + 80 + 165 + 140 + X = 540 + X$$

Step 3: Use the Overall Percentage

The student's overall percentage is **78%**. This means:

$$\frac{Total\ Marks\ Obtained}{Total\ Maximum\ Marks} \times 100 = 78$$

Substitute the values:

$$\frac{540 + X}{800} \times 100 = 78$$

Step 4: Solve for X

Divide both sides by 100:

$$\frac{540 + X}{800} = 0.78$$

Multiply both sides by 800:

$$540 + X = 0.78 \times 800$$
$$540 + X = 624$$

Subtract 540 from both sides:

$$X = 624 - 540$$
$$X = 84 \ldots Ans.$$

Question

Manoj's commission is 10% on all sales up to Rs 10,000 and 5% on all sales exceeding this. He remits Rs 75,500 to his company after deducting his commission. The total sales will come out to be

1. Rs. 78,000
2. Rs. 80,000
3. Rs. 85,000
4. Rs. 90,000

Explanations

Answer: 2. Rs. 80,000

Step 1: Define the Total Sales

Let the total sales be x.

Step 2: Calculate the Commission

Manoj's commission structure is:

- **10%** on sales up to **Rs 10,000**:

$$Commission\ on\ first\ Rs\ 10,000 = 0.10 \times 10,000 = 1,000$$

- **5%** on sales exceeding **Rs 10,000**:

$$Commission\ on\ remaining\ sales = 0.05 \times (x - 10,000)$$

Total commission:

$$Total\ Commission = 1,000 + 0.05(x - 10,000)$$

Step 3: Relate Commission to Remittance

Manoj remits **Rs 75,500** to his company after deducting his commission. This means:

$$Total\ Sales - Total\ Commission = 75,500$$

Substitute the total commission:

$$x - \left(1,000 + 0.05(x - 10,000)\right) = 75,500$$

Step 4: Simplify and solve for x

Expand the equation:

$$x - 1,000 - 0.05x + 500 = 75,500$$

Combine like terms:

$$0.95x - 500 = 75,500$$

Add 500 to both sides:

$$0.95x = 76,000$$

Divide both sides by 0.95:

$$x = \frac{76,000}{0.95} = 80,000 \ldots Ans.$$

Question

During one year, the population of a town increased by 5% and during the next year, the population decreased by 5%. If the total population is 29925 at the end of the second year, then what was the population size in the beginning of the first year?

(1) 25000
(2) 30000
(3) 33000
(4) 36000

Explanations
Answer: (2). 30000
Step 1: Define the Initial Population
Let the initial population at the beginning of the first year be **P**.

Step 2: Population After the First Year
The population increases by **5%** during the first year. The population at the end of the first year is:
$$P + 0.05P = 1.05P$$

Step 3: Population After the Second Year
The population decreases by **5%** during the second year. The population at the end of the second year is:
$$1.05P - 0.05 \times 1.05P = 1.05P \times (1 - 0.05) = 1.05P \times 0.95 = 0.9975P$$

Step 4: Use the Given Final Population
The population at the end of the second year is given as **29,925**:
$$0.9975P = 29,925$$

Step 5: Solve for P
Divide both sides by 0.9975:
$$P = \frac{29,925}{0.9975} = 30,000 \ldots Ans.$$

Question

40% of the employees in a factory are workers. All the remaining employees are executives. The annual income of each worker is Rs. 39,000. The annual income of each executive is Rs. 42,000. What is the average annual income of all employees in the factory together?

1. Rs. 40,500
2. Rs. 40,800
3. Rs. 41,000
4. Rs. 41,500

Explanations

Answer: 2. Rs. 40,800

Step 1: Define the Total Number of Employees

Let the total number of employees in the factory be E.

Step 2: Calculate the Number of Workers and Executives

- **40%** of the employees are workers:
$$Number\ of\ workers = 0.40E$$
- The remaining **60%** are executives:
$$Number\ of\ executives = 0.60E$$

Step 3: Calculate Total Income

- Annual income of each worker = **Rs. 39,000**:
$$Total\ income\ of\ workers = 39,000 \times 0.40E = 15,600E$$
- Annual income of each executive = **Rs. 42,000**:
$$Total\ income\ of\ executives = 42,000 \times 0.60E = 25,200E$$
- **Total income of all employees**:
$$15,600E + 25,200E = 40,800E$$

Step 4: Calculate Average Annual Income

The average annual income is:
$$Average\ income = \frac{Total\ income}{Total\ employees} = \frac{40,800E}{E} = 40,800 \ldots Ans.$$

Profit and Loss

Basic Terms and Definitions

1. **Cost Price (C.P)**: The price at which an article is purchased.
2. **Selling Price (S.P)**: The price at which an article is sold.
3. **Profit (or Gain)**: If Selling Price > Cost Price
$$Profit = S.P - C.P$$
4. **Loss**: If Selling Price < Cost Price
$$Loss = C.P - S.P$$
5. **Marked Price (M.P.)**: The price labelled on the product before any discount.
6. **Discount**: A reduction given on the Marked Price.

Profit and Loss Percentages

1. **Profit Percentage**
$$Profit\ \% = \left(\frac{Profit}{(C.P)}\right) \times 100$$

2. **Loss Percentage**
$$Loss\ \% = \left(\frac{Loss}{(C.P)}\right) \times 100$$

Example 1:
A shopkeeper buys an article for ₹200 and sells it for ₹250. Find the profit percentage.
Solution:
$$Profit = 250 - 200 = ₹50$$
$$Profit\ \% = \left(\frac{50}{200}\right) \times 100 = 25\%$$

Selling Price and Cost Price Formulas

1. **Selling Price (S.P) when Profit percentage is given**
$$S.P = C.P \times \left(1 + \frac{Profit\ \%}{100}\right)$$
2. **Selling Price (S.P) when Loss percentage is given**
$$S.P = C.P \times \left(1 - \frac{Loss\ \%}{100}\right)$$
3. **Cost Price (C.P) when Selling Price and Profit% is given:**

$$C.P = \left(\frac{S.P}{1 + \frac{Profit\ \%}{100}} \right)$$

4. **Cost Price (C.P) when Selling Price and Loss% is given**:

$$C.P = \left(\frac{S.P}{1 - \frac{Loss\ \%}{100}} \right)$$

Example 2:

A person sells an article for ₹1800 at a **20% profit**. Find the cost price.

Solution:

$$C.P = \left(\frac{1800}{1 + \frac{20\ \%}{100}} \right)$$

$$= \frac{1800}{1.2} = 1500 \dots Ans.$$

Discount and Marked Price

1. **Discount Formula**

$$Discount = Marked\ Price - Selling\ Price$$

2. **Discount Percentage**

$$Discount\ \% = \left(\frac{Discount}{Marked\ Price} \right) \times 100$$

3. **Successive Discounts**

   If two successive discounts of x% and y% are given, the effective discount is:

$$Effective\ Discount = x + y - \frac{xy}{100}$$

Example 3:

A shopkeeper gives two successive discounts of **20% and 10%** on an item marked at ₹5000. Find the final price.

Solution:

$$Effective\ Discount = 20 + 10 - \frac{20 \times 10}{100}$$

$$= 20 + 10 - \frac{200}{100}$$

$$= 20 + 10 - 2 = 28\%$$

$$Discount = \frac{28}{100} \times 5000 = 1400$$

$$\therefore Final\ price = 5000 - 1400 = Rs\ 3600$$

False Weight and Dishonest Shopkeeper

1. If a shopkeeper **uses less weight** but sells at cost price, the profit percentage is:

$$Profit\ \% = \left(\frac{True\ Weight - False\ Weight}{False\ Weight}\right) \times 100$$

2. If a shopkeeper **mixes cheaper items** with an expensive item and sells at the price of the expensive item, the profit percentage is:

$$Profit\ \% = \left(\frac{Cheaper\ Item\ Quantity}{Total\ Quantity}\right) \times 100$$

Example 4:

A shopkeeper uses a **900g weight** instead of 1kg and sells at cost price. Find his profit%.

$$Profit\ \% = \left(\frac{1000 - 900}{900}\right) \times 100$$

$$= \frac{100}{900} \times 100 = 11.11$$

Partnership

When two or more people invest in a business, **profit is shared in the ratio of their investments**.

1. **Formula for Partnership Profit Sharing:**

$$Profit\ Share = \frac{Invenstment\ \times Time}{Total\ Investment\ Time}$$

Example 5:

A and B invest ₹4000 and ₹6000 in a business. After one year, the total profit is ₹5000. Find A's share.

$$Total\ Investment = 4000 + 6000 = 10000$$

$$A's\ Profit = \frac{4000}{10000} \times 5000 = 2000$$

So, **A gets ₹2000,** and **B gets ₹3000.**

Shortcut Tricks for Profit and Loss

1. If an item is sold at $x\%$ **profit** and then sold again at $y\%$ **loss**, the net percentage effect is:

$$Net\ Effect = \frac{x - y - \frac{xy}{100}}{on\ Cost\ Price}$$

2. If two items are sold at the same price, one at $x\%$ **profit** and the other at $x\%$ **loss**, then there is **always a loss**, and the formula is:

$$Loss\ \% = \frac{x^2}{100}$$

3. If the price of an article increases by **x%**, the reduction in quantity to maintain the same expenditure is:

$$\frac{x}{100 + x} \times 100$$

Concept Check 15: Profit and Loss

1. *A shopkeeper buys an item for ₹800 and sells it for ₹1000. Find the profit percentage.*
2. *An item is sold at ₹600 after a 25% discount. Find the marked price.*
3. *A dishonest dealer uses **950g** weight instead of 1kg and sells at cost price. Find the profit%.*
4. *A trader makes a **25% profit** on cost price. Find his selling price if his cost price is ₹640.*
5. *A partner A invests ₹5000, and B invests ₹8000 in a business. If the profit at the end of the year is ₹3900, how much will A get?*

UGC NET PYQ Questions and Explanations on Profit and Loss:

Question

A shopkeeper purchased 10 kg of Basmati rice at the rate of Rs. 50 per kg and 15 kg of ordinary rice at the rate of Rs. 20 per kg. He mixed the two varieties of the rice and sold it for a gain of 25%. What was his sale price (Rs/kg)?

1. Rs 10 per kg
2. Rs 20 per kg
3. Rs 30 per kg
4. Rs 40 per kg

Explanations
Answer: 4. Rs 40 per kg
Step 1: Calculate the Cost Price (CP) of Each Rice

- o **Basmati rice**:
    - o Quantity = 10 kg
    - o Rate = Rs. 50 per kg
    - o Total cost = $10 \times 50 = Rs.\,500$
- o **Ordinary rice**:
    - o Quantity = 15 kg
    - o Rate = Rs. 20 per kg
    - o Total cost = $15 \times 20 = Rs.\,300$

Step 2: Calculate Total Cost Price (CP)
$$Total\ CP = 500 + 300 = Rs.\,800$$

Step 3: Calculate Total Quantity of Mixed Rice
$$Total\ quantity = 10 + 15 = 25\ kg$$

Step 4: Calculate Selling Price (SP) for 25% Gain
The shopkeeper wants a **25% profit** on the total cost price. The selling price is:
$$SP = CP + 25\%\ of\ CP$$
$$SP = 800 + 0.25 \times 800 = 800 + 200 = Rs.\,1,000$$

Step 5: Calculate Sale Price per kg
$$Sale\ price\ per\ kg = \frac{SP}{Total\ quantity} = \frac{1,000}{25} = Rs.\,40\ per\ kg$$

Question

The cost price of an article is 95% of its selling price. Find the percentage of profit or loss.

1. 5% loss
2. 5% profit
3. 5.26% profit
4. 5.5% loss

Explanations
Answer: 3. 5.26% profit
Step 1: Define the Selling Price (SP)
Let the selling price of the article be *SP*.

Step 2: Express the Cost Price (CP)

The cost price is **95% of the selling price**:

$$CP = 0.95 \times SP$$

Step 3: Calculate Profit

Profit is the difference between the selling price and the cost price:

$$Profit = SP - CP$$
$$Substitute\ CP = 0.95 \times SP:$$
$$Profit = SP - 0.95SP = 0.05SP$$

Step 4: Calculate Percentage Profit

The percentage profit is:

$$Percentage\ of\ Profit = \left(\frac{Profit}{CP}\right) \times 100$$
$$Substitute\ Profit = 0.05SP\ \ and\ CP = 0.95SP:$$
$$Percentage\ Profit = \left(\frac{0.05SP}{0.95SP}\right) \times 100 = \left(\frac{0.05}{0.95}\right) \times 100$$
$$Percentage\ of\ Profit = 5.26\% \ldots Ans.$$

Question

Which of the following is/are true?

A. *If the selling price (SP) of an article is 40 and the gain is 15%, the cost price (CP) of the article is 32.*

B. *A man bought a toy for 150 and sold it at a profit of 8%. He sold the toy for 162.*

C. *A man buys a cycle for 500, but due to some problem, he sells it for 400. He thus incurs a loss of 22%.*

D. *Cost price of an article, if its SP is 210 and the loss is 30 %, is 300.*

1. (A) Only
2. (A) and (D) Only
3. (B) and (D) Only
4. (B) and (C) Only

Explanations

Answer: 3. (B) and (D) Only

Statement A: "If the selling price (SP) of an article is 40 and the gain is 15%, the cost price (CP) of the article is 32."

- **Given:** SP = 40, Gain = 15%
- **Formula:** $SP = CP + Gain$

- o Substituting the values:

$$40 = CP + 0.15CP = 1.15CP$$

$$CP = \frac{40}{1.15} = 34.78$$

- o The cost price is **34.78**, not **32**.
- o **Statement A is false.**

Statement B:
"A man bought a toy for 150 and sold it at a profit of 8%. He sold the toy for 162."

- o **Given:** CP = 150, Profit = 8%
- o **Formula:** $SP = CP + Profit$
- o Substituting the values:

$$SP = 150 + 0.08 \times 150 = 150 + 12 = 162$$

- o The selling price is **162**, which matches the statement.
- o **Statement B is true.**

Statement C:
"A man buys a cycle for 500, but due to some problem, he sells it for 400. He thus incurs a loss of 22%."

- o **Given:** CP = 500, SP = 400
- o **Formula:** $Loss = CP - SP$
- o Substituting the values:

$$Loss = 500 - 400 = 100$$

- o **Percentage Loss:**

$$Percentage\ Loss = \left(\frac{Loss}{CP}\right) \times 100 = \left(\frac{100}{500}\right) \times 100 = 20\%$$

- o The loss is **20%**, not **22%**.
- o **Statement C is false.**

Statement D:
"Cost price of an article, if its SP is 210 and the loss is 30%, is 300."

- o **Given:** SP = 210, Loss = 30%
- o **Formula:** $SP = CP - Loss$
- o Substituting the values:

$$210 = CP - 0.30CP = 0.70CP$$

$$CP = \frac{210}{0.70} = 300$$

- o The cost price is **300**, which matches the statement.
- o **Statement D is true.**

Answer: 3. (B) and (D) Only.

Question

The cost price of two articles is same, one of them is sold at a profit of 13% while the other one is sold at a profit of 19%. If the difference between their selling price is Rs. 126, the cost of price of each article is

1. Rs.1800
2. Rs.1900
3. Rs. 2000
4. Rs. 2100

Explanations

Answer: 4. Rs. 2100

Step 1: Define the Cost Price

Let the cost price of each article be CP.

Step 2: Calculate Selling Prices

- **First article** is sold at a profit of **13%**:
$$SP1 = CP + 0.13CP = 1.13CP$$
- **Second article** is sold at a profit of **19%**:
$$SP2 = CP + 0.19CP = 1.19CP$$

Step 3: Find the Difference in Selling Prices

The difference between the selling prices is given as **Rs. 126**:
$$SP2 - SP1 = 126$$

Substitute the values of $SP1$ and $SP2$:
$$1.19CP - 1.13CP = 126$$
$$0.06CP = 126$$

Step 4: Solve for CP

Divide both sides by 0.06:
$$CP = \frac{126}{0.06} = 2{,}100 \dots Ans.$$

Question

By selling 35 eggs for Rs 30, a man loses 25%. How many eggs should he sell for Rs 144 to gain 20%.

1. 85
2. 95
3. 105
4. 115

Explanations

Answer: 3. 105

Step 1: Find the Cost Price (CP) of 35 Eggs

- o The man sells **35 eggs for Rs 30** and incurs a **25% loss**.
- o Let the cost price of 35 eggs be **CP**.
- o Selling price (SP) with a 25% loss:

$$SP = CP - 0.25CP = 0.75CP$$

- o Given $SP = 30$:

$$0.75CP = 30$$

- o Solve for CP:

$$CP = 300.75 = 40$$

- o The cost price of **35 eggs** is **Rs 40**.

Step 2: Find the Cost Price per Egg

$$Cost\ price\ per\ egg = \frac{40}{35} = \frac{8}{7}\ Rs$$

Step 3: Find the Selling Price (SP) for 20% Profit

- o To gain a **20% profit**, the selling price per egg is:

$$SP per\ egg = CP per\ egg + 0.20 \times CP per\ egg = 1.20 \times \frac{8}{7} = \frac{9.6}{7}\ Rs$$

Step 4: Calculate the Number of Eggs to Sell for Rs 144

- o Let the number of eggs to be sold for Rs 144 be **x**.
- o Total selling price for x eggs:

$$x \times \frac{9.6}{7} = 144$$

- o Solve for x:

$$x = \frac{144 \times 7}{9.6} = \frac{1008}{9.6} = 105 \dots Ans.$$

Question

A person sold an item at a loss of 7%. Had he sold the item at a gain of 7.5%, he would have received Rs. 87 more than his selling price. The cost price of the item is:

1. Rs. 500
2. Rs. 550
3. Rs. 600
4. Rs. 650

Explanations

Answer: 3. 600

Step 1: Define the Cost Price

Let the cost price of the item be **CP**.

Step 2: Calculate Selling Price at 7% Loss

- o   Selling price at a loss of 7%:

$$SP1 = CP - 0.07CP = 0.93CP$$

Step 3: Calculate Selling Price at 7.5% Gain

- o   Selling price at a gain of 7.5%:

$$SP2 = CP + 0.075CP = 1.075CP$$

Step 4: Use the Given Condition

The difference between the selling prices is **Rs. 87**:

$$SP2 - SP1 = 87$$

Substitute $SP1$ and $SP2$:

$$1.075CP - 0.93CP = 87$$
$$0.145CP = 87$$

Step 5: Solve for CP

Divide both sides by 0.145:

$$CP = 870.145 = 600 \ldots Ans.$$

Question

Which of the following statements is correct?

A. A man purchased an item at 4/5 of its selling price X and sold it at 5% more than X. His gain is 25%

B. A dealer professes to sell his goods at cost price but uses a weight of 900g for a kg weight. His gain is $11\frac{1}{9}\%$

C. If the loss is one-third of the selling price, the loss percentage is 25%.

D. By selling 100 pens, a vendor gains the selling price of 20 pens. His gain is 20%.

Choose the correct answer from the options given below.

1. A B
2. B C
3. C D
4. A D

Explanations

Answer: 2. B C

Statement A: "A man purchased an item at 4/5 of its selling price X and sold it at 5% more than X. His gain is 25%."

- **Given**:
  - Purchase price $= \frac{4}{5}X$
  - Selling price $= X + 0.05X = 1.05X$
- **Gain**:

$$Gain = Selling\ Price - Purchase\ Price = 1.05X - \frac{4}{5}X = 1.05X - 0.80X = 0.25X$$

- **Gain Percentage**:

$$Gain\ Percentage = \left(\frac{Gain}{Purchase\ Price}\right) \times 100 = \left(\frac{0.25X}{0.80X}\right) \times 100 = 31.25\%$$

- The gain is **31.25%**, not **25%**.
- **Statement A is false.**

Statement B: "A dealer professes to sell his goods at cost price but uses a weight of 900g for a kg weight. His gain is $11\frac{1}{9}\%$**. "**

- **Given**:
  - The dealer sells **900g** instead of **1000g** (1 kg).
  - The cost price (CP) of 1000g is the selling price (SP) of 900g.
- **Gain**:
  - The dealer effectively gains **100g** for every **900g** sold.
- **Gain Percentage**:

$$Gain\ Percentage = \left(\frac{Gain}{Actual\ Weight\ Sold}\right) \times 100 = \left(\frac{100}{900}\right) \times 100$$

$$= 11.1\overline{}\%$$

- o The gain is $11\frac{1}{9}\%$, which matches the statement.
- o **Statement B is true.**

Statement C: "If the loss is one-third of the selling price, the loss percentage is 25%."

- o **Given:**

$$Loss = \frac{1}{3} \times Selling\ Price\ (SP)$$

- o **Formula:**

$$Loss = Cost\ Price\ (CP) - SP$$

$$\frac{1}{3}SP = CP - SP$$

$$CP = SP + \frac{1}{3}SP = \frac{4}{3}SP$$

- o **Loss Percentage:**

$$Loss\ Percentage = \left(\frac{Loss}{CP}\right) \times 100 = \left(\frac{\frac{1}{3}SP}{\frac{4}{3}SP}\right) \times 100 = \left(\frac{1}{4}\right) \times 100 = 25\%$$

- o The loss percentage is **25%**, which matches the statement.
- o **Statement C is true.**

Statement D: "By selling 100 pens, a vendor gains the selling price of 20 pens. His gain is 20%."

- o **Given:**
  - ▪ Let the selling price of one pen be **SP**.
  - ▪ Total selling price of 100 pens = 100SP.
  - ▪ Gain = Selling price of 20 pens = 20SP.
- o **Cost Price (CP):**
  $$CP = Total\ Selling\ Price - Gain = 100SP - 20SP = 80SP$$
- o **Gain Percentage:**

$$Gain\ Percentage = \left(\frac{Gain}{CP}\right) \times 100 = \left(\frac{20SP}{80SP}\right) \times 100 = 25\%$$

- o The gain is **25%**, not **20%**.
- o **Statement D is false.**

Answer: Correct Option: 2. B and C.

Question

A person buys a mobile phone from a shop for Rs. 7800.00. The shopkeeper makes a profit of 20% at the cost price. What is the cost price of the mobile phone?

1. Rs 6500
2. Rs 6240
3. Rs 5860
4. Rs 36800

Explanations

Answer: 1. Rs 6500

Step 1: Define the Selling Price (SP)

The selling price of the mobile phone is **Rs. 7800**.

Step 2: Express the Profit

The shopkeeper makes a **20% profit** on the cost price. This means:

$$Profit = 0.20 \times CP$$

Step 3: Relate Selling Price to Cost Price

The selling price is the sum of the cost price and the profit:

$$SP = CP + Profit$$

Substitute the profit:

$$7800 = CP + 0.20CP$$
$$7800 = 1.20CP$$

Step 4: Solve for *CP*

Divide both sides by 1.20:

$$CP = \frac{7800}{1.20} = 6500 \dots Ans.$$

Question

Aman purchased some oranges at 4 oranges for Rs7 and sold them at 7 oranges for Rs13. Thus, he gained Rs30 in all. The number of oranges he bought is:

1. 252
2. 280
3. 308

4. 336

Explanations
Answer: 2. 280
Step 1: Define the Number of Oranges
Let the number of oranges Aman bought be **x**.

Step 2: Calculate the Cost Price (CP)
- o   Aman purchased **4 oranges for Rs 7**.
- o   Cost price per orange:

$$CP\ per\ orange = \frac{7}{4}\ Rs$$

- o   Total cost price for x oranges:

$$Total\ CP = x \times \frac{7}{4} = \frac{7x}{4}\ Rs$$

Step 3: Calculate the Selling Price (SP)
- o   Aman sold **7 oranges for Rs 13**.
- o   Selling price per orange:

$$SP\ per\ orange = \frac{13}{7}\ RsS$$

- o   Total selling price for x oranges:

$$Total\ SP = x \times \frac{13}{7} = \frac{13x}{7}\ Rs$$

Step 4: Calculate the Profit
- o $Profit = Total\ SP - Total\ CP$
- o   Given that the profit is **Rs 30**:

$$\frac{13x}{7} - \frac{7x}{4} = 30$$

Step 5: Solve for x
- o   Find a common denominator for the fractions:

$$LHS = \frac{13x}{7} - \frac{7x}{4} = \frac{52x - 49x}{28} = \frac{3x}{28}$$

- o   Set the equation equal to 30:

$$\frac{3x}{28} = 30$$

- o   Multiply both sides by 28:

$$3x = 840$$

$$x = \frac{840}{3} = 280 \ldots Ans.$$

$$No\ of\ arranges\ bought\ = 280$$

Question

Two lots of oranges with equal quantity, one costing Rs20 per dozen and the other costing Rs30 per dozen, are mixed together and the whole lot is sold at Rs24 per dozen. Find the profit or loss in percentage?

1. 52% profit
2. 4 % loss
3. 4 % profit
4. 52% loss

Explanations

Answer: 2. 4 % loss

Step 1: Define the Quantity

Let the number of dozens in each lot be x. Since the two lots have equal quantities, the total number of dozens in the mixture is: $2x$

Step 2: Calculate the Total Cost Price (CP)
- o **First lot**: Cost = Rs 20 per dozen
$$CP\ of\ first\ lot = 20x$$
- o **Second lot**: Cost = Rs 30 per dozen
$$CP\ of\ second\ lot = 30x$$
- o **Total CP**:
$$Total\ CP = 20x + 30x = 50x$$

Step 3: Calculate the Total Selling Price (SP)
- o The mixture is sold at Rs 24 per dozen.
- o Total SP:
$$Total\ SP = 24 \times 2x = 48x$$

Step 4: Determine Profit or Loss
- o **Profit or Loss** = Total SP - Total CP
$$48x - 50x = -2x$$
- o Since the result is negative, there is a **loss** of $Rs\ 2x$.

Step 5: Calculate Loss Percentage

o   Loss percentage is calculated as:

$$Loss\ Percentage = \left(\frac{Loss}{Total\ CP}\right) \times 100$$

o   Substitute the values:

$$Loss\ Percentage = \left(\frac{2x}{50x}\right) \times 100 = 4\% \dots Ans.$$

Question

Total cost price (C.P.) of two cars A and B of different models is Rs 5.0 lakhs. Car A is sold at a profit of 20% and car B is sold at a loss of 20%. However, the selling price of the two cars A and B remains the same.

Find the cost price (C.P.) of the two cars A and B in lakhs, respectively

1.   Rs 2.5 lakh and Rs 2.5 lakh
2.   Rs 2.4 lakh and Rs 2.6 lakh
3.   Rs 2.0 lakh and Rs 3.0 lakh
4.   Rs 2.6 lakh and Rs 2.4 lakh

Explanations

Answer: 3. Rs 2.0 lakh and Rs 3.0 lakh

Step 1: Define the Cost Prices

Let the cost price of car A be **CPA** and the cost price of car B be **CPB**.
Given:

$$CPA + CPB = 5.0\ lakhs \dots\dots (1)$$

Step 2: Express Selling Prices

o   Car A is sold at a **20% profit**:

$$SPA = CPA + 0.20CPA = 1.20CPA$$

o   Car B is sold at a **20% loss**:

$$SPB = CPB - 0.20CPB = 0.80CPB$$

Step 3: Equate Selling Prices

The selling prices of the two cars are the same:

$$SPA = SPB$$

Substitute the values:

$$1.20CPA = 0.80CPB$$

Simplify:

$$1.20CPA = 0.80CPB$$
$$\frac{CPA}{CPB} = \frac{0.80}{1.20} = \frac{2}{3}$$

$$CPA = \frac{2}{3CPB} \ldots\ldots (2)$$

Step 4: Substitute into Equation (1)

From equation (1):

$$CPA + CPB = 5.0$$

$$Substitute\ CPA = \frac{2}{3}CPB:$$

$$\frac{2}{3}CPB + CPB = 5.0$$

$$\frac{5}{3}C\,PB = 5.0$$

$$CPB = 5.0 \times \frac{3}{5} = 3.0\ lakhs$$

From equation (2):

$$CPA = \frac{2}{3}CPB = \frac{2}{3} \times 3.0 = 2.0\ lakhs$$

Answer: The cost prices of the two cars are 2.0 lakh and 3.0 lakh

Question

Statement (I): *A man sells his goods at 10% profit. If he sells his goods at 15% profit, he gets 160 more. The cost price of his goods is 4200.*

Statement (II): *A man spends 80% of his earnings. His earnings increased by 25% and his expenses increased by 20%. The man's savings thus increased by 45%.*

1. Both Statement I and Statement II are true
2. Both Statement I and Statement II are false
3. Statement I is true but Statement II is false
4. Statement I is false but Statement II is true

Explanations

Answer: 4. Statement I is false but Statement II is true

Statement I: "A man sells his goods at 10% profit. If he sells his goods at 15% profit, he gets 160 more. The cost price of his goods is 4200."

- Let the cost price (CP) of the goods be *CP*.
- Selling price at **10% profit:**

$$SP1 = CP + 0.10CP = 1.10CP$$

- o Selling price at **15% profit**:
$$SP2 = CP + 0.15CP = 1.15CP$$
- o The difference between the two selling prices is **160**:
$$SP2 - SP1 = 160$$
$$1.15CP - 1.10CP = 160$$
$$0.05CP = 160$$
$$CP = \frac{0.05}{160} = 3200$$
- o The cost price is **3200**, not **4200**.
- o **Statement I is false.**

Statement II: "A man spends 80% of his earnings. His earnings increased by 25% and his expenses increased by 20%. The man's savings thus increased by 45%."
- o Let the man's initial earnings be **E**.
- o Initial expenses:
$$Expenses = 0.80E$$
- o Initial savings:
$$Savings = E - 0.80E = 0.20E$$
- o After a **25% increase**, new earnings:
$$Enew = E + 0.25E = 1.25E$$
- o After a **20% increase**, new expenses:
Expensesnew=0.80E+0.20×0.80E=0.96EExpensesnew =0.80E+0.20×0.80E=0.96E
- o New savings:
$$Savingsnew = 1.25E - 0.96E = 0.29E$$
- o Increase in savings:
$$Increase\ in\ savings = 0.29E - 0.20E = 0.09E$$
- o Percentage increase in savings:
$$Percentage\ increase = \left(\frac{0.09E}{0.20E}\right) \times 100 = 45\%$$
- o The savings increased by **45%**, which matches the statement.
- o **Statement II is true.**

Answer: Statement I is false, but **Statement II is true.**

Question

The selling price of 30 fans is equal to the purchase price of 25 fans. What is the profit or loss in percentage?

1. *A gain of* $16\frac{2}{3}\%$
2. *A loss of* 15%
3. *A loss of* $16\frac{2}{3}\%$
4. *No gain, no loss*

Explanations

Answer: 3. *A loss of* $16\frac{2}{3}\%$

Step 1: Define the Cost Price (CP) and Selling Price (SP)
- o Let the cost price of one fan be **CP**.
- o Let the selling price of one fan be **SP**.

Step 2: Use the Given Condition

The selling price of **30 fans** is equal to the purchase price of **25 fans**:

$$30 \times SP = 25 \times CP$$

Simplify:

$$30SP = 25CP$$

$$SP = \frac{25CP}{30} = \frac{5CP}{6}$$

Step 3: Determine Profit or Loss
- o Since $SP = \frac{5CP}{6}$, the selling price is **less than** the cost price. This indicates a **loss**.
- o Loss per fan:

$$Loss = CP - SP = CP - \frac{5CP}{6} = \frac{CP}{6}$$

Step 4: Calculate Loss Percentage

$$Loss\ Percentage = \left(\frac{Loss}{CP}\right) \times 100$$

Substitute the loss:

$$Loss\ Percentage = \left(\frac{\frac{CP}{6}}{CP}\right) \times 100 = \frac{1}{6} \times 100 = 16.6\% \ldots Ans.$$

Question

The owner of a mobile phone charges his customer 25% more than the cost price. If a customer paid 8,000/- for a mobile phone, then what was the cost price of the mobile?

1. Rs.5600
2. Rs. 6000
3. Rs.6400
4. Rs.7000

Explanations

Answer: 3. Rs.6400

Step 1: Define the Cost Price (CP)

Let the cost price of the mobile phone be **CP**.

Step 2: Express the Selling Price (SP)

The owner charges **25% more** than the cost price. Therefore:

$$SP = CP + 0.25CP = 1.25CP$$

Step 3: Use the Given Selling Price

The customer paid **Rs 8,000** for the mobile phone:

$$1.25CP = 8000$$

Step 4: Solve for *CP*

Divide both sides by 1.25:

$$CP = \frac{8000}{1.25} = 6400$$

Interest (Simple and Compound)

Understanding Interest

Interest is the extra amount paid for borrowing money or earned on an investment. It is calculated based on the principal amount, rate of interest, and time.

There are two types of interest:

1. **Simple Interest (SI)** – Interest is calculated only on the principal.
2. **Compound Interest (CI)** – Interest is calculated on the principal and on accumulated interest.

Simple Interest (SI)

Formula for Simple Interest:

$$SI = \frac{P \times R \times T}{100}$$

Where:

- P = Principal (Initial amount)
- R = Rate of interest per annum
- T = Time in years

Amount (Total Money Paid or Received):

$$A = P + SI$$

Example 1:

A sum of ₹5000 is deposited at an annual interest rate of **6%** for **3 years**. Find the simple interest and total amount.

Solution:

$$SI = \frac{(5000 \times 6 \times 3)}{100} = \frac{90000}{100} = ₹900$$
$$A = 5000 + 900 = ₹5900$$

Compound Interest (CI)

Unlike SI, **Compound Interest** is calculated on the principal and previously accumulated interest.

Formula for Compound Interest:

$$A = P \times \left(1 + \frac{R}{100}\right)^T$$
$$CI = A - P$$

Where:

- A = *Final Amount after T years*
- P = *Principal Amount*
- R = *Rate of Interest per annum*
- T = *Time in years*

CI for Different Compounding Intervals

1. **Annually**:

$$A = P \times \left(1 + \frac{R}{100}\right)^T$$

2. **Half-Yearly (Semi-Annually)**:

$$A = P \times \left(1 + \frac{R}{2 \times 100}\right)^{2T}$$

3. **Quarterly**:

$$A = P \times \left(1 + \frac{R}{4 \times 100}\right)^{4T}$$

4. **Monthly**:

$$A = P \times \left(1 + \frac{R}{12 \times 100}\right)^{12T}$$

Example 2:

₹4000 is deposited at a **10% annual interest rate** for **2 years**. Find the compound interest.

Solution:

$$A = P \times \left(1 + \frac{R}{100}\right)^T$$

$$A = 4000 \times \left(1 + \frac{10}{100}\right)^2$$

$$= 4000 \times (1.1)^2$$

$$= 4000 \times 1.21 = ₹4840$$

$$CI = 4840 - 4000 = ₹840$$

Difference Between SI and CI

For **2 years**, the difference between **CI and SI** is:

$$Difference = \frac{P \times R^2}{100^2}$$

For **3 years**, the difference is:

$$Difference = \frac{P \times R^2}{100^2} + \frac{P \times R^3}{100^3}$$

Example 3:

A sum of ₹5000 is deposited for **2 years** *at* **10%** ***per annum***. Find the difference between SI and CI.

Solution:

$$SI = \frac{5000 \times 10 \times 2}{100} = 1000$$

$$CI = 5000 \times \left(1 + \frac{10}{100}\right)^2 = 5000 \times 1.21 = 6050$$

$$Difference = 6050 - 6000 = ₹50$$

Growth and Depreciation Formula

For Population or Value Growth:

$$A = P \times \left(1 + \frac{R}{100}\right)^T$$

For Depreciation (Decrease in Value):

$$A = P \times \left(1 - \frac{R}{100}\right)^T$$

Example 4:

A machine costs ₹50000 and depreciates by **10% per year**. Find its value after **3 years**.

$$A = 50000 \times \left(1 - \frac{10}{100}\right)^3$$
$$= 50000 \times (0.9)^3$$
$$= 50000 \times 0.729 = ₹36450 \ldots Ans.$$

Compound Interest with Varying Rates

When the rate of interest is different for different years:

$$A = P \times \left(1 + \frac{R_1}{100}\right) \times \left(1 + \frac{R_2}{100}\right) \times \left(1 + \frac{R_3}{100}\right)$$

Example 5:

₹6000 is deposited for **3 years** at interest rates of **5%, 10%, and 15%** for each year. Find the amount.

$$A = 6000 \times \left(1 + \frac{5}{100}\right) \times \left(1 + \frac{10}{100}\right) \times \left(1 + \frac{15}{100}\right)$$
$$= 6000 \times 1.05 \times 1.10 \times 1.15$$
$$= 6000 \times 1.323 = ₹7938$$

Shortcut Tricks for Interest

1. **For two years, CI and SI difference is:**

$$Difference = \frac{P \times R^2}{100^2}$$

2. **CI is greater than SI when time $> 1\ year$.**
3. **For long-term investments, always use CI instead of SI.**
4. **For successive percentage increase/decrease, use:**

$$A = P \times \left(1 + \frac{x}{100}\right) \times \left(1 + \frac{y}{100}\right)$$

5. **For double the money in CI, use the rule:**

$$T = \frac{72}{R}$$

Example: At **12% interest rate**, money doubles in $\frac{72}{12} = $ **6 years**.

Concept Check 16: Interest

1. *Find the simple interest on ₹5000 for 4 years at a 6% interest rate.*
2. *A sum of ₹8000 is deposited at 10% CI per annum for 2 years. Find the final amount.*
3. *The population of a city is 120000 and increases by 5% annually. Find the population after 2 years.*
4. *₹7000 is invested for 3 years at a 5% per annum varying rate (5%, 6%, and 7%). Find the amount.*
5. *What will be the difference between CI and SI for ₹10000 at 12% per annum for 2 years?*

UGC NET PYQ Questions and Explanations on Interests:

Question

Find the sum of money which will amount to Rs 26010 in 6 months at the rate of 8% per annum when interest is compounded quarterly.

1. Rs 24500
2. Rs 25000
3. Rs 25600
4. Rs 26000

Explanations
Answer: 2. Rs 25000

Step 1: Understand the Given Information
- **Amount (A)** = Rs 26,010

- o **Time (t)** = 6 months = 0.5 years
- o **Rate of interest (r)** = 8% per annum
- o **Compounding frequency** = Quarterly (4 times a year)

Step 2: Formula for Compound Interest

The formula for compound interest is:

$$A = P\left(1 + \frac{r}{n}\right)^{t}$$

Where:

- o P = Principal (initial sum of money)
- o r = Annual interest rate (in decimal)
- o n = Number of times interest is compounded per year
- o t = Time in years

Step 3: Substitute the Values

- o A=26,010
- o r=8%=0.08
- o n=4 (since interest is compounded quarterly)
- o t=0.5 years

Substitute these values into the formula:

$$26{,}010 = P\left(1 + \frac{0.08}{4}\right)^{4\times0.5}$$

Step 4: Simplify the Equation

$$26{,}010 = P(1 + 0.02)^2$$
$$26{,}010 = P(1.02)^2$$
$$26{,}010 = P \times 1.0404$$

Step 5: Solve for PP

$$P = 26{,}0101.0404 = 25{,}000 \dots Ans.$$

Question

A sum of Rs. 1.0 Lakh is invested for 1 year at an interest rate of 10% per annum compounded half-yearly. The compound interest is

1. Rs. 6150
2. Rs. 10250
3. Rs. 10500
4. Rs. 11000

Explanations
Answer: 2. Rs. 10250

Step 1: Understand the Given Information
- **Principal (P)** = Rs 1,00,000
- **Rate of interest (r)** = 10% per annum
- **Time (t)** = 1 year
- **Compounding frequency** = Half-yearly (2 times a year)

Step 2: Formula for Compound Interest
The formula for compound interest is:

$$A = P\left(1 + \frac{r}{n}\right)^{nt}$$

Where:
- A = Amount after interest
- P = Principal
- r = Annual interest rate (in decimal)
- n = Number of times interest is compounded per year
- t = Time in years

Step 3: Substitute the Values
- $P=1,00,000$
- $r=10\%=0.10$
- $n=2$ (since interest is compounded half-yearly)
- $t=1$ year

Substitute these values into the formula:

$$A = 1,00,000\left(1 + \frac{0.10}{2}\right)^{2\times1}$$

Step 4: Simplify the Equation
$$A = 1,00,000(1 + 0.05)^2$$
$$A = 1,00,000(1.05)^2$$
$$A = 1,00,000 \times 1.1025 = 1,10,250$$

Step 5: Calculate Compound Interest
$$Compound\ Interest = A - P = 1,10,250 - 1,00,000 = 10,250 \ldots Ans.$$

Question

A person borrowed Rs. 1024 for two years at 50% interest per annum but payable half-yearly. If the interest was compound interest, then how much amount would he have to pay back at the end of the loan period?

1. Rs. 2048
2. Rs. 2500
3. Rs. 5344
4. Rs. 5184

Explanations

Answer: 2. Rs. 2500

Step 1: Understand the Given Information

- **Principal (P)** = Rs 1,024
- **Rate of interest (r)** = 50% per annum
- **Time (t)** = 2 years
- **Compounding frequency** = Half-yearly (2 times a year)

Step 2: Formula for Compound Interest

The formula for compound interest is:

$$A = P\left(1 + \frac{r}{n}\right)^{nt}$$

Step 3: Substitute the Values

- $P = 1{,}024$
- $r = 50\% = 0.50$
- $n = 2$ (since interest is compounded half-yearly)
- $t = 2$ years

Substitute these values into the formula:

$$A = 1{,}024\left(1 + \frac{0.50}{2}\right)^{2\times2}$$

Step 4: Simplify the Equation

$$A = 1{,}024(1 + 0.25)4$$
$$A = 1{,}024(1.25)4$$
$$A = 1{,}024 \times 2.44140625 = 2{,}500 \dots Ans.$$

Question (Simple)

A sum of money becomes 34800 in 2 years and 42,000 in 5 years at simple interest per annum. Find the rate of interest and the sum of money respectively

1. 6%, 40,000
2. 7%, 30.000
3. 8%, 30,000
4. 5%, 35,000

Explanations

Answer: 3. 8%, 30,000

Step 1: Understand the Given Information
- The sum becomes **Rs 34,800** in **2 years.**
- The sum becomes **Rs 42,000** in **5 years.**
- The interest is **simple interest.**

Step 2: Formula for Simple Interest

The formula for simple interest is:

$$A = P + SI$$

Where:
- A = Amount after interest
- P = Principal
- SI = Simple Interest

The simple interest formula is:

$$SI = P \times r \times t$$

Where:
- r = Rate of interest (in decimal)
- t = Time in years

Step 3: Set Up Equations

For **2 years**:

$$34,800 = P + P \times r \times 2$$
$$34,800 = P(1 + 2r) \ldots\ldots (1)$$

For **5 years**:

$$42,000 = P + P \times r \times 5$$
$$42,000 = P(1 + 5r) \ldots\ldots (2)$$

Step 4: Divide Equations (2) and (1)

Divide equation (2) by equation (1):

$$\frac{42{,}000}{34{,}800} = \frac{P(1 + 5r)}{P(1 + 2r)}$$

Simplify:

$$\frac{42{,}000}{34{,}800} = \frac{1 + 5r}{1 + 2r}$$

$$\frac{35}{29} = \frac{1 + 5r}{1 + 2r}$$

Cross-multiply:

$$35(1 + 2r) = 29(1 + 5r)$$

Expand:

$$35 + 70r = 29 + 145r$$

Rearrange:

$$35 - 29 = 145r - 70r$$

$$6 = 75r$$

$$r = \frac{6}{75} = 0.08 = 8\% \ldots Ans.$$

Step 5: Find the Principal (P)

Substitute r=8%=0.08 into equation (1):

$$34{,}800 = P(1 + 2 \times 0.08)$$

$$34{,}800 = P(1 + 0.16)$$

$$34{,}800 = 1.16P$$

$$P = \frac{34{,}800}{1.16} = 30{,}000 \ldots Ans.$$

The rate of interest is **8%**, and the sum of money (principal) is **Rs 30,000**.

Question

A man invests Rs 1550 in two parts, one part at the rate of 8% interest and another part at the rate of 6%. If the total interest earned in one year is Rs 106, find the amount invested at each rate of interest, respectively.

1. Rs 650 and Rs 900
2. Rs 700 and Rs 850
3. Rs 750 and Rs 800
4. Rs 800 and Rs 750

Explanations

Answer: 1. Rs 650 and Rs 900

Step 1: Define the Variables

Let:

- x = Amount invested at **8%**
- $1550-x$ = Amount invested at **6%**

Step 2: Calculate the Interest

- Interest from the first part (8%):

$$Interest1 = 0.08x$$

- Interest from the second part (6%):

$$Interest2 = 0.06(1550 - x)$$

Step 3: Total Interest

The total interest earned in one year is **Rs 106**:

$$Interest1 + Interest2 = 106$$

Substitute the values:

$$0.08x + 0.06(1550 - x) = 106$$

Step 4: Simplify and solve for x

Expand the equation:

$$0.08x + 93 - 0.06x = 106$$

Combine like terms:

$$0.02x + 93 = 106$$

Subtract 93 from both sides:

$$0.02x = 13$$

Divide both sides by 0.02:

$$x = \frac{13}{0.02} = 650$$

Step 5: Find the Amount Invested at Each Rate

- Amount invested at **8%**:

$$x = 650 \dots Ans.$$

- Amount invested at **6%**:

$$1550 - x = 1550 - 650 = 900 \dots Ans.$$

Final Answer: The amounts invested at **8%** and **6%** are **Rs 650** and **Rs 900**, respectively.

Question

A certain sum of money becomes 28800 in 2 years at 20% per annum of compound interest (Compounded annually). The sum of money is:

1. 24000
2. 22000
3. 21000
4. 20000

Explanations

Answer: 4. 20000

Step 1: Understand the Given Information
- **Amount (A)** = Rs 28,800
- **Time (t)** = 2 years
- **Rate of interest (r)** = 20% per annum
- **Compounding frequency** = Annually

Step 2: Formula for Compound Interest
The formula for compound interest is:

$$A = P\left(1 + \frac{r}{100}\right)^t$$

Step 3: Substitute the Values
- $A = 28,800$
- $r = 20\%$
- $t = 2$ years

Substitute these values into the formula:

$$28,800 = P\left(1 + \frac{20}{100}\right)^2$$

Step 4: Simplify the Equation

$$28,800 = P(1 + 0.20)^2$$
$$28,800 = P(1.20)^2$$
$$28,800 = P \times 1.44$$

Step 5: Solve for P

$$P = 28,800 \div 1.44 = 20,000 \ldots Ans.$$

Question (Simple)

In what time will a sum of money double itself at the rate of 12.5% per annum simple interest?

1. 10 years
2. 8 years
3. 6 years
4. 12 years

Explanations

Answer: 2. 8 years

Step 1: Understand the Given Information

- o Let the **principal (P)** be P.
- o The **amount (A)** after doubling will be $2P$.
- o **Rate of interest (r)** = 12.5% per annum
- o **Time (t)** = ?

Step 2: Formula for Simple Interest

The formula for simple interest is:

$$A = P + SI$$

The simple interest formula is:

$$SI = P \times r \times t$$

Step 3: Substitute the Values

Since the amount doubles:

$$A = 2P$$

Substitute into the simple interest formula:

$$2P = P + P \times r \times t$$

Simplify:

$$2P = P(1 + r \times t)$$

Divide both sides by P:

$$2 = 1 + r \times t$$
$$1 = r \times t$$

Step 4: Solve for t

$$Given\ r = 12.5\% = 0.125$$
$$1 = 0.125 \times t$$
$$t = \frac{1}{0.125} = 8 \dots Ans.$$

Question (Simple)

A man deposited some amount of money in a bank at some simple rate of interest for 3 years. Had he deposited the money at 2% higher rate of interest, he would have fetched Rs 360 more. Find the amount deposited in the bank.

Rs 6200

Rs 7000

Rs 6500

Rs 6000

Explanations

Answer: 4. Rs 6000

Step 1: Define the Variables

Let:

- P = Principal (amount deposited)
- r = Original rate of interest (in percentage)
- t = Time = 3 years

Step 2: Calculate Simple Interest

- **Original Simple Interest (SI)**:
$$SI = P \times r \times t = P \times r \times 3$$
- **New Simple Interest (SI')** at a **2% higher rate**:
$$SI' = P \times (r + 2) \times 3$$

Step 3: Use the Given Condition

The difference between the two simple interests is **Rs 360**:
$$SI' - SI = 360$$

Substitute the values:
$$P \times (r + 2) \times 3 - P \times r \times 3 = 360$$

Simplify:
$$3P(r + 2) - 3Pr = 360$$
$$3Pr + 6P - 3Pr = 360$$
$$6P = 360$$

Step 4: Solve for P

$$P = \frac{360}{6} = 60 \dots Ans.$$

Question (Simple)

Any amount deposited in the bank in two years amounts to Rs. 1008/- and in 3 1/2 years it becomes Rs 1164/-.

Find the bank deposit amount and annual interest rate.

1. Rs. 700, 12%
2. Rs. 800, 13%
3. Rs. 750, 13%
4. Rs. 850, 13.5%

Explanations

Answer: 2. Rs. 800, 13%

Step 1: Understand the Given Information

- The amount after **2 years** = Rs 1,008
- The amount after **3.5 years** = Rs 1,164
- The interest is **simple interest.**

Step 2: Formula for Simple Interest

The formula for simple interest is:

$$A = P + SI$$

The simple interest formula is:

$$SI = P \times r \times t$$

Step 3: Set Up Equations

For **2 years**:

$$1,008 = P + P \times r \times 2$$
$$1,008 = P(1 + 2r) \dots \dots (1)$$

For **3.5 years**:

$$1,164 = P + P \times r \times 3.5$$
$$1,164 = P(1 + 3.5r) \dots \dots (2)$$

Step 4: Divide Equations (2) and (1)

Divide equation (2) by equation (1):

$$\frac{1,164}{1,008} = \frac{P(1 + 3.5r)}{P(1 + 2r)}$$
$$\frac{1,164}{1,008} = \frac{(1 + 3.5r)}{1 + 2r}$$
$$\frac{97}{84} = \frac{1 + 3.5r}{1 + 2r}$$

$$97(1 + 2r) = 84(1 + 3.5r)$$
$$97 + 194r = 84 + 294r$$
$$97 - 84 = 294r - 194r$$
$$13 = 100r$$
$$\mathbf{13 = 100r}$$
$$r = \frac{13}{100} = 0.13 = 13\% \ldots Ans.$$

Step 5: Find the Principal (PP)

Substitute r=13%=0.13 into equation (1):

$$1{,}008 = P(1 + 2 \times 0.13)$$
$$1{,}008 = P(1 + 0.26)$$
$$1{,}008 = 1.26P$$
$$P = \frac{1{,}008}{1.26} = 800$$

Final Answer: The bank deposit amount is **Rs 800**, and the annual interest rate is **13%**.

Question (Simple and Compound)

The difference between the compound interest and simple interest on a principal amount for 2 years at 10% per annum is Rs 5431. Find the principal amount.

1. Rs 54310
2. Rs 108620
3. Rs 453100
4. Rs 543100

Explanations

Answer: 4. Rs 543100

Step 1: Understand the Given Information
- **Time (t)** = 2 years
- **Rate of interest (r)** = 10% per annum
- **Difference between compound interest (CI) and simple interest (SI)** = Rs 5,431

Step 2: Formulas for Simple Interest and Compound Interest
- **Simple Interest (SI):**

$$SI = P \times r \times t$$

- o **Compound Interest (CI):**

$$CI = P(1 + r100)t - P$$

Step 3: Calculate the Difference Between CI and SI

The difference between CI and SI is given by:

$$CI - SI = P\left(1 + \frac{r}{100}\right)^t - P - P \times r \times t$$

Substitute $t=2$ and $r=10\%$:

$$CI - SI = P\left(1 + \frac{10}{100}\right)^2 - P - P \times 0.10 \times 2$$

Simplify:

$$CI - SI = P(1.10)^2 - P - 0.20P$$
$$CI - SI = P(1.21) - P - 0.20P$$
$$CI - SI = 1.21P - 1.20P$$
$$CI - SI = 0.01P$$

Step 4: Use the Given Difference

The difference between CI and SI is **Rs 5,431**:

$$0.01P = 5,431$$
$$P = \frac{5,431}{0.01} = 543,100$$

Question (Simple and Compound)

The simple interest on a certain principal amount for 4 years at 10% per annum is half of the compound interest on Rs 1000 for 2 years at 20% per annum. Find the principal amount.

1. 500
2. 450
3. 650
4. 550

Explanations
Answer: 4. 550

Step 1: Understand the Given Information

- o **Simple Interest (SI):**
    - Principal $= P$
    - Time = 4 years

- Rate = 10% per annum
  o **Compound Interest (CI):**
    - Principal = Rs 1,000
    - Time = 2 years
    - Rate = 20% per annum
  o The simple interest is **half** of the compound interest:

$$SI = \frac{1}{2} CI$$

Step 2: Calculate Compound Interest (CI)

The formula for compound interest is:

$$CI = P\left(1 + \frac{r}{100}\right)^t - P$$

Substitute the values for CI:

$$CI = 1000\left(1 + \frac{20}{100}\right)^2 - 1000$$
$$CI = 1000(1.20)^2 - 1000$$
$$CI = 1000 \times 1.44 - 1000$$
$$CI = 1440 - 1000 = 440$$

Step 3: Calculate Simple Interest (SI)

The formula for simple interest is:

$$SI = P \times r \times t$$

Substitute the values for SI:

$$SI = P \times 0.10 \times 4 = 0.40P$$

Step 4: Relate SI and CI

$$Given\ that\ SI = \frac{1}{2} CI$$
$$0.40P = \frac{1}{2} \times 440$$
$$0.40P = 220$$
$$P = \frac{220}{0.40} = 550 \ ...\ Ans.$$

Question

Salary of a person decreases by 10% every year and his bonus increases by 24% every year. If his salary and bonuses at the end of 2020 were Rs. 8000 and Rs. 2500 respectively. find the difference between his total earnings in March 2020 and March 2022.

1.   165, increase
2.   176, increase
3.   180, decrease
4.   176, decrease

Explanations
Answer: 4. 176, decrease
Given:
  o   Salary at the end of 2020 = Rs. 8000
  o   Bonus at the end of 2020 = Rs. 2500
  o   The salary decreases by 10% every year.
  o   The bonus increases by 24% every year.

We need to find the difference between his total earnings in March 2020 and March 2022.

Earnings in March 2020:
We are told his salary and bonus at the end of 2020 (which is also the total at March 2020) were Rs. 8000 and Rs. 2500, respectively.
So, his total earnings in March 2020 =

$$Total\ earnings\ 2020 = 8000 + 2500 = 10500$$

Earnings in March 2022:
To find his earnings in March 2022, we will apply the changes over 2 years (2021 and 2022).

Salary after 1 year (end of 2021):
Salary decreases by 10% every year. So, after 1 year:

$$Salary\ in\ 2021 = 8000 \times (1 - 0.10) = 8000 \times 0.90 = 7200$$

Bonus after 1 year (end of 2021):
Bonus increases by 24% every year. So, after 1 year:

$$Bonus\ in\ 2021 = 2500 \times (1 + 0.24) = 2500 \times 1.24 = 3100$$

Salary after 2 years (end of 2022):
Salary continues to decrease by 10% each year. So, after 2 years:

$$Salary\ in\ 2022 = 7200 \times (1 - 0.10) = 7200 \times 0.90 = 6480$$

Bonus after 2 years (end of 2022):
Bonus continues to increase by 24% each year. So, after 2 years:

$$Bonus\ in\ 2022 = 3100 \times (1 + 0.24) = 3100 \times 1.24 = 3844$$

Total earnings in March 2022:
Now, we can calculate the total earnings in March 2022:

$$Total\ earnings\ in\ 2022 = 6480 + 3844 = 10324$$

Difference in total earnings:

Now, let's find the difference between total earnings in March 2020 and March 2022:

$$Difference = 10500 - 10324 = 176 \dots Ans.$$

Question (Simple)

An amount deposited at 5% simple interest becomes Rs. 1512 in 4 years. How will much the same amount become in 2 1/2 years at 10% simple interest per annum?

1. 1,475
2. 1,575
3. 1,675
4. 1,875

Explanations
Answer: 2. 1,575
Step 1: Find the Principal Amount
Given:

- Amount after 4 years = Rs 1,512
- Rate of interest = 5% per annum
- Time = 4 years

The simple interest formula is:

$$SI = P \times r \times t$$

Substitute the values:

$$1,512 = P + P \times 0.05 \times 4$$
$$1,512 = P(1 + 0.20)$$
$$1,512 = 1.20P$$
$$P = \frac{1,512}{1.20} = 1,260$$

Step 2: Calculate the Amount After 2.5 Years at 10% Interest
Now, use the principal $P=1,260$ to find the amount after **2.5 years** at **10% simple interest**.

- $r=10\%=0.10$
- $t=2.5$ years

Calculate the simple interest:

$$SI = P \times r \times t = 1,260 \times 0.10 \times 2.5 = 315$$

Calculate the amount:

$$A = P + SI = 1,260 + 315 = 1,575 \dots Ans.$$

Question

The price of an article A increases by Rs40 every year while the price of article B increases by Rs15 every year. If in 2015, the price of the article A was Rs420 and that of article B was Rs630, then in which year the article A will cost Rs40 more than article B?

1. 2022
2. 2023
3. 2025
4. 2024

Explanations

Answer: 3. 2025

Step 1: Define the Prices
- o **Article A**:
  - Initial price in 2015 = Rs 420
  - Annual increase = Rs 40
  - Price after n years = 420+40n
- o **Article B**:
  - Initial price in 2015 = Rs 630
  - Annual increase = Rs 15
  - Price after n years = 630+15n

Step 2: Set Up the Equation

We need to find the year when Article A costs **Rs 40 more** than Article B:

$$420 + 40n = 630 + 15n + 40$$
$$420 + 40n = 670 + 15n$$
$$25n = 250$$
$$n = 10$$

Step 3: Find the Year
- o Starting year = 2015
- o n=10 years later = **2025**

Question

An amount of Rs 8500 becomes Rs 9500 in 3 years' time at some simple rate of interest. How much the amount of 10,200 will become in 5 years at the same rate of simple interest?

1. Rs 11800

2. Rs 12000
3. Rs 12200
4. Rs 12500

Explanations

Answer: 3. Rs 12200

Step 1: Find the Rate of Interest

- **Principal (P)** = Rs 8,500
- **Amount (A)** = Rs 9,500
- **Time (t)** = 3 years

The simple interest formula is:

$$A = P + SI$$
$$SI = P \times r \times t$$

Substitute the values:

$$9,500 = 8,500 + 8,500 \times r \times 3$$
$$1,000 = 25,500r$$
$$r = \frac{1,000}{25,500} = \frac{2}{51} = 0.0392$$

Step 2: Calculate the Amount for Rs 10,200

- **Principal (P)** = Rs 10,200
- **Time (t)** = 5 years
- **Rate (r)** = $\frac{2}{51}$

The simple interest is:

$$SI = 10,200 \times \frac{2}{51} \times 5 = 10,200 \times \frac{10}{51} = 2,000$$

The amount is:

$$A = 10,200 + 2,000 = 12,200 \ldots Ans.$$

Question

A person invested 5000 in each of the years 2005, 2010, 2015 and 2020. The investment of the person doubles every five years. What will be the total amount, the person will receive in 2025?

1. 1,35,000
2. 1,30,000
3. 1,50,000
4. 1,20,000

Explanations

Answer: 3. 1,50,000

Given Information:

- o A person invests ₹**5000** in each of the years **2005, 2010, 2015, and 2020**.
- o The investment **doubles every 5 years**.
- o We need to find the total amount in **2025**.

Step-by-Step Calculation:

1. **Investment in 2005**:
    - o Doubles every 5 years:
        - 2010 → ₹**10,000**
        - 2015 → ₹**20,000**
        - 2020 → ₹**40,000**
        - 2025 → ₹**80,000**
2. **Investment in 2010**:
    - o Doubles every 5 years:
        - 2015 → ₹**10,000**
        - 2020 → ₹**20,000**
        - 2025 → ₹**40,000**
3. **Investment in 2015**:
    - o Doubles every 5 years:
        - 2020 → ₹**10,000**
        - 2025 → ₹**20,000**
4. **Investment in 2020**:
    - o Doubles every 5 years:
        - 2025 → ₹**10,000**

Total Amount in 2025:

$$80,000 + 40,000 + 20,000 + 10,000 = 1,50,000 \ldots Ans.$$

Question (Simple and Compound)

A man deposits Rs 5000 in a bank at the rate of 12% simple interest for 2 years. He also deposits another amount of Rs 5000 in another bank at the same rate of 12% compound interest, compounded annually. Find the difference between the simple interest and compound interest generated on the amount after 2 years

1. Rs 72
2. Rs 1200

3. Rs 1272
4. Rs 272

Explanations

Answer: 1. Rs 72

We need to calculate the difference between **Simple Interest (SI)** and **Compound Interest (CI)** on a principal of ₹**5000** at an interest rate of **12% per annum** for **2 years**.

Step 1: Calculate Simple Interest (SI)
Formula for Simple Interest:

$$SI = P \times R \times \frac{T}{100}$$

Where:
- P=5000 (Principal)
- R=12% (Rate of Interest per annum)
- T=2 years (Time)

$$SI = \frac{5000 \times 12 \times 2}{100}$$

$$SI = \frac{\mathbf{120000}}{\mathbf{100}} = \mathbf{1200}$$

Step 2: Calculate Compound Interest (CI)
Formula for Compound Interest:

$$A = P \times \left(1 + \frac{R}{100}\right)^T$$

Where:
- A is the final amount
- P=5000
- R=12%
- T=2 years

$$A = 5000 \times \left(1 + \frac{12}{100}\right)^2$$
$$= 5000 \times (1.12)^2$$
$$= 5000 \times 1.2544$$
$$A = 6272$$
$$CI = A - P = 6272 - 5000 = 1272$$

Step 3: Find the Difference

$$Difference = CI - SI = 1272 - 1200 = 72 \dots Ans.$$

Discounting

Understanding Discount

A **discount** is a reduction in price offered on a product to attract buyers. It is usually calculated as a percentage of the **Marked Price (M.P.)**.

Types of Discounts

1. **Trade Discount**: Given by wholesalers to retailers on bulk purchases.
2. **Cash Discount**: Given to customers for **quick payment** or **cash payment**.
3. **Successive Discount**: Multiple discounts applied one after another.
4. **Banker's Discount**: Used in financial transactions, including promissory notes.

Basic Discount Formula

$$Discount = Marked\ Price - Selling\ Price$$

$$Discount\ \% = \left(\frac{Discount}{Marked\ Price}\right) \times 100$$

$$Discount\ Amount = Marked\ Price\ (MP) \times \frac{Discount\ Percentage}{100}$$

Example 1:

A shopkeeper marks an item at ₹1000 and gives a 20% discount. Find the selling price.

Solution:

$$Discount = 1000 \times \frac{20}{100} = 200$$

$$Selling\ Price\ (SP) = Marked\ Price\ (MP) - Discount$$

$$Selling\ Price\ (SP) = 1000 - 200 = ₹800$$

Successive Discounts

If two successive discounts of $x\%$ **and** $y\%$ are given, the **effective discount** is:

$$Effective\ Discount = x + y - \frac{xy}{100}$$

If two successive discounts are applied, say **D1**% **and** **D2**%, the **total discount** is calculated as:

$$Total\ Discount = D1 + D2 - \frac{D1 \times D2}{100}$$

Example 2:

A mobile is marked at ₹8000. The shopkeeper offers **two successive discounts of 20% and 10%**. Find the final price.

Solution:

$$Effective\ Discount = 20 + 10 - \frac{20 \times 10}{100}$$

$$= 30 - \frac{200}{100} = 30 - 2 = 28\%$$

$$Selling\ Price = 8000 - \frac{28}{100} \times 8000$$

$$= 8000 - 2240 = ₹5760$$

Single Discount Equivalent to Successive Discounts

If **n** successive discounts are given, the **final price** is:

$$Final\ Price = M.P. \times \left(1 - \frac{x_1}{100}\right) \times \left(1 - \frac{x_2}{100}\right) \times \ldots \times \left(1 - \frac{x_n}{100}\right)$$

Banker's Discount (BD)

In banking and finance, **discounting of bills** is a common practice. A bill of exchange (promissory note) is paid **before its maturity date** with a discount.

Banker's Discount Formula:

$$BD = \frac{Face\ Value \times Rate \times Time}{100}$$

Banker's Gain (BG):

$$BG = BD - True\ Discount\ (TD)$$

Example 3:

A bill of ₹5000 is to be paid after 1 year, and the bank gives a **10% discount**. Find the discounted amount.

Solution:

$$BD = \frac{5000 \times 10 \times 1}{100} = ₹500$$

$$Net\ Amount\ Paid = 5000 - 500 = ₹4500$$

Shortcut Tricks for Discounting

1. **For successive discounts, use the formula:**

$$Effective\ Discount = x + y - \frac{xy}{100}$$

2. **For three successive discounts, extend the formula:**

$$Effective\ Discount = x + y + z - \frac{xy}{100} - \frac{yz}{100} - \frac{xz}{100} + \frac{xyz}{100^2}$$

3. **If an article is sold at a discount and the profit percentage is given, use:**

$$C.P = \frac{S.P}{1 + \frac{Profit\ \%}{100}}$$

Concept Check 17: Discounting

1. *A product has a **marked price of ₹4000** and is sold after a **30% discount**. Find the selling price.*
2. *A shopkeeper offers **three successive discounts of 10%, 20%, and 30%**. Find the final discount percentage.*
3. *A bill of ₹10,000 is due in **2 years**. If the discount rate is **8% per annum**, find the banker's discount.*
4. *A cycle marked at ₹5000 is sold at ₹4250. Find the percentage discount.*
5. *A retailer marks an item at **₹8000** and offers a **15% trade discount and 5% cash discount**. Find the final price.*

UGC NET PYQ Questions and Explanations on Discounts:

Question

Two successive discounts of 10% and 15% are equivalent to a single discount of-

1. 23.5%
2. 25%
3. 18.5%
4. 22.5%

Explanations
Answer: 1. 23.5%

We need to find the **equivalent single discount** when two successive discounts of **10% and 15%** are applied.

Step 1: Formula for Successive Discounts

When two successive discounts of **x%** and **y%** are applied, the equivalent single discount is given by:

$$Effective\ Discount = x + y - \frac{xy}{100}$$

Where:

- x=10%
- y=15%

Step 2: Apply the Formula

$$Equivalent\ Discount = 10 + 15 - \frac{10 \times 15}{100}$$

$$= 10 + 15 - \frac{150}{100}$$

$$= 25 - 1.5 = 23.5\% \ldots Ans.$$

Question

If a discount of 6% on the marked price of an item results in its selling price being Rs 235, then at what price should the item be sold to allow a discount of 15%?

1. Rs 199.5
2. Rs 206.5
3. Rs 212.5
4. Rs 215

Explanations

Answer: 3. Rs 212.5

We need to find the **new selling price** when a **15% discount** is applied, given that a **6% discount** results in a **selling price of ₹235**.

Step 1: Find the Marked Price (M.P.)

The **formula to find Marked Price (M.P.)** from Selling Price (S.P.) and Discount is:

$$M.P = \frac{S.P.}{1 - \frac{Discount}{\%100}}$$

Substituting values:

$$M.P = \frac{235}{1 - \frac{6}{100}}$$

$$\frac{235}{0.95} = 250$$

Step 2: Find the New Selling Price with a 15% Discount

Using the formula:

$$S.P = M.P \times \left(1 - \frac{Discount\ \%}{100}\right)$$

$$S.P = 250 \times \left(1 - \frac{15}{100}\right)$$

$$= 250 \times 0.85$$

$$= 212.5 \dots Ans.$$

Question

A shopkeeper first increased the price of an item by 12% and then announces a discount of 20%. The actual discount on the original price is:

1. 12.6%
2. 10.4%
3. 14.2%
4. 12%

Explanations

Answer: 2. 10.4%

We need to find the **actual discount** on the original price when:

- The price is **first increased by 12%**.
- Then, a **20% discount** is applied.

Step 1: Formula for Net Effect of Increase and Discount

$$Net\ Change = x - y - \frac{xy}{100}$$

Where

- $x=12$ (Increase)
- $y=20\%$ (Discount)

Step 2: Apply the Formula

$$Net\ Discount = 12 - 20 - \frac{12 \times 20}{100}$$

$$= 12 - 20 - \frac{240}{100}$$

$$= 12 - 20 - 2.4$$

$$= -10.4\% \dots Ans.$$

Question

Which of the following statements are true?

(A). A single discount equivalent to successive discounts of 20%, 10% and 5% is 35%

(B). If an article is sold for Rs 209/- after two successive discounts of 12% and 5%, then the original price of the article is 250/-

(C). If a shopkeeper gives successive discount of 5% twice on the marked price of Rs 80/-, the selling price of the article is 75/-

(D). The difference between a single discount of 35% and two consecutive discounts of 20% on a certain bill is 22/-, then the total amount of the bill is 2200/-

1.   ABC
2.   AC
3.   BD
4.   CD

Explanations

Answer: 3. BD

(A) A single discount equivalent to successive discounts of 20%, 10%, and 5% is 35%.

Solution: To find the equivalent single discount for successive discounts, we use the formula:

$$Single\ Discount = 1 - (1 - d1)(1 - d2)(1 - d3)$$
$$Where\ d1 = 20\% = 0.20,\ d2 = 10\% = 0.10, and\ d3 = 5\% = 0.05.$$
$$Single\ Discount = 1 - (1 - 0.20)(1 - 0.10)(1 - 0.05)$$
$$Single\ Discount = 1 - (0.80)(0.90)(0.95)$$
$$Single\ Discount = 1 - 0.684 = 0.316\ or\ 31.6\%.$$

The equivalent single discount is **31.6%**, not 35%.

Statement (A) is false.

(B) If an article is sold for Rs 209/- after two successive discounts of 12% and 5%, then the original price of the article is Rs 250/-.

Solution: Let the original price be PP. After a 12% discount, the price becomes:

$$P1 = P(1 - 0.12) = 0.88P.$$

After a further 5% discount, the price becomes:

$$P2 = P1(1 - 0.05) = 0.88P \times 0.95 = 0.836P.$$

The selling price is Rs 209/-, so:

$$0.836P = 209.$$

Solving for P:

$$P = \frac{209}{0.836} = 250.$$

The original price is indeed Rs 250/-.
Statement (B) is true.

(C) If a shopkeeper gives successive discounts of 5% twice on the marked price of Rs 80/-, the selling price of the article is Rs 75/-.
Solution: Let the marked price be Rs 80/-. After the first 5% discount:

$$P1 = 80(1 - 0.05) = 80 \times 0.95 = 76.$$

After the second 5% discount:

$$P2 = 76(1 - 0.05) = 76 \times 0.95 = 72.2.$$

The selling price is Rs 72.2/-, not Rs 75/-.
Statement (C) is false.

(D) The difference between a single discount of 35% and two consecutive discounts of 20% on a certain bill is Rs 22/-, then the total amount of the bill is Rs 2200/-.
Solution: Let the total amount of the bill be P.

- Single discount of 35%:

$$Discount = 0.35P.$$

- Two consecutive discounts of 20%:

$$Discount = P - P(1 - 0.20)(1 - 0.20) = P - 0.64P = 0.36P.$$

- The difference between the two discounts is Rs 22/-:

$$0.36P - 0.35P = 0.01P = 22.$$

Solving for P:

$$P = \frac{22}{0.01} = 2200.$$

The total amount of the bill is Rs 2200/-.
Statement (D) is true.

Final Answer: True Statements: (B) and (D).

Question

Three successive discounts of 10%, 20% and 30% on the marked price of an item are equivalent to a single discount of

1. 60%

2. 50.4%
3. 54.6%
4. 49.6%

Explanations

Answer: 4. 49.6%

To find the equivalent single discount for three successive discounts of 10%, 20%, and 30%, we use the formula for successive discounts:

$$Single\ Discount = 1 - (1 - d1)(1 - d2)(1 - d3)$$

Where:

- $d1 = 10\% = 0.10$
- $d2 = 20\% = 0.20$
- $d3 = 30\% = 0.30$

Step-by-Step Calculation:

1. Calculate the remaining fraction after each discount:
   - After the first discount of 10%, the remaining fraction is:
     $$1 - 0.10 = 0.90.$$
   - After the second discount of 20%, the remaining fraction is:
     $$0.90 \times (1 - 0.20) = 0.90 \times 0.80 = 0.72.$$
   - After the third discount of 30%, the remaining fraction is:
     $$0.72 \times (1 - 0.30) = 0.72 \times 0.70 = 0.504.$$
2. The equivalent single discount is:
   $$Single\ Discount = 1 - 0.504 = 0.496\ or\ 49.6\% \ldots Ans.$$

Question

If the selling price of Rs. 623 results in a discount of 11% on the market price of an item, at what price should the item be sold to offer a discount of 19%?

1. Rs.557
2. Rs.567
3. Rs.577
4. Rs.587

Explanations

Answer: 2. Rs.567

We need to find the **new selling price** when a **19% discount** is applied, given that an **11% discount** results in a **selling price of ₹623**.

Step 1: Find the Marked Price (M.P.)

The **formula to find Marked Price (M.P.)** from Selling Price (S.P.) and Discount is:

$$M.P = \frac{S.P.}{1 - \dfrac{Discount\%}{100}}$$

Substituting values:

$$M.P = \frac{623}{1 - \dfrac{11}{100}}$$

Step 2: Find the New Selling Price with a 19% Discount

Using the formula:

$$S.P = M.P \times \left(1 - \frac{Discount\,\%}{100}\right)$$

$$S.P = 700 \times \left(1 - \frac{19}{100}\right)$$

$$= 700 \times 0.81$$

$$= 567 \dots Ans.$$

Question

A Person sells an item at a discount of 40% and still makes a profit of 20%. By what percentage was the marked price of the item more than the cost price of the item?

1. 50%
2. 100%
3. 150%
4. 120%

Explanations

Answer: 2. 100%

Step 1: Define the Variables

- o   Let the **cost price (CP)** be CP.
- o   Let the **marked price (MP)** be MP.

Step 2: Calculate the Selling Price (SP)

- o   The item is sold at a **40% discount** on the marked price:

$$SP = MP - 0.40MP = 0.60$$

- o   The person makes a **20% profit** on the cost price:

$$SP = CP + 0.20CP = 1.20CP$$

Step 3: Equate the Selling Prices

$$0.60MP = 1.20CP$$

$$MP = \frac{1.20CP}{0.60} = 2CP$$

Step 4: Calculate the Percentage Increase

The marked price is **twice** the cost price, so the percentage increase is:

$$\frac{MP - CP}{CP} \times 100 = \frac{2CP - CP}{CP} \times 100 = 100\% \ ... \ Ans.$$

Question

The cost price of an article is 75% of its marked price for sale. How much percent does the tradesman gain after allowing a discount of 15%?

1. 20%
2. $13\frac{1}{3}\%$
3. 10%
4. $15\frac{2}{3}\%$

Explanations

Answer: 2. $12\frac{1}{3}\%$

We need to find the **profit percentage** when:

- o   The **Cost Price (C.P.)** is **75% of the Marked Price (M.P.)**.
- o   A **15% discount** is given on M.P.

Step 1: Assume Marked Price (M.P.)

Let **M.P. = ₹100** (for easy calculation).

Step 2: Calculate Cost Price (C.P.)

$$C.P. = 75\% \ of \ M.P.$$

$$C.P. = \frac{75}{100} \times 100 = 75$$

Step 3: Calculate Selling Price (S.P.) after Discount

Since a **15% discount** is given:

$$S.P. = M.P. \times \left(1 - \frac{15}{100}\right)$$
$$= 100 \times 0.85$$
$$= \mathbf{85}$$

Step 4: Find Profit Percentage

$$Profit\ \% = \left(\frac{S.P. - C.P.}{C.P.}\right) \times 100$$
$$= \left(\frac{85 - 75}{75}\right) \times 100$$
$$= \left(\frac{10}{75}\right) \times 100 = \mathbf{13.33\%..Ans.}$$

Question

If the population of a town decreases by 25% and 40% in two successive years, what shall be the decrease in the percentage of population after 2 years?

1. 61%
2. 55%
3. 65%
4. 62%

Explanations

Answer: 2. 55%

We need to find the **total percentage decrease in population** when:
- o   The population decreases by **25% in the first year.**
- o   The population further decreases by **40% in the second year.**

Step 1: Formula for Successive Percentage Decrease

$$Total\ Decrease = x + y - \frac{x \times y}{100}$$

Where:
- o   x=25% (First-year decrease)
- o   y=40% (Second-year decrease)

Step 2: Apply the Formula

$$Total\ Decrease = 25 + 40 - \frac{25 \times 40}{100}$$
$$= 25 + 40 - \frac{1000}{100}$$

$$= 25 + 40 - 10 = \mathbf{55\%} \dots \textit{Ans.}$$

Question

Two Shopkeepers 'A' and 'B' sell certain kinds of machines at the same list price. However, shopkeeper "A" allows two successive discounts of 20% and 15%, and shopkeeper 'B' allows two successive discounts of 10% and 25%. **Which of the following statements is correct?**

1. A offers more discount
2. B offers more discount
3. Both A' and B'offers the same discount
4. A offers a 35% discount and 'B' offers a 30% discount

Explanations

Answer: 2. B offers more discount

We need to determine which shopkeeper offers a higher discount when:

- **Shopkeeper A** gives **two successive discounts of 20% and 15%.**
- **Shopkeeper B** gives **two successive discounts of 10% and 25%.**

Step 1: Formula for Successive Discounts

For two successive discounts **x%** and **y%**, the equivalent single discount is:

$$Equivalent\ Discount = x + y - \frac{x \times y}{100}$$

Step 2: Calculate Discounts

For Shopkeeper A:

$$Discount = 20 + 15 - \frac{20 \times 15}{100}$$
$$= 20 + 15 - \frac{300}{100}$$
$$= 20 + 15 - 3 = 32\% \dots \textit{Ans.}$$

For Shopkeeper B:

$$Discount = 10 + 25 - \frac{10 \times 25}{100}$$
$$= 10 + 25 - \frac{250}{100}$$
$$= 10 + 25 - 2.5 = 32.5\% \dots \textit{Ans.}$$

Step 3: Compare Discounts

- o Shopkeeper A offers a total discount of 32%.
- o Shopkeeper B offers a total discount of 32.5%.

Since **B offers a slightly higher discount than A**

Question

A vendor marks all his goods at 50% above the cost price and then offers a discount of 25% on the marked prices. What is his profit on the sales?

1. 25%
2. 12.50%
3. 22.50%
4. 20.50%

Explanations
Answer: 2. 12.50%
We need to find the **profit percentage** when:
- o The vendor **marks goods 50% above the cost price**.
- o He then offers a **25% discount** on the marked price.

Step 1: Assume Cost Price (C.P.)
Let **C.P. = ₹100** (for easy calculation).

Step 2: Calculate Marked Price (M.P.)
Since the vendor marks the goods **50% above the cost price**:

$$M.P. = C.P. \times \left(1 + \frac{50}{100}\right)$$
$$= 100 \times 1.50 = \mathbf{150}$$

Step 3: Calculate Selling Price (S.P.) After Discount
Since the vendor gives a **25% discount**:

$$S.P. = M.P. \times \left(1 - \frac{25}{100}\right)$$
$$= 150 \times 0.75 = \mathbf{112.50}$$

Step 4: Find Profit Percentage

$$Profit\ \% = \left(\frac{S.P. - C.P.}{C.P.}\right) \times 100$$
$$= \left(\frac{112.50 - 100}{100}\right) \times 100$$

$$= \left(\frac{12.50}{100}\right) \times 100 = \mathbf{12.50\%} \dots \boldsymbol{Ans.}$$

Question

Statement I: The single discount equivalent to a series discount of 10 %, 30% and 50% is 68.5%

Statement II: The single discount equivalent to a series discount of 10 %, 20 % and 40 % is 43.2%

1. Both Statement I and Statement II are true
2. Both Statement I and Statement II are false
3. Statement I is true but Statement II is false
4. Statement I is false but Statement Il is true

Explanations

Answer: 3. Statement I is true but Statement II is false

Step 1: Formula for Successive Discounts

For three successive discounts **x%**, **y%**, and **z%**, the equivalent single discount is:

$$Equivalent\ Discount = x + y + z - \frac{xy}{100} - \frac{yz}{100} - \frac{xz}{100} + \frac{xyz}{10000}$$

Step 2: Verify Statement I

Given discounts: **10%, 30%, and 50%**

Equivalent Discount

$$= 10 + 30 + 50 - \frac{10 \times 30}{100} - \frac{30 \times 50}{100} - \frac{10 \times 50}{100} + \frac{10 \times 30 \times 50}{10000}$$

$$= 10 + 30 + 50 - 3 - 15 - 5 + 1.5 = \mathbf{68.5\%} \dots \boldsymbol{Ans.}$$

Statement I is True.

Step 3: Verify Statement II

Given discounts: **10%, 20%, and 40%**

Equivalent Discount

$$= 10 + 20 + 40 - \frac{10 \times 20}{100} - \frac{20 \times 40}{100} - \frac{10 \times 40}{100} + \frac{10 \times 20 \times 40}{10000}$$

$$= 10 + 20 + 40 - 2 - 8 - 4 + 0.8 = \mathbf{56.8\%} \dots \boldsymbol{Ans.}$$

Statement II is False (since 43.2% is incorrect, actual value is 56.8%).

Question

A person buys 3 items of Rs. 1500 each and 2 items of Rs. 1800 each from a shopping mall. On the total bill a discount of 10% is given. What is the average cost of the items?

      (1) 1650
      (2) 1458
      (3) 1658
      (4) 1550

Explanations

Answer: 2. 1458

We need to find the **average cost per item** after a **10% discount** when:
- A person buys **3 items of ₹1500 each**.
- A person buys **2 items of ₹1800 each**.

Step 1: Calculate Total Cost Before Discount

$$Total\ Cost = (3 \times 1500) + (2 \times 1800)$$
$$= 4500 + 3600 = 8100$$

Step 2: Apply 10% Discount

$$Final\ Cost = 8100 \times \left(1 - \frac{10}{100}\right)$$
$$= 8100 \times 0.90 = \mathbf{7290}$$

Step 3: Find Average Cost Per Item

Total number of items:

$$3 + 2 = 5$$
$$Average\ Cost = \frac{7290}{5} = \mathbf{1458} \ ...\ \textbf{\textit{Ans.}}$$

Question

At what percentage above the cost price must an article be marked so as to gain 8% after allowing a customer a discount of 10%?

      (1) 18%
      (2) 20%
      (3) 28%
      (4) 10.8%

Explanations

Answer: 2. 20%

We need to determine **at what percentage above the cost price** an article must be **marked** to ensure an **8% profit** after giving a **10% discount**.

Step 1: Assume Cost Price (C.P.)

Let **C.P. = ₹100** (for easy calculation).

Step 2: Find Selling Price (S.P.)

Since the shopkeeper wants **8% profit**, the selling price is:

$$S.P. = C.P. \times \left(1 + \frac{Profit\ \%}{100}\right)$$

$$S.P. = 100 \times \left(1 + \frac{8}{100}\right)$$

$$= 100 \times 1.08 = 108$$

Step 3: Find Marked Price (M.P.)

Since a **10% discount** is given on the **Marked Price (M.P.)**, the relation is:

$$S.P. = M.P. \times \left(1 - \frac{Discount\ \%}{100}\right)$$

$$108 = M.P. \times \left(1 - \frac{10}{100}\right)$$

$$108 = M.P. \times 0.90$$

$$M.P. = \frac{108}{0.90} = 120$$

Step 4: Find Percentage Increase Over Cost Price

$$Percentage\ Increase = \left(\frac{M.P. - C.P.}{C.P.}\right) \times 100$$

$$= \left(\frac{120 - 100}{100}\right) \times 100$$

$$= \left(\frac{20}{100}\right) \times 100 = 20\% \ ... Ans.$$

CHAPTER 4

Speed, Time, & Distance, Boat and Stream and Time & Work

Speed, Time, & Distance, Boat and Stream and Time & Work

In competitive exams like UGC NET Paper I, mathematical reasoning plays a crucial role in assessing candidates' problem-solving abilities. Among the important topics, **Speed, Time & Distance, Boat and Stream, and Time & Work** stand out due to their frequent appearance in past year question papers (PYQs). These topics test a candidate's ability to analyze and apply fundamental mathematical concepts in real-world scenarios.

- **Speed, Time & Distance** problems help in understanding motion, relative speed, and travel-based calculations.
- **Boat and Stream** problems enhance problem-solving skills by introducing variations like upstream and downstream movements, requiring conceptual clarity on relative speed.
- **Time & Work** problems test efficiency and productivity concepts, which are directly relevant to management and planning skills.

This chapter will cover all essential formulas, shortcuts, and methods to solve these problems efficiently. We will also focus on solving numerous **previous year questions (PYQs)** to ensure conceptual clarity and improve accuracy. Understanding these topics not only helps in scoring well in **UGC NET Paper I** but also enhances logical thinking, which is crucial for any teaching and research-based profession.

Speed, Time, & Distance

Speed, Time, and Distance (STD) is one of the fundamental topics in mathematical reasoning, commonly tested in competitive exams like **UGC NET Paper I**. It involves the relationship between speed, time, and distance, which can be used to solve problems on motion, trains, boats, and relative speed.

Basic Formula

The fundamental formula that governs this topic is:

$$Speed = \frac{Distance}{Time}$$

Using this, we can derive:
- **Distance** = Speed × Time
- **Time** = Distance ÷ Speed

Speed is typically measured in **km/hr** or **m/sec**.

Conversion of Speed Units

- To convert **km/hr to m/sec**, multiply by **(5/18)**

$$1km\ per\ hr\ = \frac{5}{18}\ m\ per\ sec$$

- To convert **m/sec to km/hr**, multiply by **(18/5)**

$$1\ m\ per\ sec = \frac{18}{5}\ km\ per\ hr$$

Types of Speed, Time & Distance Problems

1. Average Speed

If a journey is covered in two parts at different speeds, then **Average Speed** is given by:

$$Average\ Speed = \frac{2xy}{x + y}$$

where **x** and **y** are two different speeds for equal distances.

Example:

A car travels at **40 km/hr** for half the journey and **60 km/hr** for the other half. Find the average speed.

$$Average\ Speed = \frac{2 \times 40 \times 60}{40 + 60} = \frac{4800}{100} = 48\ kilometers\ per\ hour$$

2. Relative Speed

- **Same direction:**

$$Relative\ Speed = (Speed1 - Speed2)$$

- **Opposite direction:**

$$Relative\ Speed = (Speed1 + Speed2)$$

Example:

Two trains moving at **50 km/hr** and **30 km/hr** in the same direction. Find their relative speed.

$$Relative\ Speed = (50 - 30) = 20\ kilometers\ per\ hour$$

3. Train-Based Problems

- When a train crosses a **stationary object** (pole, man, signal), the distance covered = **length of the train**

$$Time = \frac{Length\ of\ Train}{Speed}$$

- When a train crosses a **platform or bridge**, the distance covered = **length of train + length of platform**

$$Time = \frac{Length\ of\ Train + length\ of\ platform}{Speed}$$

Example:

A **200m long** train crosses a pole in **10 sec**. Find its speed.

$$Speed = \frac{200}{10} = 20\ meters\ per\ second = \frac{20 \times 18}{5} = 72\ km\ per\ hour$$

Example:

A train **250 meters** long crosses a platform of **500 meters** in **50 seconds**. Find the speed of the train in **kilometers per hour**.

Solution:

- **Total Distance Covered = Length of Train + Length of Platform**

$$250 + 500 = 750\ meters$$

- **Time Taken = 50 seconds**
- **Speed (in meters per second)**

$$Speed = \frac{Distance}{Time} = \frac{750}{50} = 15\ meters\ per\ second$$

- **Convert meters per second to kilometers per hour:**

$$15 \times \frac{18}{5} = 54\ kilometers\ per\ hour$$

4. Meeting Point Problem

If two objects start from two different points **A** and **B** towards each other, the time taken to meet is:

$$Time = \frac{Distance\ between\ A\ and\ B}{Sum\ of\ their\ speeds}$$

Example:

Two persons start from two places **50 km apart** towards each other at **5 km/hr** and **10 km/hr**. When will they meet?

$$Time = \frac{50}{5 + 10} = \frac{50}{15} = 3.33 \; hours \, (3 \; hours \; 20 \; minutes)$$

5. Circular Track Problems

If two people run around a circular track of **length L** at speeds **S_1** and **S_2**,

- o **Meeting time (Same Direction):**

$$Time = \frac{L}{S1 - S2}$$

- o **Meeting time (Opposite Direction):**

$$Time = \frac{L}{S1 + S2}$$

Concept Check 18: Speed, Time, & Distance

1. *A man travels **600 km** at **60 km/hr** and returns at **40 km/hr**. Find the average speed.*
2. *A train of **250m** crosses a platform of **500m** in **50 sec**. Find its speed.*
3. *Two trains, **120m** and **180m** long, cross each other in **18 sec** while moving in opposite directions. Find their speed if one train moves at **30 km/hr**.*

UGC NET PYQ Questions and Explanations on Speed, Time, & Distance:

Question

The speed of an electric train is 25% more than that of a steam engine train. What is the time taken by the electric train to cover a distance which the steam engine train takes 4 hours 25 minutes to cover?

1. $3\frac{1}{10} \; hr$
2. $3\frac{11}{15} \; hr$
3. $3\frac{11}{12} \; hr$
4. $3\frac{8}{15} \; hr$

Explanations

Answer: (4). $3\frac{8}{15}$ hr

Let the speed of the steam engine train be **S** kilometers per hour.

Then, the speed of the electric train is **25% more**, which means:

$$Speed\ of\ electric\ train = S + \frac{25}{100}S = \frac{125}{100}S = \frac{5}{4}S$$

The time taken by a train to cover a certain distance is given by:

$$Time = \frac{Distance}{Speed}$$

Since the **distance remains the same**, we can use the inverse ratio of speeds to find the time taken by the electric train:

Time taken by electric train

$$= Time\ taken\ by\ steam\ train \times \frac{Speed\ of\ steam\ train}{Speed\ of\ electric\ train}$$

Substituting the values:

$$Time\ taken\ by\ electric\ train = 4\ hours\ 25\ minutes \times \frac{4}{5}$$

Convert **4 hours 25 minutes** into hours:

$$4 + \frac{25}{60} = 4 + \frac{5}{12} = \frac{48}{12} + \frac{5}{12} = \frac{53}{12}\ hours$$

Now, multiplying by **4 per 5**:

$$\frac{53}{12} \times \frac{4}{5} = \frac{53 \times 4}{12 \times 5} = \frac{212}{60} = \frac{53}{15} = 3\frac{8}{15}\ hours \ldots Ans.$$

Question

Two trains A and B moving with speeds of 45 km/hour and 36 km/hour, respectively cross a 1.2 km long bridge in 2 minutes and 3 minutes, respectively. What is the ratio of the lengths of train A and train B?

1. 1:3
2. 2:3
3. 1:2
4. 2:1

Explanations

Answer: 3. 1:2

We are given two trains, **A** and **B**, moving at speeds of **45 kilometers per hour** and **36 kilometers per hour**, respectively. Both trains cross a **1.2-kilometer-long bridge**, and we need to determine the ratio of their lengths.

Step 1: Convert Speed to Meters per Second

Since speed is given in **kilometers per hour**, we convert it to **meters per second** using the formula:

$$1\ kilometer\ per\ hour = \frac{5}{18}\ meters\ per\ second$$

For Train **A**:

$$45 \times \frac{5}{18} = \frac{225}{18} = 12.5\ meters\ per\ second$$

For Train **B**:

$$36 \times \frac{5}{18} = \frac{180}{18} = 10\ meters\ per\ second$$

Step 2: Use Distance Formula

The total distance covered by each train while crossing the bridge is:

$$Distance = Speed \times Time$$

For Train **A** (Time = 2 minutes = 120 seconds):

$$Distance_A = 12.5 \times 120 = 1500\ meters$$

For Train **B** (Time = 3 minutes = 180 seconds):

$$Distance_B = 10 \times 180 = 1800\ meters$$

Each train covers a total distance equal to **(Length of Train + Length of Bridge)** while crossing.

$$Length\ of\ Train + 1.2\ km = Total\ Distance$$

Since **1.2 km = 1200 meters**, we solve for the lengths:

For Train **A**:

$$L_A + 1200 = 1500 \Rightarrow L_A = 1500 - 1200 = 300\ meters$$

For Train **B**:

$$L_B + 1200 = 1800 \Rightarrow L_B = 1800 - 1200 = 600\ meters$$

Step 3: Find the Ratio of Lengths

$$\frac{L_A}{L_B} = \frac{300}{600} = \frac{1}{2}$$

Thus, the ratio of the lengths of Train A to Train B is **1:2**.

Question

A man travels three-fifth of a distance AB at a speed of 3a and the remaining at the speed of 2b. If he goes from B to A and returns at a speed of 5 in the same time then:

1. $\dfrac{1}{a} + \dfrac{1}{b} = \dfrac{1}{c}$

2. $a + b = c$

3. $\dfrac{1}{a} + \dfrac{1}{b} = \dfrac{2}{c}$

4. $\dfrac{1}{a} + \dfrac{1}{b} = \dfrac{1}{2c}$

Explanations

Answer: 3. $\dfrac{1}{a} + \dfrac{1}{b} = \dfrac{2}{c}$

We are given that a man travels:

- **Three-fifth** of the distance **AB** at a speed of **3a**.
- The **remaining two-fifth** of the distance at a speed of **2b**.

On his return journey, he travels **from B to A and back** at a speed of **5** in the **same total time**.

Step 1: Calculate Time for Forward Journey

Let **D** be the total distance from **A to B**.

Time Taken for First Part (Three-fifth of Distance)

$$Time = \frac{Distance}{Speed}$$

$$Time1 = \frac{\frac{3}{5}D}{3a} = \frac{3D}{5} \times \frac{1}{3a} = \frac{D}{5a}$$

Time Taken for Second Part (Two-fifth of Distance)

$$Time2 = \frac{\frac{2}{5}D}{2b} = \frac{2D}{5} \times \frac{1}{2b} = \frac{D}{5b}$$

Total Time for A to B Journey

$$T = \frac{D}{5a} + \frac{D}{5b}$$

Step 2: Calculate Time for Return Journey

For the return journey from **B to A and back**, total distance covered = **2D**, and speed = **5**.

$$T' = \frac{2D}{5}$$

Since the time taken for the forward and return journey is the same:

$$\frac{D}{5a} + \frac{D}{5b} = \frac{2D}{5c}$$

Cancel **D** from both sides:

$$\frac{1}{5a} + \frac{1}{5b} = \frac{2}{5c}$$

Multiply by **5** on both sides:

$$\frac{1}{a} + \frac{1}{b} = \frac{2}{c} \ldots \textbf{\textit{Ans.}}$$

Question

A person travels from X to Y at a speed of 30 km/hr and returns from Y to X by increasing his speed by 50%. His average speed during the journey is:

1. 37.5 km/hr
2. 37 km/hr
3. 36 km/hr
4. 38 km/hr

Explanations

Answer: 3. 36 km/hr

The formula for **average speed** when a journey is covered in two parts with different speeds is:

$$Average\ Speed = \frac{2xy}{x + y}$$

where:

- **x** = speed from **X to Y** = **30 kilometers per hour**
- **y** = speed from **Y to X** (increased by 50%)

Step 1: Calculate the Return Speed

Since the speed increases by **50%**, we calculate:

$$y = 30 + \frac{50}{100} \times 30 = 30 + 15 = 45\ kilometers\ per\ houry$$

Step 2: Apply the Average Speed Formula

$$Average\ Speed = \frac{2 \times 30 \times 45}{30 + 45}$$

$$= \frac{2 \times 1350}{75} = \frac{2700}{75} = 36\ kilometers\ per\ hour \ldots \textbf{\textit{Ans.}}$$

Question

A 200 m long train is travelling at a constant speed of 20 m/s. How long will it take to completely cross a 1000 m long railway platform?

1. 1 minute
2. 1.5 minute

3. 2 minutes

4. 2.5 minutes

Explanations

Answer: 1. 1 minute

We are given:

- o **Length of the train = 200 meters**
- o **Length of the platform = 1000 meters**
- o **Speed of the train = 20 meters per second**

Step 1: Total Distance to be Covered

When a train crosses a platform, the total distance it needs to travel is:

$$Total\ Distance = Length\ of\ Train + Length\ of\ Platform$$
$$= 200 + 1000 = 1200\ meters$$

Step 2: Use the Time Formula

$$Time = \frac{Distance}{Speed}$$
$$= \frac{1200}{20} = 60\ seconds$$

Convert **60 seconds** to **minutes**:

$$60\ seconds = 1\ minute$$

Question

A school boy, travelling at 3 km/hr, reaches his school 28 minutes late but when he travels at 5 km/h, he reaches his school 28 minutes early. What distance does he travel every day to reach the school?

1. 6 km
2. 8 km
3. 7 km
4. 9 km

Explanations

Answer: 3. 7km

We are given:

- o When the boy travels at **3 kilometers per hour**, he reaches **28 minutes late**.
- o When he travels at **5 kilometers per hour**, he reaches **28 minutes early**.

Thus, the total **time difference** between these two cases is:

$$28 + 28 = 56 \; minutes = \frac{56}{60 \; hours} = \frac{14}{15 \; hours}$$

Let **D** be the distance to the school.

Step 1: Use the Time Formula

Time taken when speed is **3 km per hour**:

$$T1 = \frac{D}{3}$$

Time taken when speed is **5 km per hour**:

$$T2 = \frac{D}{5}$$

Since the difference in time between these two cases is **14 per 15 hours**, we write:

$$\frac{D}{3} - \frac{D}{5} = \frac{14}{15}$$

Step 2: Solve for Distance (D)

Find the LCM of **3 and 5**, which is **15**, and rewrite the equation:

$$\frac{5D}{15} - \frac{3D}{15} = \frac{14}{15}$$

$$\frac{2D}{15} = \frac{14}{15}$$

Multiply both sides by **15**:

$$2D = 14$$

$$D = \frac{14}{2}$$

$$D = 7 \; ... \textbf{Ans.}$$

Question

A ship is approaching towards a shore, when it is 32 miles from the shore, a plane having speed 15 times that of the ship is sent to deliver supplies. How far from seashore does the sea plane catches up with the ship?

1. 30 miles
2. 25 miles

3. 15 miles
4. 10 miles

Explanations

Answer: 1. 30 Miles.

Let the speed of the ship be **S** miles per hour.
The speed of the plane is **15S** miles per hour.
The ship is **32 miles away** from the shore when the plane starts.
Let the **distance from the shore** where the plane catches up with the ship be **d** miles.
The distance traveled by the ship while the plane reaches it is **(32 - d)** miles.
Since both the ship and the plane start at the same time and meet at the same point, the time taken by both must be the same.

Step 1: Use the Time Formula

$$Time = \frac{Distance}{Speed}$$

For the **ship**:

$$Time = \frac{32 - d}{S}$$

For the **plane**:

$$Time = \frac{d}{15S}$$

Since the time is the same for both:

$$\frac{32 - d}{S} = \frac{d}{15S}$$

Cancel **S** from both sides:

$$32 - d = \frac{d}{15}$$

Step 2: Solve for d

Multiply both sides by **15** to eliminate the fraction:

$$15(32 - d) = d$$
$$480 - 15d = d$$
$$480 = 16d$$
$$d = \frac{480}{16} = 30 \dots \textbf{\textit{Ans.}}$$

Question

If a person travels in a car at a speed of 36 km/hour, then he will reach his destination on time. He covers half the journey in (4/5) time. What should be his speed for the remaining part of the journey so that he reaches his destination on time?

1. 80 km/hour
2. 75 km/hour
3. 90 km/hour
4. 85 km/hour

Explanations

Answer: 3. 90 km/hour

We are given:

- The person **travels at 36 kilometers per hour** and reaches on time.
- He covers **half the journey** in **four-fifths (4/5) of the total time**.
- We need to find the required speed for the **remaining journey** so that he reaches on time.

Step 1: Define Variables

Let:

- **D** be the total distance.
- **T** be the total time required to reach the destination.
- **D/2** is the half-distance.

Step 2: Time Taken for First Half

Time taken for the first half:

$$T1 = \frac{Distance}{Speed} = \frac{\frac{D}{2}}{36}$$

Since it is given that this takes **four-fifths of the total time (4T/5)**:

$$\frac{D}{2} \times \frac{1}{36} = \frac{4T}{5}$$

Multiplying both sides by **36**:

$$\frac{D}{72} = \frac{4T}{5}$$

Multiplying both sides by **72**:

$$D = \frac{4T}{5} \times 72$$

$$D = \frac{288T}{5}$$

Thus, total time **T** is:

$$T = \frac{D}{36}$$

Setting equal:

$$\frac{D}{36} = \frac{288T}{5D}$$

So, the remaining time is:

$$T2 = T - \frac{4T}{5} = \frac{T}{5}$$

Step 3: Find the Required Speed

For the second half:

$$Speed = \frac{Remaining\ Distance}{Remaining\ Time} = \frac{\frac{D}{2}}{\frac{T}{5}}$$

$$= \frac{D}{2} \times \frac{5}{T}$$

$$= \frac{5D}{2T} =$$

$$Since\ T = \frac{D}{36}, substitute:$$

$$= \frac{5D}{2 \times \left(\frac{D}{36}\right)}$$

$$= \frac{5D \times 36}{2D}$$

$$= \frac{180}{2} = 90 \ .... Ans.$$

Question

Travelling in a train, a man notices 13 telephone poles in two minutes. If the two successive telephone poles are known to be 125 m a part, then the train is travelling at a speed of:

1. 40 km/hr
2. 42 km/hr
3. 45 km/hr
4. 48 km/hr

Explanations

Answer: 3. 45 km/hr

We are given:

- The man notices **13 telephone poles** in **2 minutes**.
- The distance between **two successive poles** is **125 meters**.

Step 1: Calculate the Total Distance Covered

Since there are **13 poles**, the number of **gaps** between them is:

$$Number\ of\ gaps = 13 - 1 = 12$$

Each gap is **125 meters**, so the total distance covered by the train in **2 minutes** is:

$$Total\ Distance = 12 \times 125 = 1500\ meters$$

Step 2: Convert Time to Hours

We are given **2 minutes**, so convert it to hours:

$$2\ minutes = \frac{2}{60} = \frac{1}{30}\ hours$$

Step 3: Calculate the Speed

Using the formula:

$$Speed = \frac{Distance}{Time}$$

$$= \frac{1500}{\frac{1}{30}}$$

$$= 1500 \times 30 = 45000\ meters\ per\ hour$$

Convert meters per hour to kilometres per hour:

$$\frac{45000}{1000} = 45\ kilometers\ per\ hour\ ...Ans.$$

Question

A person travels from X to Y at a speed of 50 km/hr and returns from Y to X by increasing his speed by 50%. His average speed during the journey is-

1. 62.5 km/hr
2. 60 km/hr
3. 62 km/hr
4. 64 km/hr

Explanations
Answer: 2. 60 km/hr

We use the formula for **average speed** when a journey is covered in two parts with different speeds:

$$Average\ Speed = \frac{2xy}{x + y}$$

where:
- ○ **x** = Speed from **X to Y** = **50 kilometers per hour**
- ○ **y** = Speed from **Y to X**, which is **increased by 50%**

Step 1: Calculate the Return Speed
Since the speed increases by **50%**, we calculate:

$$y = 50 + \frac{50}{100} \times 50 = 50 + 25 = 75\ kilometers\ per\ hour$$

Step 2: Apply the Average Speed Formula

$$Average\ Speed = \frac{2 \times 50 \times 75}{50 + 75}$$

$$= \frac{2 \times 3750}{125} = \frac{7500}{125} = 60\ kilometers\ per\ hour\ ...Ans.$$

Question

A 500m long train running at a speed of 100m/s crosses a tunnel in 10s. What is the length?

1. 200m
2. 500m
3. 800m
4. 1000m

Explanations
Answer: 2. 200m

We are given:
- ○ **Length of the train = 500 meters**
- ○ **Speed of the train = 100 meters per second**
- ○ **Time taken to cross the tunnel = 10 seconds**

We need to find the **length of the tunnel**.

Step 1: Use the Distance Formula

When a train crosses a tunnel, the total distance covered is:

$$Total\ Distance = Length\ of\ Train + Length\ of\ Tunnel$$

Using the formula:

$$Distance = Speed \times Time$$
$$Total\ Distance = 100 \times 10 = 1000\ meters$$

Step 2: Find the Length of the Tunnel

$$Length\ of\ Tunnel = Total\ Distance - Length\ of\ Train$$
$$= 1000 - 500 = 500\ meters \ldots Ans.$$

Question

A person travels 365 km in 8 hours in two stages. In the first part of the journey, he travels by bus at the speed of 40 km/hour and in the second part of the journey, he travels by train at the speed of 55 km/hour. How much distance did he travel by train?

1. 165 km
2. 170 km
3. 200 km
4. 164 km

Explanations

Answer: 1. 165 km

We are given:

- **Total distance** = 365 kilometers
- **Total time** = 8 hours
- **Speed in the first part (by bus)** = 40 kilometers per hour
- **Speed in the second part (by train)** = 55 kilometers per hour

Let **x** be the distance traveled by **train**.

Then, the remaining distance traveled by **bus = (365 - x) kilometers**.

Step 1: Use the Time Formula

We use the formula:

$$Time = \frac{Distance}{Speed}$$

Total time taken:

$$\frac{365 - x}{40} + \frac{x}{55} = 8$$

Step 2: Solve for xxx

Multiply by **220** (LCM of 40 and 55) to eliminate fractions:

$$(365 - x) \times \frac{220}{40} + x \times \frac{220}{55} = 8 \times 220$$

$$(365 - x) \times 5.5 + x \times 4 = 1760$$

Expanding:

$$2007.5 - 5.5x + 4x = 1760$$

$$2007.5 - 1.5x = 1760$$

$$2007.5 - 1760 = 1.5x$$

$$247.5 = 1.5x$$

$$x = \frac{247.5}{1.5} = 165 \; kilometers \ldots Ans.$$

Question

Two friends A and B live 140 km apart. They both drive in a straight line towards each other to meet. If A drives at 80 km/h and B drives at 40 km/hr, then how many kilometres apart will they be exactly 45 minutes before they meet?

1. 70 km
2. 90 km
3. 100 km
4. 80 km

Explanations

Answer: 2. 90 km

We are given:

- o   **Total Distance between A and B = 140 km**
- o   **Speed of A = 80 km per hour**
- o   **Speed of B = 40 km per hour**
- o   **Time before meeting = 45 minutes (0.75 hours)**

Step 1: Calculate the Time to Meet

Since both A and B are moving towards each other, their **combined speed** is:

$$Combined \; Speed = 80 + 40 = 120 \; km \; per \; hour$$

Time taken to meet:

$$Time \; to \; Meet = \frac{Total \; Distance}{Combined \; Speed}$$

$$= \frac{140}{120} = \frac{7}{6} \; hours = 70 \; minutes$$

Step 2: Find Distance Covered in 45 Minutes

We need to find how far A and B travel **45 minutes (0.75 hours) before they meet**.

Distance covered in **45 minutes**:

$$Distance = Speed \times Time$$
$$= 120 \times 0.75 = 90 \; km \; ... Ans.$$

Question

Two railway stations A and B are 380 km apart. Train- 1 leaves station A at 7:00 A M moving with a speed of 80 km/hour towards B. After half an hour Train- 2 leaves station B towards A moving with speed of 90 km/hour. At what time, the two trains will cross each other?

1. 8:45AM
2. 9:00AM
3. 9:30AM
4. 10:15AM

Explanations

Answer: 3. 9:30AM

We are given:

- **Distance between Station A and B = 380 km**
- **Train-1** starts from **A at 7:00 AM** with a speed of **80 km per hour**
- **Train-2** starts from **B at 7:30 AM** with a speed of **90 km per hour**

We need to find the time when both trains will **cross each other**.

Step 1: Find the Head Start of Train-1

Train-1 **leaves 30 minutes earlier** than Train-2.

- In **30 minutes = 0.5 hours**, Train-1 covers:

$$Distance = Speed \times Time$$
$$= 80 \times 0.5 = 40 \; km$$

So, at **7:30 AM**, Train-1 is **40 km** ahead.

The **remaining distance** between the two trains at 7:30 AM is:

$$380 - 40 = 340 \; km$$

Step 2: Use the Relative Speed Formula

Since both trains are moving towards each other, their **relative speed** is:

$$Relative\ Speed = 80 + 90 = 170\ km\ per\ hour$$

The time taken to meet:

$$Time = \frac{Remaining\ Distance}{Relative\ Speed}$$

$$= \frac{340}{170} = 2\ hours$$

Step 3: Find the Meeting Time

- Train-2 started at **7:30 AM**.
- Adding **2 hours**, the trains will meet at:

$$7:30 + 2:00 = 9:30\ AM\ ...\ Ans.$$

Question

A salesman travels from Delhi to Ambala at 30 km/h and returns at 90 km/h. If the total time taken is 8 hours, find the total distance covered by him.

1. 480 km
2. 240 km
3. 360 km
4. 280 km

Explanations

Answer: 3. 360 km

We are given:

- **Speed from Delhi to Ambala = 30 km per hour**
- **Speed from Ambala to Delhi = 90 km per hour**
- **Total time taken for the entire journey = 8 hours**
- We need to find the **total distance covered**.

Step 1: Let the One-Way Distance be DDD

Since the distance from **Delhi to Ambala** and **Ambala to Delhi** is the same, let:

- **One-way distance = D**

The time taken for the first journey (Delhi → Ambala):

$$T1 = \frac{D}{30}$$

The time taken for the return journey (Ambala → Delhi):

$$T2 = \frac{D}{90}$$

Total time for both journeys:

$$T1 + T2 = 8$$
$$\frac{D}{30} + \frac{D}{90} = 8$$

Step 2: Solve for D

Find the LCM of **30 and 90**, which is **90**. Convert fractions:

$$\frac{3D}{90} + \frac{D}{90} = 8$$
$$\frac{4D}{90} = 8$$

Multiply both sides by **90**:

$$4D = 720$$
$$D = 180$$

Since the total distance covered includes **both onward and return journeys**:

$$Total\ Distance = 2D = 2 \times 180 = 360\ km\ ...\ Ans.$$

Question

A train running at a speed of 90 km/hr starts slowing down at a constant rate of decrease in speed of 2.5 m/s. What is the distance covered by the train before it comes to a halt?

1. 500 m
2. 750 m
3. 250 m
4. 125 m

Explanations

Answer: 4. 125 m

We are given:

- **Initial speed (u) = 90 km per hour**
- **Final speed (v) = 0** (since the train comes to a halt)
- **Acceleration (a) = -2.5 m/s^2** (since the train is slowing down)
- We need to find the **distance covered (s)** before coming to rest.

Step 1: Convert Speed to m/s

Since **1 km/h = 5/18 m/s**, we convert **90 km/h** to m/s:

$$u = 90 \times \frac{5}{18} = 25 \ meter\ per\ second$$

Step 2: Use the Equation of Motion

Using the kinematic equation:

$$v2 = u2 + 2as$$

Substituting the given values:

$$0 = 25^2 + 2(-2.5)s$$
$$0 = 625 - 5s$$
$$5s = 625$$
$$s = \frac{625}{5} = 125 \ ... Ans.$$

Question

A train moving at a speed of 63 km/hr enters a railway station and crosses the platform in 20 s. If the length of the train is 100 m, what is the length of the platform?

1. 150 m
2. 200 m
3. 250 m
4. 300 m

Explanations

Answer: 3. 250 m

We are given:

- **Speed of the train = 63 kilometers per hour**
- **Time taken to cross the platform = 20 seconds**
- **Length of the train = 100 meters**
- We need to find the **length of the platform**.

Step 1: Convert Speed to Meters per Second

Since **1 kilometer per hour = 5 per 18 meters per second**, we convert **63 kilometers per hour** to meters per second:

$$Speed = 63 \times \frac{5}{18} = 17.5 \ meters\ per\ second$$

Step 2: Use the Distance Formula

Total distance covered by the train while crossing the platform:

$$Distance = Speed \times Time$$
$$= 17.5 \times 20 = \mathbf{350\ meters}$$

Since the total distance covered includes both the **length of the train** and the **length of the platform**, we have:

$$Length\ of\ Train + Length\ of\ Platform = 350$$
$$100 + Length\ of\ Platform = 350$$
$$Length\ of\ Platform = 350 - 100 = 250\ meters \ldots Ans.$$

Question

A passenger train running at the speed of 75 km/hr leaves the railway station 9 hours after a goods train leaves and overtakes it in 6 hours. The speed of the goods train is

1. 35 km/hr
2. 32 km/hr
3. 30 km/hr
4. 28 km/hr

Explanations

Answer: 3. 30 km/hr

We are given:

- **Speed of the passenger train = 75 kilometers per hour**
- **Passenger train leaves 9 hours after the goods train**
- **Passenger train overtakes the goods train in 6 hours**
- We need to find the **speed of the goods train.**

Step 1: Distance Covered by the Goods Train Before the Passenger Train Starts

Let the speed of the goods train be **x kilometers per hour**.

Since the goods train has a **9-hour head start**, the distance it covers in that time is:

$$Distance\ covered\ by\ goods\ train\ in\ 9\ hours = 9x$$

Step 2: Distance Covered by Both Trains in 6 Hours

When the passenger train starts, it takes **6 hours** to overtake the goods train.

- **Distance covered by passenger train in 6 hours**:
$$Distance = Speed \times Time$$
$$= 75 \times 6 = 450\ kilometers$$

- o **Distance covered by goods train in 6 hours**:

$$= x \times 6 = 6x = x$$

Since both trains have covered the same total distance when they meet:

$$9x + 6x = 450$$
$$15x = 450$$
$$x = \frac{450}{15} = 30 \ kilometers \ per \ hour \ ... Ans.$$

Question

A man travels from his home to his office at a speed of 4 km/h and reaches his office 30 minutes late. If his speed had been 6 km/h. he would have reached office 5 minutes early.

Find the distance of his office from his home.

1. 8.5 km
2. 7 km
3. 8 km
4. 9 km

Explanations

Answer: 2. 7 km

We are given:

- o The man travels at **4 kilometers per hour** and reaches **30 minutes late**.
- o If he had traveled at **6 kilometers per hour**, he would have reached **5 minutes early**.
- o We need to find the **distance between his home and office**.

Step 1: Define Variables

Let the **actual time** he should take to reach his office be **T hours**.

Let the **distance** to his office be **D kilometers**.

Case 1: When he travels at 4 km/h

The time taken:

$$T + \frac{30}{60} = T + \frac{1}{2}$$
$$\frac{D}{4} = T + \frac{1}{2}$$

Case 2: When he travels at 6 km/h

The time taken:

$$T - \frac{5}{60} = T - \frac{1}{12}$$

Step 2: Solve for D

Since both equations are equal to **T**, we equate them:

$$\frac{D}{4} - \frac{1}{2} = \frac{D}{6} + \frac{1}{12}$$

Multiply throughout by **12** to eliminate fractions:

$$3D - 6 = 2D + 1$$
$$3D - 2D = 6 + 1$$
$$D = 7 \ldots Ans.$$

Question

Two trains are moving in same direction at 60 km/hr and 45 km/hr. The faster train passes a girl sitting in the slower train in 15 seconds. The length of the faster train is-

1. 22.5 m
2. 225 m
3. 62.5 m
4. 165 m

Explanations

Answer: 3. 62.5 m

We are given:

- **Speed of the faster train = 60 kilometers per hour**
- **Speed of the slower train = 45 kilometers per hour**
- **Time taken to pass the girl = 15 seconds**
- We need to find the **length of the faster train**.

Step 1: Find the Relative Speed

Since both trains are moving in the **same direction**, the relative speed is:

$$Relative\ Speed = Speed\ of\ Faster\ Train - Speed\ of\ Slower\ Train$$
$$= 60 - 45 = 15$$

Convert **15 kilometers per hour** to **meters per second**:

$$15 \times \frac{5}{18} = \frac{75}{18} = 4.167\ meters\ per\ second$$

Step 2: Use the Distance Formula

The distance covered by the faster train while passing the girl is equal to the **length of the faster train.**

$$Distance = Speed \times Time$$
$$= 4.167 \times 15 = \textbf{62.5 } \textbf{\textit{meters}} \dots \textbf{\textit{Ans.}}$$

Question

Which of the following statements are correct?

- A. *If A's speed is more than B's speed, then to travel the same distance, A will take more time than B*
- B. *Two speeds, 1500 m/min and 90 km/hr are equal*
- C. *By walking at a speed of 18 km/hr, the distance covered in 2 minutes and 30 seconds is 750 meters*

1. A and B only
2. B and C only
3. A and C only
4. C only

Explanations

Answer: 2. B and C only

Statement A: *"If A's speed is more than B's speed, then to travel the same distance, A will take more time than B."*

- o This statement is **incorrect** because if A's speed is more than B's speed, A will take **less time** to cover the same distance, not more.
- o **Corrected statement:** If A's speed is more than B's speed, then A will take **less time** than B to cover the same distance.

Thus, **Statement A is incorrect.**

Statement B: *"Two speeds, 1500 meters per minute and 90 kilometers per hour are equal."*

- o Convert **90 kilometers per hour** to **meters per minute**:
$$90 \times \frac{1000}{60} = 90 \times 16.67 = 1500 \; meters \; per \; minute$$
- o Since both speeds are **equal, Statement B is correct.**

Statement C: *"By walking at a speed of 18 kilometers per hour, the distance covered in 2 minutes and 30 seconds is 750 meters."*

- o Convert **18 kilometers per hour** to **meters per second**:
$$18 \times \frac{5}{18} = 5 \; meters \; per \; second$$

- o   Convert **2 minutes and 30 seconds** to **seconds**:
$$2 \times 60 + 30 = 150 \; seconds$$
- o   Calculate the **distance covered**:
$$Distance = Speed \times Time$$
$$= 5 \times 150 = 750 \; meters \ldots Ans.$$
- o   Since the calculation is **correct, Statement C is correct.**

Boat and Stream

Boat and Stream problems are based on the relative motion of a boat in **still water, upstream, and downstream**. These types of questions are common in **UGC NET Paper I** and other competitive exams.

Basic Terms & Concepts
1.   **Still Water Speed**: The speed of the boat when the water is not moving (i.e., in a lake or pond).
2.   **Stream or Current Speed**: The speed of the water flow in a river or stream.
3.   **Upstream**: When the boat moves **against the current** (i.e., opposite to the flow of water).
4.   **Downstream**: When the boat moves **with the current** (i.e., in the same direction as the flow of water).

Key Formulas
Let:
- o   **B** = Speed of boat in still water
- o   **S** = Speed of the stream (current)
- o   **U** = Upstream speed
- o   **D** = Downstream speed

1. Downstream Speed (Boat moving with the current)
$$D = B + S$$
The effective speed increases because the boat moves in the same direction as the stream.

2. Upstream Speed (Boat moving against the current)
$$U = B - S$$

The effective speed decreases because the stream opposes the boat's movement.

3. Finding the Speed of Boat and Stream

- **Boat's speed in still water:**

$$B = \frac{D + U}{2}$$

- **Stream's speed:**

$$S = \frac{D - U}{2}$$

4. Time, Speed, and Distance Formula

$$Time = \frac{Distance}{Speed}$$

Use this formula for both upstream and downstream calculations.

Types of Problems

1. Finding the Time Taken to Travel Upstream or Downstream
Example:
A boat's speed in still water is **10 kilometers per hour**, and the stream's speed is **2 kilometers per hour**.
Find the time taken to travel **24 kilometers** upstream.
Solution:

- **Upstream Speed** = 10−2=8kilometers per hour
- **Time** = Distance ÷ Speed

$$T = \frac{24}{8} = 3 \; hours$$

2. Finding the Distance Covered
Example:
A boat travels **upstream for 4 hours** at **6 kilometers per hour**.
How far has it traveled?
Solution:

$$Distance = Speed \times Time = 6 \times 4 = 24 \; kilometers$$

3. Finding the Speed of the Stream

Example:

A boat takes **3 hours** to travel **21 kilometers downstream** and **7 hours** to return the same distance upstream. Find the speed of the stream.

Solution:

- **Downstream Speed** $= 21 \div 3 = 7$ *kilometers per hour*
- **Upstream Speed** $= 21 \div 7 = 3$ *kilometers per hour*
- **Stream's speed**:

$$S = \frac{D - U}{2} = \frac{7 - 3}{2} = 2 \text{ kilometers per hour}$$

4. Finding the Speed of the Boat in Still Water

Example:

A boat goes **30 kilometers downstream in 3 hours** and returns upstream in **5 hours**.

Find the speed of the boat in still water.

Solution:

- **Downstream Speed** $= 30 \div 3 = 10$ *kilometers per hour*
- **Upstream Speed** $= 30 \div 5 = 6$ *kilometers per hour*
- **Boat's speed in still water**:

$$B = \frac{D + U}{2} = \frac{10 + 6}{2} = 8 \text{ kilometers per hour}$$

Concept Check 19: Boat and Stream

1. A boat's speed in still water is **12 kilometers per hour**. If the speed of the stream is **4 kilometers per hour**, find how long it will take to travel **32 kilometers downstream**.

2. A boat takes **5 hours** to travel **30 kilometers upstream** and **3 hours** to travel the same distance downstream. Find the speed of the stream.

3. A man rows **30 kilometers downstream in 2 hours** and the same distance upstream in **3 hours**. Find his speed in still water.

UGC NET PYQ Questions and Explanations on Boat and Stream:

Question

Suppose a man swims 12 km upstream and 20 km downstream in a river in 4 hours. If he swims 18 km upstream and 10 km downstream also in 4 hours, then the speed at which he swims in the still water is.

1. 4 km /hr
2. 6 km /hr
3. 8 km /hr
4. 10 km /hr

Explanations

Answer: 3. 8 km /hr

We are given:

- **Upstream Distance 1 = 12 km**
- **Downstream Distance 1 = 20 km**
- **Total Time for First Case = 4 hours**
- **Upstream Distance 2 = 18 km**
- **Downstream Distance 2 = 10 km**
- **Total Time for Second Case = 4 hours**

We need to find the **speed of the man in still water**.

Step 1: Define Variables

Let:

- **B** = Speed of the man in still water (in km per hour)
- **S** = Speed of the stream (in km per hour)
- **Upstream Speed** = B−S
- **Downstream Speed** = B+S

Using the **time formula**:

$$Time = \frac{Distance}{Speed}$$

Step 2: Write Equations

For the first case:

$$\frac{12}{B - S} + \frac{20}{B + S} = 4$$

For the second case:

$$\frac{18}{B-S} + \frac{10}{B+S} = 4$$

Step 3: Solve the Equations

Let:

$$x = B - S, y = B + S$$

So the equations become:

$$\frac{12}{x} + \frac{20}{y} = 4$$

$$\frac{18}{x} + \frac{10y}{= 4}$$

Multiply both equations by **xy** to eliminate fractions:

$$12y + 20x = 4xy$$

$$18y + 10x = 4xy$$

Since both equations equal **4xy**, we set them equal to each other:

$$12y + 20x = 18y + 10x$$

Rearrange:

$$20x - 10x = 18y - 12y$$

$$10x = 6y$$

$$\frac{x}{y} = \frac{6}{10} = \frac{3}{5}$$

$$Since\ x = B - S\ and\ y = B + S, we\ substitute:$$

$$\frac{(B-S)}{(B+S)} = \frac{3}{5}$$

Cross-multiply:

$$5(B - S) = 3(B + S)$$

$$5B - 5S = 3B + 3S$$

$$5B - 3B = 5S + 3S$$

$$2B = 8S$$

$$B = 4S$$

Step 4: Find B

Using the equation:

$$\frac{12}{B-S} + \frac{20}{B+S} = 4$$

Substituting B=4S:

$$12(4S - S) + \frac{20}{4S + S} = 4$$

$$\frac{12}{3S} + \frac{20}{5S} = 4$$

$$\frac{4}{S} + \frac{4}{S} = 4$$

$$\frac{8}{S} = 4 = 2$$

Since B=4S:

$$B = 4 \times 2 = 8 \ km \ per \ hour \ ... Ans.$$

Question

The speed of a boat in still water is 10 Km/hr (10 Kmph). If it can travel 26 Km downstream and 14 Km upstream in the same time, the speed of the stream is:

1. 4.5 Km/hr
2. 5 Km/hr
3. 3 Km/hr
4. 4 Km/hr

Explanations

Answer: 3. 3 Km/hr

We are given:

- **Speed of the boat in still water (B) = 10 kilometers per hour**
- **Distance travelled downstream = 26 kilometers**
- **Distance traveled upstream = 14 kilometers**
- **Time taken for both journeys is the same**
- We need to find the **speed of the stream (S).**

Step 1: Define Upstream and Downstream Speeds

- **Downstream Speed** $= B + S = 10 + S$ *kilometers per hour*
- **Upstream Speed** $= B - S = 10 - S$ *kilometers per hour*

Since the time taken for both journeys is the same:

$$\frac{Distance \ Downstream}{Speed \ Downstream} = \frac{Distance \ Upstream}{Speed \ Upstream}$$

$$\frac{26}{10 + S} = \frac{14}{10 - S}$$

Step 2: Cross Multiply

$$26(10 - S) = 14(10 + S)$$
$$260 - 26S = 140 + 14S$$
$$260 - 140 = 26S + 14S$$
$$120 = 40S$$

$$S = \frac{120}{40} = 3 \ kilometers \ per \ hour \ ... Ans.$$

Question

A motorboat covers a certain distance downstream in 5 h but takes 6 h to return upstream to the starting point. If the speed to the stream is 4 km/h, then what is the speed of the motor boat in still water?

1. 40 km/h
2. 42 km/h
3. 44 km/h
4. 46 km/h

Explanations

Answer: 3. 44 km/h

We are given:

- **Downstream time = 5 hours**
- **Upstream time = 6 hours**
- **Speed of the stream (S) = 4 kilometers per hour**
- We need to find the **speed of the motorboat in still water (B)**.

Step 1: Define Upstream and Downstream Speeds

- *Downstream Speed* $= B + S = B + 4$
- *Upstream Speed* $= B - S = B - 4$

Since the distance traveled in both cases is the same, we use the formula:

$$Distance = Speed \times Time$$

Setting the distances equal for both cases:

$$5(B + 4) = 6(B - 4)$$

Step 2: Solve for B

Expanding both sides:

$$5B + 20 = 6B - 24$$

Rearrange:

$$5B - 6B = -24 - 20$$
$$-B = -44$$
$$B = 44 \dots Ans.$$

Question

The speed of a boat in still water is 5 km/hr and the speed of the stream is 1 km/hr. A man rows to a place at a distance of 24 km and comes back to the starting point. Find the total time taken by him.

1. 8 hr
2. 10 hr
3. 12 hr
4. 15 hr

Explanations

Answer: 2. 10 hr

We are given:

- **Speed of the boat in still water (B) = 5 kilometers per hour**
- **Speed of the stream (S) = 1 kilometer per hour**
- **Distance one way = 24 kilometers**
- We need to find the **total time taken for the round trip**.

Step 1: Calculate Upstream and Downstream Speeds

- $Downstream\ Speed = B + S = 5 + 1 = 6\ kilometers\ per\ hour$
- $Upstream\ Speed = B - S = 5 - 1 = 4\ kilometers\ per\ hour$

Step 2: Calculate Time for Downstream and Upstream

Using the formula:

$$Time = \frac{Distance}{Speed}$$

Time Taken for Downstream:

$$TimeDown = \frac{24}{6} = 4\ hours$$

Time Taken for Upstream:

$$TimeUp = \frac{24}{4} = 6\ hours$$

Step 3: Find Total Time

$$Time\ total = Time\ down + Time\ up$$
$$= 4 + 6 = 10\ hours\ ...\ Ans.$$

Question

In a river from a fixed location, two identical boats start moving upstream and downstream, respectively. The speed of the water current in the river is 3 km/hour. If the speed of each of the boats in still water is 15 km/hour, the separation between the boats after 12 minutes will be

1. 3.6 km

2. 5.6 km

3. 6.0 km

4. 7.2 km

Explanations

Answer: 3. 6.0 km

We are given:

- o   *Speed of each boat in still water* (B) $=$ 15 *kilometers per hour*
- o   *Speed of the water current* (S) $=$ 3 *kilometers per hour*
- o   *Time elapsed* $=$ 12 *minutes* $= \frac{12}{60}$ *hours* $= \frac{1}{5}$ *hours*

We need to find the **separation between the two boats after 12 minutes**.

Step 1: Determine Upstream and Downstream Speeds

- o   **Downstream Speed** $= B + S = 15 + 3 = 18$ *kilometers per hour*
- o   **Upstream Speed** $= B - S = 15 - 3 = 12$ *kilometers per hour*

Step 2: Calculate Distance Traveled by Each Boat

Using the formula:

$$Distance = Speed \times Time$$

Distance traveled by the downstream boat:

$$Ddown = 18 \times \frac{1}{5} = \frac{18}{5} = 3.6 \; kilometers$$

Distance traveled by the upstream boat:

$$Dup = 12 \times \frac{1}{5} = \frac{12}{5} = 2.4 \; kilometers$$

Step 3: Calculate the Separation Between Boats

$$Separation = Ddown + Dup$$
$$= 3.6 + 2.4 = 6.0 \; kilometers \ldots Ans.$$

Time and Work

Time and Work is an important topic in mathematical reasoning, commonly tested in **UGC NET Paper I** and other competitive exams. It focuses on the relationship between **work, time, and efficiency**.

Basic Formula: The fundamental formula that governs this topic is:

$$Work\ Done = Rate\ of\ Work \times Time$$

Using this, we derive:

- o **Work Efficiency = 1 / Time Taken**
- o **Total Work = LCM of time taken by different workers**

Types of Time & Work Problems

1. Work Done by One Person

If a person **A** can complete a task in **X days**, then the **work done by A in one day** is:

$$\frac{1}{X}$$

Example:
If A can complete a task in **10 days**, then A's **one-day work** is:

$$\frac{1}{10}$$

2. Work Done by Multiple People

If **A** can complete a task in **X days** and **B** can complete the same task in **Y days**, then their combined **one-day work** is:

$$\frac{1}{X} + \frac{1}{Y}$$

Example:
If A can do a task in **10 days** and B in **15 days**, their combined **one-day work** is:

$$\frac{1}{10} + \frac{1}{15} = \frac{3}{30} + \frac{2}{30} = \frac{5}{30} = \frac{1}{6}$$

So, together they complete the work in **6 days**.

3. Work Efficiency Ratio

If **A** is twice as efficient as **B**, then:
- o A takes **half** the time as B.
- o If B takes **X days**, then A takes **X/2 days**.

Example:
If B takes **12 days**, A will take:

$$\frac{12}{2} = 6 \ days$$

4. Work and Number of Workers

If **more workers** are added, work gets completed **faster**.

$$Work\ Done \propto Number\ of\ Workers$$

Example:
If 4 workers complete a task in **12 days**, then **8 workers** will take:

$$\frac{12 \times 4}{8} = 6\ days$$

5. Work and Time Inversely Proportional

$$Time \propto \frac{1}{Efficiency}$$

If **A is twice as efficient as B**, then **A takes half the time**.

6. Special Cases

1. Alternate Workdays

If **A and B** work on alternate days, the total work done is:

$$(A's\ one - day\ work\ + B's\ one - day\ work) \times half\ the\ days$$

2. Work with Leave Days

If **A works for X days and takes Y days off**, the total work is calculated by adjusting for the actual working days.

Concept Check 20: Time and Work

1. *A can complete a work in **12 days**, B can complete it in **18 days**. If both work together, how many days will they take?*
2. *A is **twice as efficient as B**. If A can finish a task in **8 days**, how many days will they take together?*
3. *12 men can complete a task in **10 days**. How many men are required to complete it in **6 days**?*

UGC NET PYQ Questions and Explanations on Time and Work:

Question

Ayush and Bilal can do a job in 'D' days. If Ayush can alone do the job in D+3 days and Bilal alone can do the job in D+12 days, find the value of D.

1. 9
2. 8
3. 6
4. 5

Explanations

Answer: 3. 6

We are given:

- o **Ayush alone completes the work in $D + 3$ days**
- o **Bilal alone completes the work in $D + 12$ days**
- o **Both Ayush and Bilal together complete the work in D days**

We need to find the value of D.

Step 1: Express Work Done per Day

- *Work done by Ayush in one day* $= \dfrac{1}{D+3}$
- *Work done by Bilal in one day* $= \dfrac{1}{D+12}$
- *Work done by both together in one day* $= \dfrac{1}{D}$

Since both works together:

$$\frac{1}{D + 3} + \frac{1}{D + 12} = \frac{1}{D}$$

Step 2: Solve for DDD

$$Take\ the\ LCM\ of\ (D + 3)\ and\ (D + 12)$$

$$\frac{(D + 12) + (D + 3)}{(D + 3)(D + 12)} = \frac{1}{D}$$

$$\frac{2D + 15}{(D + 3)(D + 12)} = \frac{1}{D}$$

Cross multiply:

$$(2D + 15)D = (D + 3)(D + 12)$$

Expand:

$$2D^2 + 15D = D^2 + 12D + 3D + 36$$

$$2D^2 + 15D = D^2 + 15D + 36$$

Cancel $15D$ from both sides:

$$2D^2 = D^2 + 36$$

$$2D^2 - D^2 = 36$$

$$D^2 = 36$$

$$D = 6 \dots Ans.$$

Question

A man and a boy completed a piece of work in 10 days and were a paid Rs. 10,000. The man was 50% more efficient than the boy. What is the difference in the daily wages of the man and the boy?

1. Rs. 100
2. Rs. 500
3. Rs. 400
4. Rs. 200

Explanations

Answer: 4. Rs. 200

We are given:

- o A **man** and a **boy** together complete the work in **10 days**.
- o They are paid **Rs. 10,000** in total.
- o The **man is 50% more efficient** than the boy.
- o We need to find the **difference in their daily wages**.

Step 1: Define Efficiency

Let the efficiency of the **boy** be **x units of work per day**.

Since the **man is 50% more efficient**, his efficiency will be:

$$Man's\ efficiency = x + \frac{50}{100}x = 1.5x$$

Total efficiency of both together:

$$Total\ efficiency = x + 1.5x = 2.5x$$

Step 2: Find Total Work

Since both complete the work in **10 days**, total work done is:

$$Total\ Work = Total\ Efficiency \times Total\ Days$$
$$= 2.5x \times 10 = 25x$$

Step 3: Find Individual Work Contribution

- o **Work done by the man = Man's efficiency × Days**
$$= 1.5x \times 10 = 15x$$
- o **Work done by the boy = Boy's efficiency × Days**
$$= x \times 10 = 10x$$

Step 4: Find Individual Wages

Since the **total payment is Rs. 10,000**, payment is distributed based on their work done:

- o **Man's earnings**:
$$\frac{15x}{25x} \times 10000 = \frac{15}{25} \times 10000 = 6000$$
- o **Boy's earnings**:
$$\frac{10x}{25x} \times 10000 = \frac{10}{25} \times 10000 = 4000$$

Step 5: Find Daily Wages

Since they worked for **10 days**:

- o ***Man's daily wage*** $= \frac{6000}{10} = 600$
- o ***Boy's daily wage*** $= \frac{4000}{10} = 400$

Difference in daily wages:
$$600 - 400 = 200$$

Question

A man can do a work in 10 days. The man along with a boy can do the same work in 8 days.

What is the ratio of efficiencies of work of the man and the boy?

1. 2:1
2. 3:1
3. 4:1
4. 5:1

Explanations

Answer: 3. 4:1

We are given:

- o **A man alone** can complete the work in **10 days**.
- o **A man and a boy together** can complete the same work in **8 days**.
- o We need to find the **ratio of the efficiency of the man and the boy**.

Step 1: Define Efficiency

- o The efficiency of a worker is the **amount of work done per day**.
- o If a person completes a task in **X days**, then the **work done per day (efficiency) is $\frac{1}{X}$**.

Efficiency of the Man:

$$Man's\ efficiency = \frac{1}{10\ (since\ he\ completes\ the\ work\ in\ 10\ days)}$$

Efficiency of the Man and the Boy Together:

$$Combined\ efficiency = \frac{1}{8\ (since\ they\ complete\ the\ work\ in\ 8\ days)}$$

Step 2: Find Efficiency of the Boy

Since both work together:

$$Man's\ efficiency + Boy's\ efficiency = Combined\ efficiency$$

$$\frac{1}{10} + Boy's\ efficiency = \frac{1}{8}$$

Solving for the **boy's efficiency**:

$$Boy's\ efficiency = \frac{1}{8} - \frac{1}{10}$$

Find LCM of **8 and 10**, which is **40**:

$$\frac{5}{40} - \frac{4}{40} = \frac{1}{40}$$

$$So,\ \boldsymbol{Boy's\ efficiency} = \frac{1}{40}$$

Step 3: Find the Ratio of Efficiencies

Ratio of Man's efficiency to Boy's efficiency $= \frac{1}{10} : \frac{1}{40}$

Multiply both by **40** to simplify:

$$\left(\frac{1}{10} \times 40\right) : \left(\frac{1}{40} \times 40\right)$$

$$4 : 1 \ldots Ans.$$

Question

'A' takes twice as much time as 'B' to complete a work and 'C' does it in the same time as both 'A' and 'B' together do it. If all three of them work together and complete the work in 5 days, then the time taken by 'B' to complete the work alone is:

1. 12 days
2. 14 days
3. 15 days
4. 18 days

Explanations

Answer: 3. 15 days

We are given:

- **A takes twice as much time as B** to complete the work.
  - *This means if **B takes x days**, then **A takes 2x days**.*
- **C completes the work in the same time as A and B together**.
  - $$This\ means\ C\ takes\ \frac{2x \cdot x}{2x + x} = \frac{2x^2}{3x} = \frac{2x}{3}$$
- **A, B, and C together complete the work in 5 days**.
- We need to find the **time taken by B alone**.

Step 1: Work Efficiency of Each Person

Efficiency (Work done per day) is given by:

$$Efficiency = \frac{1}{Time\ taken}$$

$$A's\ efficiency = \frac{1}{2x}$$

$$B's\ efficiency = \frac{1}{x}$$

$$C's\ efficiency = \frac{1}{\frac{2x}{3}} = \frac{3}{2x}$$

Since all three complete the work together in **5 days**, we set up the equation:

$$\frac{1}{2x} + \frac{1}{x} + \frac{3}{2x} = \frac{1}{5}$$

Step 2: Solve for x

Taking **LCM of 2x and x**:

$$\frac{1}{2x} + \frac{2}{2x} + \frac{3}{2x} = \frac{1}{5}$$

$$\frac{1 + 2 + 3}{2x} = \frac{1}{5}$$

$$\frac{6}{2x} = \frac{1}{5}$$

$$\frac{3}{x} = \frac{1}{5}$$

$$x = 15 \ldots Ans.$$

Question

Forty-five (45) people can do a piece of work in 16 days. Six days after he started his work, 30 more people joined his work. Now how many days will they together take to complete the remaining work?

1. 5 1/2
2. 7 days
3. 5 days
4. 6 days

Explanations

Answer: 4. 6 days

We are given:

- o   **45 people** can complete the work in **16 days**.
- o   **After 6 days, 30 more people** join, making the total workers **45 + 30 = 75**.
- o   We need to find how many more days they will take to complete the remaining work.

Step 1: Find Total Work

Total work is measured in **man-days** (work done by one person in one day).

$$Total\ Work = Number\ of\ People \times Number\ of\ Days$$
$$= 45 \times 16 = 720\ \textit{units of work}$$

Step 2: Find Work Done in 6 Days

In **6 days**, 45 people work, so the work completed is:

$$Work\ Done = 45 \times 6 = 270$$
$$Remaining\ Work = 720 - 270 = 450\ units$$

Step 3: Find Time Required with 75 Workers

After 6 days, the workforce increases to **75 people**.

The time required to complete the remaining work:

$$Time = \frac{Remaining\ Work}{Total\ Workers}$$
$$= \frac{450}{75} = 6\ \textit{days} \dots \textit{Ans}.$$

Question

15 men working 8 hours per day complete a piece of work in 18 days. To complete the same work in 6 days, working 12 hours a day, the number of men required will be:

1.   24 men
2.   26 men

3. 28 men
4. 30 men

Explanations

Answer: 4. 30 men

We are given:

- **15 men** working **8 hours per day** complete the work in **18 days**.
- We need to find how many men are required to complete the **same work** in **6 days**, working **12 hours per day**.

Step 1: Find Total Work in Terms of Man-Hours

Total work is measured in **man-hours**:

$$Total\ Work = Number\ of\ Men \times Hours\ per\ Day \times Days$$
$$= 15 \times 8 \times 18$$
$$= \mathbf{2160\ man-hours}$$

Step 2: Find Required Number of Men

Let the required number of men be **x**.

The new workforce works for **12 hours per day** and must finish in **6 days**:

$$Total\ Work = x \times 12 \times 6$$
$$2160 = x \times 72$$
$$x = \frac{2160}{72} = \mathbf{30} \ldots \textbf{\textit{Ans}}.$$

Question

60 persons consume 300 kg of wheat in 40 days. In how many days will 25 persons consume 100 kg of wheat?

1. 28 days
2. 30 days
3. 32 days
4. 35 days

Explanations

Answer: 3. 32 days

We are given:

- **60 persons** consume **300 kg** of wheat in **40 days**.
- We need to find how many days **25 persons** will take to consume **100 kg** of wheat.

Step 1: Find Consumption Rate

The total consumption rate per day for **60 persons**:

$$Consumption\ per\ day = \frac{300}{40} = 7.5\ kg\ per\ day$$

Since **60 persons** consume **7.5 kg per day**, the **per person** consumption rate per day:

$$Per\ person\ per\ day\ consumption = \frac{7.5}{60} = 0.125\ kg\ per\ person\ per\ day$$

Step 2: Find Time for 25 Persons to Consume 100 kg

Total wheat to be consumed = **100 kg**.

Total daily consumption of **25 persons**:

$$Total\ daily\ consumption = 25 \times 0.125 = 3.125\ kg\ per\ day$$

Time required:

$$Time = \frac{Total\ Wheat}{Daily\ Consumption}$$

$$= \frac{100}{3.125} = \mathbf{32\ days} \ldots \textbf{Ans}.$$

Question

5 pumps working 18 hours a day empty a tank in 12 days. How many hours per day should 6 pumps work to empty a tank in 9 days?

1. 19 hours
2. 20 hours
3. 21 hours
4. 22 hours

Explanations

Answer: 2. 20 hours

We are given:

- **5 pumps** working **18 hours per day** empty a tank in **12 days**.
- We need to find how many **hours per day** should **6 pumps** work to empty the tank in **9 days**.

Step 1: Find Total Work in Terms of Pump-Hours

Total work is measured in **pump-hours**:

$$Total\ Work = Number\ of\ Pumps \times Hours\ per\ Day \times Days$$

$$= 5 \times 18 \times 12 = 1080\ pump - hours$$

Step 2: Find Required Hours per Day for 6 Pumps in 9 Days

Let the required number of hours per day be **x**.

The new workforce works for **9 days** with **6 pumps**, so:

$$Total\ Work = 6 \times x \times 9$$
$$1080 = 6 \times 9 \times x$$
$$1080 = 54x$$
$$x = \frac{1080}{54} = \mathbf{20} \ldots \boldsymbol{Ans.}$$

Question

A man can do a piece of work in 8 days and another man can do the same work in 10 days. How long should it take both A and B working together but independently?

$$1.\ 6\ days, \quad 2.\ 4\frac{4}{9}, \quad 3.\ 4\frac{1}{5}, \quad 4.\ 5\frac{1}{2}$$

Explanations

Answer:

We are given:

- **A alone can complete the work in 8 days**.
- **B alone can complete the work in 10 days**.
- We need to find how long **A and B together** will take.

Step 1: Work Efficiency of A and B

Efficiency (work done per day) is given by:

$$Efficiency = \frac{1}{Time\ taken}$$

$$\boldsymbol{A's\ efficiency} = \frac{1}{8} \ (A\ completes\ \mathbf{1/8th}\ of\ the\ work\ per\ day)$$

$$\boldsymbol{B's\ efficiency} = \frac{1}{10} (B\ completes\ \mathbf{1/10th}\ of\ the\ work\ per\ day)$$

Total work done per day when **A and B work together**:

$$\frac{1}{8} + \frac{1}{10}$$

Taking **LCM of 8 and 10**, which is **40**:

$$\frac{5}{40} + \frac{4}{40} = \frac{9}{40}$$

This means **A and B together** complete **9/40** of the work per day.

Step 2: Find the Total Time Taken

Time required to complete the whole work:

$$Total\ Time = \frac{1}{Work\ done\ per\ day}$$

$$= \frac{1}{\frac{9}{40}} = \frac{40}{9} = 4\frac{4}{9}\ days \ldots Ans.$$

Question

Working 9 hours a day, 12 persons complete a work in 25 days. Working 6 hours a day, 15 persons can do the same work in

1. 28 days
2. 29 days
3. 30 days
4. 32 days

Explanations

Answer: 3. 30 days

We are given:

- **12 persons** working **9 hours per day** complete the work in **25 days**.
- We need to find how many days **15 persons** working **6 hours per day** will take to complete the same work.

Step 1: Find Total Work in Terms of Person-Hours

Total work is measured in **person-hours**:

$$Total\ Work = Number\ of\ Persons \times Hours\ per\ Day \times Days$$
$$= 12 \times 9 \times 25$$
$$= 2700\ person\ hours$$

Step 2: Find Required Days for 15 Persons Working 6 Hours per Day

Let the required number of days be **x**.

The new workforce works **15 persons** for **6 hours per day**, so:

$$Total\ Work = 15 \times 6 \times x$$
$$2700 = 15 \times 6 \times x$$
$$2700 = 90x$$
$$x = \frac{2700}{90} = 30 \ldots Ans.$$

Question

Ram can finish a work in 18 days. Shyam is twice as efficient as Ram. If both of them start the work together, how many days it will take them to finish the work?

1. 6 days
2. 8 days
3. 9 days
4. 12 days

Explanations

Answer: 1. 6 Days.

We are given:

- **Ram alone** can complete the work in **18 days.**
- **Shyam is twice as efficient as Ram**, meaning Shyam takes **half the time of Ram** to complete the same work.

Thus, **Shyam alone** can complete the work in:

$$\frac{18}{2} = 9 \ days$$

We need to find how long **Ram and Shyam together** will take.

Step 1: Work Efficiency of Ram and Shyam

Efficiency (work done per day) is given by:

$$Efficiency = \frac{1}{Time \ taken}$$

$$Ram's \ efficiency = \frac{1}{18} \ (Ram \ completes \ \textbf{1/18th} \ of \ the \ work \ per \ day)$$

$$Shyam's \ efficiency = \frac{1}{9} \ (Shyam \ completes \ \textbf{1/9th} \ of \ the \ work \ per \ day)$$

Total work done per day when **Ram and Shyam work together**:

$$\frac{1}{18} + \frac{1}{9}$$

Taking **LCM of 18 and 9**, which is **18**:

$$\frac{1}{18} + \frac{2}{18} = \frac{3}{18} = \frac{1}{6}$$

This means **Ram and Shyam together** complete **1/6th** of the work per day.

Step 2: Find the Total Time Taken

Time required to complete the whole work:

$$Total \ Time = \frac{1}{Work \ done \ per \ day}$$

$$1 = \frac{1}{\frac{1}{6}} = 6\ days\ ...Ans.$$

Question

A person X can do a piece of work worth Rs 3000 in 6 days: But he engages an assistant Y. and Completes the work in 4 days. Find the share of the assistant Y in completing the work.

1. 800
2. 1000
3. 1500
4. 1200

Explanations

Answer: 2. 1000

We are given:

- o **Person X** can complete the work alone in **6 days**.
- o With the help of **assistant Y**, the work is completed in **4 days**.
- o The total payment for the work is **Rs. 3000**.
- o We need to find **Y's share** in the payment.

Step 1: Work Efficiency of X and Y

Efficiency (work done per day) is given by:

$$Efficiency = \frac{1}{Time\ taken}$$

$$X's\ efficiency = \frac{1}{6}\ (X\ completes\ \textbf{1/6th}\ of\ the\ work\ per\ day)$$

X and Y together complete the work in **4 days**, so their combined efficiency is:

$$\frac{1}{4}\ (since\ they\ complete\ 1\ full\ work\ in\ 4\ days)$$

Since,

$$Efficiency\ of\ (X\ +\ Y) = \frac{1}{4}$$

We can write:

$$\frac{1}{6} + Y's\ efficiency = \frac{1}{4}$$

Step 2: Find Y's Efficiency

Solving for **Y's efficiency**:

$$Y's\ efficiency = \frac{1}{4} - \frac{1}{6}$$

Find LCM of **4 and 6**, which is **12**:

$$\frac{3}{12} - \frac{2}{12} = \frac{1}{12}$$

So, **Y's efficiency** = $\frac{1}{12}$, meaning **Y alone can complete the work in 12 days**.

Step 3: Find Y's Share in the Payment

Work is shared in proportion to the work done.

$$Total\ work\ =\ 1\ unit$$

$$X's\ total\ work\ in\ 4\ days\ = \frac{4}{6} = \frac{2}{3}$$

$$Y's\ total\ work\ in\ 4\ days\ = \frac{4}{12} = \frac{1}{3}$$

Since Y does **1/3rd** of the total work, his share in the payment is:

$$\frac{1}{3} \times 3000 = \mathbf{1000} \ldots Ans.$$

Question

A man X. can complete $\frac{1}{3}$ of a job in 5 days and another man Y can complete $\frac{2}{5}$ of the job in 10 days. In how many days both X & Y together can complete the job?

$$1.\ 9\frac{3}{8}, \qquad 2.\ 8\frac{3}{8}, \qquad 3.\ 9\frac{3}{5}, \qquad 4.\ 7\frac{7}{9}$$

Explanations

Answer: 1. $9\frac{3}{8}$

We are given:

- X can complete $\frac{1}{3}$ of the job in **5 days**.
- Y can complete $\frac{2}{5}$ of the job in **10 days**.
- We need to find how many days both **X and Y together** can complete the whole job.

Step 1: Find the Efficiency (Work per Day)

Work done per day by X:

If **X completes** $\frac{1}{3}$ **of the job in 5 days**, then his **one-day work** is:

$$\frac{1}{3} \div 5 = \frac{1}{15}$$

Work done per day by Y:

If **Y completes** $\frac{2}{5}$ **of the job in 10 days**, then his **one-day work** is:

$$\frac{2}{5} \div 10 = \frac{2}{50} = \frac{1}{25}$$

Step 2: Find Their Combined Work per Day

Total work done per day by **X and Y together**:

$$\frac{1}{15} + \frac{1}{25}$$

Find the **LCM of 15 and 25**, which is **75**:

$$\frac{5}{75} + \frac{3}{75} = \frac{8}{75}$$

Thus, X and Y together complete $\frac{8}{75}$ *of the work in* **one day**.

Step 3: Find Total Time Taken

Total time to complete the **entire work**:

$$Total\ Time = \left(\frac{1}{\frac{8}{75}}\right) = \frac{75}{8} = 9\frac{3}{8}\ days \ldots Ans.$$

Question

A and B can together complete a task in 20 hours. after 5 hours A leaves. B takes 45 hours to finish the remaining task. How many hours would A have taken to complete the entire task. if he worked alone from the beginning?

1. 30 hours
2. 40 hours
3. 48 hours
4. 60 hours

Explanations

Answer: 1. 30 hours

We are given:

- **A and B together** complete the task in **20 hours.**
- **After 5 hours, A leaves**, and **B alone takes 45 hours** to complete the remaining task.
- We need to find **how many hours A alone would take to complete the entire task.**

Step 1: Work Done by A and B Together in 5 Hours

Since **A and B together** complete the whole work in **20 hours**, their **one-hour work** is:

$$\frac{1}{20} \ (work\ done\ per\ hour)$$

Thus, in **5 hours**, they complete:

$$5 \times \frac{1}{20} = \frac{5}{20} = \frac{1}{4}$$

So, $\frac{1}{4}$ of the total work is completed in **5 hours**.

Step 2: Work Left for B Alone

The remaining work after **5 hours**:

$$1 - \frac{1}{4} = \frac{3}{4}$$

B takes **45 hours** to complete ¾ of the work, so **B's efficiency (work per hour)** is:

$$\left(\frac{\frac{3}{4}}{45}\right) = \frac{3}{180} = \frac{1}{60}$$

So, **B alone can complete the entire work in**:

$$\frac{1}{\frac{1}{60}} = 60\ hours$$

Step 3: Find A's Efficiency

Since **A and B together complete the work in 20 hours**, their combined efficiency is:

$$\frac{1}{20}$$

*Since we found that **B's efficiency is** $\frac{1}{60}$, A's efficiency is:*

$$\frac{1}{20} - \frac{1}{60}$$

Find LCM of **20 and 60**, which is **60**:

$$\frac{3}{60} - \frac{1}{60} = \frac{2}{60} = \frac{1}{30}$$

So, **A alone can complete the entire work in**:

$$\frac{1}{\frac{1}{30}} = 30\ hours \ldots Ans.$$

Question

A takes twice as much time as B takes and thrice as much as C to complete a job. By working together, A, B and C can complete the job in 4 hours. Find the time taken by each of them separately to complete the job. i.e. the time taken by A, B, and C respectively to complete the job.

1. (24, 12, 8)
2. (12, 8, 24)
3. (8, 12, 24)
4. (8, 16, 24)

Explanations

Answer: 1. (24, 12, 8)

We are given:

- **A takes twice the time of B.**
- **A takes thrice the time of C.**
- **A, B, and C together complete the job in 4 hours.**
- We need to find the individual time taken by **A, B, and C** to complete the job alone.

Step 1: Define Variables

Let:

- **Time taken by C alone** = x hours.
- **Time taken by A alone = 3 times C's time** = 3x hours.
- **Time taken by B alone** = $\frac{3x}{2}$ **hours** (since A takes twice the time of B).

Thus, we have:

$$A's\ time \; = \; 33x$$
$$B's\ time \; = \; 3x/2$$
$$C's\ time \; = \; x$$

Step 2: Work Done Per Hour

Work done per hour by each person is:

$$\frac{1}{A's\ time} + \frac{1}{B's\ time} + \frac{1}{C's\ time} = \frac{1}{4}$$

Substituting values:

$$\frac{1}{3x} + \frac{2}{3x} + \frac{1}{x} = \frac{1}{4}$$

Find LCM of **3x, 3x, and x**, which is **3x**:

$$\frac{1}{3x} + \frac{2}{3x} + \frac{3}{3x} = \frac{1}{4}$$

$$\frac{6}{3x} = \frac{1}{4}$$

$$\frac{2}{x} = \frac{1}{4}$$

$$x = 8 \dots Ans.$$

Thus, **C's time = 8 hours**.

Now, we find **A and B's time**:

$$A = 3x = 3(8) = \textbf{24 hours} \dots \textbf{\textit{Ans.}}$$

$$B = \frac{3x}{2} = \frac{3(8)}{2} = \textbf{12 hours} \dots \textbf{\textit{Ans.}}$$

Final Answer: The time taken by **A, B, and C** to complete the job alone is **(24, 12, 8) hours**.

Question

Gopal can do a piece of work in 3 days while Ravi can do the sane work in 4 days. The wage for the full work is Rs. 3500/-. If they both work together to complete the work, then find the earnings of Ravi?

1. 1300
2. 1500
3. 1600
4. 1650

Explanations

Answer: 2. 1500

We are given:

- **Gopal alone** can complete the work in **3 days**.
- **Ravi alone** can complete the work in **4 days**.
- **Total wage for the full work = Rs. 3500**.
- We need to find **Ravi's earnings** if they both work together.

Step 1: Work Efficiency of Gopal and Ravi

Efficiency (work done per day) is given by:

$$Efficiency = \frac{1}{Time\ taken}$$

$$\textbf{\textit{Gopal's efficiency}} = \frac{1}{3} \ (\textit{Gopal completes \textbf{1/3rd} of the work per day})$$

$$\textit{Ravi's efficiency } = \frac{1}{4} = (\textit{Ravi completes } \textbf{1/4th} \textit{ of the work per day})$$

Total work done per day when **Gopal and Ravi work together**:

$$\frac{1}{3} + \frac{1}{4}$$

Find LCM of **3 and 4**, which is **12**:

$$\frac{4}{12} + \frac{3}{12} = \frac{7}{12}$$

Thus, **Gopal and Ravi together** complete **7/12th** of the work per day.

Step 2: Find Their Individual Work Share

Since the total work is **1 unit**, the share of work done by Ravi:

$$Ravi's\ share = Ravi'\frac{s\ efficiency}{Total\ efficiency} = \left(\frac{\frac{1}{4}}{\frac{7}{12}}\right)$$

$$= \frac{1}{4} \times \frac{12}{7} = \frac{12}{28} = \frac{3}{7}$$

$$So,\ Ravi\ completes\ \frac{3}{7}\ \textit{\textbf{of the total work}}.$$

Step 3: Find Ravi's Earnings

Since the total wage is **Rs. 3500**, Ravi's share in the payment is:

$$\frac{3}{7} \times 3500 = \textbf{1500} \dots \textit{\textbf{Ans}}.$$

CHAPTER 5

Types of reasoning: Number series, Letter series, Codes and Relationships

Types of Reasoning:

The concept of mathematical reasoning refers to the process of determining the truth value of given statements. Reasoning is a way of assessment of thinking ability and solving a problem in a logical pattern. These reasoning statements are common in competitive exams like UGC NTA NET. Knowing the right tricks to solve the questions could become effortless and fun to solve. The reasoning supports identifying the potential problem-solving ability in all aspiring candidates by assessing verbal and non-verbal thinking.

Logical Reasoning:

Logical reasoning uses rational, systemic steps based on mathematical procedures to conclude a problem. We can draw conclusions based on given facts and mathematical principles. Inductive reasoning is non-rigorous logical reasoning, and statements are generalized. On the other hand, deductive reasoning is rigorous logical reasoning, and the statements are considered true if the assumptions entering the deduction are true. Two types of logical reasoning can be distinguished from formal deduction: abduction and induction. In the presence of a precondition or premise, a conclusion or logical consequence, as well as a rule or material condition that implies the conclusion. In terms of mathematics, reasoning can be of two major types which are:

Inductive Reasoning:

This type of reasoning is based on observing patterns. Based on observing a pattern, inductive reasoning can determine the next successive terms in a sequence. An inductive conclusion is referred to as a conjecture. **Inductive reasoning** is non-rigorous logical reasoning, and statements are generalized.

      i.   Letter Series

    ii.   Number Series
    iii. Pattern Questions
    iv. Codes Relationships

Deductive Reasoning:

Unlike inductive reasoning, deductive reasoning is valid proof. It is how geometric proofs are written. An individual uses deductive reasoning to draw conclusions based on previously known information. Deductive reasoning is rigorous logical reasoning, and the statements are considered true if the assumptions entering the deduction are true. So, in maths, deductive reasoning is considered more critical than inductive reasoning.

Example:
- o **Statement:** Pythagorean Theorem holds for any right-angled triangle.
- o **Reasoning:** If triangle XYZ is a right triangle, it will follow Pythagorean Theorem.

Abductive Reasoning: Abductive reasoning consists of making observations and seeking the hypothesis that best fits or explains the observations. Predicting the best outcome is based on a list of incomplete observations.

Example: If you see an abandoned bowl of hot soup on the table, you can use abduction to conclude the owner of the soup is likely returning soon.

Other Forms of Reasoning:

Analogical Reasoning:

Analogical reasoning is a type of reasoning in which two situations, examples, or domains are related. The knowledge derived from one situation can infer new information about the other when such a common system can be found.

Examples: Europa might have life because it has an atmosphere that contains oxygen, just like the Earth.

Verbal Reasoning:

The ability to understand concepts expressed through language is known as verbal reasoning. It is our ability to extract meaning and information from the text, think constructively, and apply logic. Some important topics under Verbal Reasoning are:

- **Analogy,**
- **Classification,**
- **Coding-Decoding,**
- **Blood Relation,**
- **Venn Diagram,**
- **Calendar,**
- **Clocks,**
- **Direction and Distance,**
- **Decision Making,**
- **Input-Output,**
- **Puzzles** and so on.

Non-Verbal Reasoning:

The questions in a non-verbal reasoning test are based on mathematical concepts such as symmetry, rotation, mirroring, shape, size and direction and involve diagrams rather than words. Non-verbal reasoning skills benefit science subjects, maths, engineering, computing, and design. These types of questions are not being asked in the UGC NET exam these days.

Series:

The study of series is a significant part of calculus and its generalization and mathematical analysis. Questions on number series are frequently asked in most exams. It's a crucial topic in the case of UGC NET. Almost 1-2 Questions come in the exam on this topic. In the series type question, it could be:

- o   Number Series:
- o   Letter Series:
- o   Mixed Series:
- o   Continuous Series:

Number Series:

In mathematics, a number series is a sequence of numbers. The number series questions require us to identify the rules that lead to creating a number series. There are many kinds of series, and many types of questions may appear in these series. As a rule of thumb, these questions are based on numerical sequences that follow a logical rule or pattern derived from elementary arithmetic concepts. The pattern must be analysed from a particular series. We are then asked to predict the next number in the sequence following the same rule. Some numbers are incorrectly placed in the series of numbers, and you need to identify or correct them.

Types of Number Series:

The following is a list of the questions that may be asked:

I. Addition Series:

In this type of number series reasoning, specific numbers based on some patterns are added to get the next number.

Question: 3, 6, 11, 18, 27, ?, 51
Solution: The series can be solved as follows.

$$3 + 3 = 6$$
$$6 + 5 = 11$$
$$11 + 7 = 18$$
$$18 + 9 = 27$$
$$27 + 11 = 38$$

$$38 + 13 = 51$$

Therefore, 38 is the correct answer.

II. Subtraction Series:

In this type of number series reasoning, specific numbers based on some patterns are subtracted to get the next number.

Question 2: 50, 45, 40, 35, 30, ?
Solution: The series can be solved as follows.

$$50 - 5 = 45$$
$$45 - 5 = 40$$
$$40 - 5 = 35$$
$$35 - 5 = 30$$
$$30 - 5 = 25$$

III. Multiplication Series:

In this type of number series reasoning, a particular number pattern is multiplied to get the next number.

Question: 1, 3, 9, 27, 81, ?
Solution: The series can be solved as follows.

$$1 \times 3 = 1$$
$$3 \times 3 = 9$$
$$9 \times 3 = 27$$
$$27 \times 3 = 81$$
$$81 \times 3 = 243$$

Therefore, 243 is the correct answer.

IV. Division Series:

In this type of number series reasoning, a particular number pattern is divided to get the next number.

Question: 4096, 1024, 256, ?, 16, 4
Solution: The series can be solved as follows.

$$4096 \div 4 = 1024$$
$$1024 \div 4 = 256$$
$$256 \div 4 = 64$$
$$64 \div 4 = 16$$
$$16 \div 4 = 4$$

Therefore, 64 is the correct answer.

V. Square Series:

In this type of number series reasoning, each number is a perfect square of a particular number pattern.

Question: 0, 1, 4, 9, 16, 25, ?, 49,...?
Solution: They are the squares of whole numbers:

$$0 (= 0 \times 0)$$
$$1 (= 1 \times 1)$$
$$4 (= 2 \times 2)$$
$$9 (= 3 \times 3)$$
$$16 (= 4 \times 4)$$
$$25 (= 5 \times 5)$$
$$36 (= 6 \times 6)$$
$$49 (= 7 \div 7)$$
$$64 (= 8 \times 8)$$

Ans. 36 and 64

VI. Cube Series:

In this type of number series reasoning, each number is a perfect cube of a particular number pattern.

Question: 1, 8, 27, 64,.?.,216,.?.
Solution: They are the cubes of the counting numbers

$$1 (= 1 \times 1 \times 1)$$
$$8 (= 2 \times 2 \times 2)$$
$$27 (= 3 \times 3 \times 3)$$
$$64 (= 4 \times 4 \times 4)$$
$$125 (= 5 \times 5 \times 5)$$
$$216 (= 6 \times 6 \times 6)$$
$$343 (= 7 \times 7 \times 7)$$

Ans. 125 and 343

VII. Fibonacci Series:

In this type of number series reasoning, the next number is the addition of two previous numbers.

Question: 0, 1, 1, 2, 3, 5, 8, 13, 21, 34, ...?

Solution: Fibonacci Sequences are found by adding the two numbers preceding them.

The 2 is calculated by adding the two numbers before it $(1 + 1)$
The 21 is calculated by adding the two numbers before it $(8 + 13)$
In the above sequence, the next number would be 55 $(21 + 34)$

VIII. Alternating Series:

In this type of number series reasoning, multiple number patterns are used alternatively to form a series.

Question: 2, 29, 4, 25, 6, ?, 8, 17

Solution: The series can be solved as follows.

$$2 + 2 = 4$$
$$4 + 2 = 6$$
$$6 + 2 = 8$$

Similarly

$$29 - 4 = 25$$
$$25 - 4 = 21$$
$$21 - 4 = 17$$

Ans. 21.

IX. Mixed Operator Series:

In this type of number series reasoning, multiple operators are applied to get the next number in the series. That is where these days, UGC NET is asking.

Question: Select the number that doesn't belong in the series 10, 22, 69, 280, 480

Solution: 480 is the wrong number and has to be replaced by 1405.

$$9 \times 1 + 1 = 10$$
$$10 \times 2 + 2 = 22$$
$$22 \times 3 + 3 = 69$$
$$69 \times 4 + 4 = 280$$
$$280 \times 5 + 5 = 1405$$

Ans. 1405.

X. Arranging Number:

In this type of number series reasoning, candidates need to rearrange numbers as specified and answer the given questions.

Question: After the number 381576 is arranged in ascending order, how many digits will remain the same?
Solution:

The original number form is: 3 8 1 5 7 6
The ascending order is: 1 3 5 6 7 8
The only number that remains unchanged is number 7.

TIPS FOR PASSING A NUMBER SERIES TEST QUESTION

- **Tip:** Start from the left and look for patterns or sequences based on number increases or decreases.
- **Tip:** Look for patterns that include addition, subtraction, multiplication or division.
- **Tip:** Be aware that the increase or decrease in the number series/sequence may involve odd or even number increases/decreases.
- **Tip:** The most effective way to practice numerical reasoning tests is to try our Rapid Fire on Number series under timed conditions.

Concept Check 21: Number Series

1. 4, 9, 16, 25, ?
2. 3, 6, 11, 18, 27, ?
3. 2, 6, 12, 20, 30, ?
4. 81, 27, 9, 3, ?
5. 1, 1, 2, 3, 5, 8, ?

UGC NET PYQ Questions and Explanations on Number Series:

Question

Find the number that can replace question mark (?) in the series given below:

21,22,26,35,51, ?

1. 62
2. 66

3. 86

4. 76

Explanation:

Answer: 4. 76

Step 1: Find the difference between consecutive terms

- $22 - 21 = 1$
- $26 - 22 = 4$
- $35 - 26 = 9$
- $51 - 35 = 16$

The differences are: **1, 4, 9, 16**

These are **square numbers**:

$$1^2, 2^2, 3^2, 4^2$$

Step 2: Identify the next difference

Following the pattern, the next term should be increased by $5^2 = 25$

Step 3: Find the missing number

$$51 + 25 = 76 \dots Ans.$$

Question

Find the number that can replace the question mark (?) in the series given below:

$$3, 8, 15, 24, 35, 48, ?$$

1. 58

2. 63

3. 60

4. 61

Explanation:

Answer: 2 63

Step 1: Find the difference between consecutive terms

$$8 - 3 = 5$$
$$15 - 8 = 7$$
$$24 - 15 = 9$$
$$35 - 24 = 11$$
$$48 - 35 = 13$$

- The differences are: **5, 7, 9, 11, 13**
- The differences are increasing by **+2** each time.
- The next difference should be **13 + 2 = 15**
- The missing number is: $48 + 15 = 63 \dots Ans.$

Question

The tenth term in the following sequence: 1, 5, 14, 30, 55...

1. 155
2. 175
3. 285
4. 385

Explanation:

Answer: 4. 385

Find the differences between consecutive terms:

$$5 - 1 = 4$$
$$14 - 5 = 9$$
$$30 - 14 = 16$$
$$55 - 30 = 25$$

- The differences are: **4, 9, 16, 25**
- These are **square numbers**: $2^2, 3^2, 4^2, 5^2$
- We extend the sequence:

$$55 + 6^2 = 55 + 36 = 91$$
$$91 + 7^2 = 91 + 49 = 140$$
$$140 + 8^2 = 140 + 64 = 204$$
$$204 + 9^2 = 204 + 81 = 285$$
$$285 + 10^2 = 285 + 100 = 385 \ldots Ans.$$

Question

Find the number that can replace the question mark (?) in the series given below:

$$4, 27, 16, 125, 36, ?, 64, 729$$

1. 343
2. 81
3. 49
4. 161

Explanation:

Answer: 1. 343

- Observing the sequence, we see alternating terms:
- The pattern alternates between **squares (even positions)** and **cubes (odd positions)**:

$$4(2^2)$$

$$27(3^3)$$
$$16(4^2)$$
$$125(5^3)$$
$$36(6^2)$$
$$\mathbf{343(7^3)}$$
$$64(8^2)$$
$$729(9^3)$$

Question

Which of the statements (A)-(D) are true in the context of number series I and II given below

$$\textit{Series I}: 6, 24, x, 720, 5040$$
$$\textit{Series II}: 432, 250, 128, y, 16$$

- A. The sum of x and y is 164
- B. x exceeds the double of y by 12
- C. Both x and y are exactly divisible by 6
- D. Either x or y is a perfect square

1. AB
2. BC
3. AD
4. ABC

Explanation:

Answer: 2. BC

Series I: 6, 24, x, 720, 5040

- o We observe the pattern:

$$6 = 3! = 3 \times 2 \times 1 = 6$$
$$24 = 4! = 4 \times 3 \times 2 \times 1 = 24$$
$$x = 5! = 5 \times 4 \times 3 \times 2 \times 1 = 120$$
$$720 = 6! = 6 \times 5 \times 4 \times 3 \times 2 \times 1 = 720$$
$$5040 = 7! = 7 \times 6 \times 5 \times 4 \times 3 \times 2 \times 1 = 5040$$

- o The pattern follows factorials: $3!, 4!, 5!, 6!, 7!$
- o Since the missing number corresponds to $5!$:

Series II: 432, 250, 128, y, 16

$$432 = 6^3 \times 2$$
$$250 = 5^3 \times 2$$
$$128 = 4^3 \times 2$$
$$y = 3^3 \times 2 = 54$$

$$16 = 2^3 \times 2$$

Analyse the Statements

A. *The sum of x and y is 164* **FALSE**

$$\text{The sum of } x \text{ and } y \text{ is } 174$$

B. *x exceeds the double of y by 12* **TRUE**

$$2y = 2 \times 54 = 108 \text{ and } 120 - 108$$
$$= 12. \text{ Hence, } x \text{ exceeds the double of } y \text{ by } 12$$

C. *Both x and y are exactly divisible by 6* **TRUE**

$$120/6 = 20 \text{ and } 54/6 = 9$$

D. *Either x or y is a perfect square* **FALSE**

$$x = 120 \text{ \textbf{is not} a perfect square.}$$
$$y = 54 \text{ \textbf{is not} a perfect square.}$$

Question

Find the next term of the series 16, 125, 25, 64, 36, 27, 49,-

(1) 64

(2) 81

(3) 216

(4) 8

Explanation:

Answer: 4. 8

Identify the Pattern:

- 16: 4^2
- 125: 5^3
- 25: 5^2
- 64: 4^3
- 36: 6^2
- 27: 3^3
- 49: 7^2

We see two separate patterns:

- **Even-positioned terms** (1st, 3rd, 5th, 7th): Perfect squares
- **Odd-positioned terms** (2nd, 4th, 6th, 8th): Perfect cubes
- The missing term (8th position) follows the cube pattern:
  - $8 = 2^3$

Question

What will be the eleventh term in the following sequence?

$$-\frac{3}{2}, \frac{3}{4}, -\frac{3}{8}, \frac{3}{16}, -\frac{3}{32}, \ldots\ldots?$$

1. $\dfrac{3}{1024}$

2. $-\dfrac{3}{1024}$

3. $3/2048$

4. $-\dfrac{3}{2048}$

Explanation:

Answer:

$$4. -\frac{3}{2048}$$

Step 1: Identify the Pattern

1. **Signs:** The terms alternate between negative and positive:
$$-, +, -, +, -, \ldots$$
   This means the sign of the $n-th$ term is $(-1)^n$.
2. **Numerator:** The numerator is always **3**.
3. **Denominator:** The denominator follows a geometric progression:
$$2, 4, 8, 16, 32, \ldots$$

Each denominator is double the previous one, so the denominator for the $n-th$ term is $2n$.

Step 2: General Formula

Combining the observations, the $n-th$ term of the sequence is:

$$a_n = (-1)^n \cdot \frac{3}{2^n}$$

Step 3: Calculate the 11th Term

For the 11th term ($n = 11$):

$$a_{11} = (-1)^{11} \cdot \frac{3}{2^{11}}$$

$$a_{11} = -1 \cdot \frac{3}{2048}$$

$$a_{11} = -\frac{3}{2048} \ldots Ans.$$

Question

Find the next term in the series..... $275, 7Y7, 14X9, 23W11, 34V13, (?)$

(1) 27U24

(2) 45015

(3) 47U15

(4) 47U14

Explanation:

Answer: (3) 47U15

Step 1: Break Down the Series

The series consists of terms in the format: **Number, Letter, Number**. Let's separate each term into its components:

1. **275** → 2, 7, 5
2. **7Y7** → 7, Y, 7
3. **14X9** → 14, X, 9
4. **23W11** → 23, W, 11
5. **34V13** → 34, V, 13

Step 2: Analyze the Components

(a) First Number Sequence:

- The first numbers in each term are:

$$2,7,14,23,34, \ldots$$

- The differences between consecutive terms are:

$$7 - 2 = 5, \quad 14 - 7 = 7, \quad 23 - 14 = 9, \quad 34 - 23 = 11, \ldots$$

- The differences themselves form a sequence: **5, 7, 9, 11, …**, which increases by **2** each time.
- The next difference will be **13**.
- Therefore, the next first number is:

$$34 + 13 = 47$$

(b) Letter Sequence:

- The letters in each term are:

$$-, Y, X, W, V, \ldots$$

- The letters are moving backward in the alphabet:

$$Y, X, W, V, \ldots$$

- The next letter will be **U**.

(c) Second Number Sequence:

- The second numbers in each term are:

$$5, 7, 9, 11, 13, \ldots$$

- This is an arithmetic sequence increasing by **2** each time.
- The next number will be:

$$13 + 2 = 15$$

Step 3: Combine the Components

The next term will have:

- First number: **47**
- Letter: **U**
- Second number: **15**

Thus, the next term is **47U15**...Ans.

Question

Identify the term 'X' in the following series (Dec 2019)

$$3, 2, 11, 14, 27, 34, 51, X$$

1. 62,   2. 69,   3. 60,   4. 71,

Explanation:

Answer. 1. 62

The sequence differs through this expression:

$$Pattern: n^2 + 2, n^2 - 2, n^2 + 2, n^2 - 2, and\ so\ on...$$
$$Now, if\ we\ put\ n\ =\ 1\ in\ n^2 + 2, we\ get:$$
$$(1)^2 + 2\ =\ 3, which\ is\ the\ first\ term.$$
$$Similarly, if\ we\ put\ n\ =\ 2\ in\ n^2 - 2, we\ get:$$
$$(2)^2 - 2\ =\ 2, which\ is\ the\ second\ term.$$
$$Again\ if\ we\ put\ n\ =\ 3\ in\ n^2 + 2, we\ get:$$
$$(3)^2 + 2\ =\ 11, which\ is\ the\ third\ term,$$
$$Similarly, if\ we\ put\ n\ =\ 4\ in\ n^2 - 2, we\ get:$$
$$(4)^2 - 2\ =\ 14, which\ is\ the\ fourth\ term.$$
$$Again\ if\ we\ put\ n\ =\ 5\ in\ n^2 + 2, we\ get:$$
$$(5)^2 + 2\ =\ 27, which\ is\ the\ fifth\ term,$$
$$Similarly, if\ we\ put\ n\ =\ 6\ in\ n^2 - 2, we\ get:$$
$$(6)^2 - 2\ =\ 34, which\ is\ the\ sixth\ term.$$
$$Again\ if\ we\ put\ n\ =\ 7\ in\ n^2 + 2, we\ get:$$
$$(7)^2 + 2\ =\ 51, which\ is\ the\ seventh\ term,$$
$$Similarly, if\ we\ put\ n\ =\ 8\ in\ n^2 - 2, we\ get:$$
$$(8)^2 - 2\ =\ 62, the\ eighth\ and\ the\ required\ term.$$
$$So, x\ =\ 62.$$

Question

The smallest integer greater than 1, which is simultaneously a square and a cube of certain integer (Dec 2019)

1. 8,   2. 9,   3. 36,   4. 64,

Explanation:
Answer. 4. 64
The number 8 is the cube of the integer 2, but it is not the square.
The number 9 is the square of integer 3 but is not the cube.
The number 36 is the square of integer 6 but is not the cube.
64 is the square of integer 8 and the cube of integer 4.
So the answer, if listed, must be 64

Question

Complete the following series (Oct 2020)
$$9,11,15,23,39, \underline{\quad\quad}?$$

1. 71,   2. 65,   3. 44,   4. 68,

Explanation:
Answer. 1. 71

$$9,11,15,23,39, \underline{\quad\quad}$$
$$9 + 2 = 11 \ (Square)$$
$$11 + 4 = 15$$
$$15 + 8 = 23$$
$$23 + 16 = 39$$
$$\mathbf{39 + 32 = 71 \ Ans.}$$

Question

What number would replace question mark (?) in the series given below?
$$1,7,16,28,43,61,82, ?$$

1. 102
2. 143
3. 106
4. 110

Explanation:

Answer. 3. 106
Step 1: Calculate the Differences
First, compute the differences between consecutive terms:

$$7 - 1 = 6$$
$$16 - 7 = 9$$
$$28 - 16 = 12$$
$$43 - 28 = 15$$
$$61 - 43 = 18$$
$$82 - 61 = 21$$

The differences are:

$$6, 9, 12, 15, 18, 21$$

Step 2: Analyze the Differences
- The differences themselves form a sequence:
$$6, 9, 12, 15, 18, 21$$
- This sequence increases by **3** each time.
- The next difference will be:
$$21 + 3 = 24$$

Step 3: Compute the Next Term
Add the next difference to the last term in the series:

$$82 + 24 = 106 \ldots Ans.$$

Question

Identify the numbers that occur in the series 0, 7, 26, 63, 124....

    A. 344
    B. 511
    C. 215
    D. 730

1. A and B only
2. B and C only
3. C and D only
4. A and D only

Explanation:
Answer. 2. B and C only
The pattern follows the formula:

$$n^3 - 1$$

where n increases sequentially:

- *First term*: $1^3 - 1 = 0$
- *Second term*: $2^3 - 1 = 7$
- *Third term*: $3^3 - 1 = 26$
- *Fourth term*: $4^3 - 1 = 63$
- *Fifth term*: $5^3 - 1 = 124$
- *Sixth term*: $6^3 - 1 = 216 - 1 = 215 \dots Correct$
- *Seventh term*: $7^3 - 1 = 343 - 1 = 342$
- *Eighth term*: $8^3 - 1 = 512 - 1 = 511 \dots Correct$
- *Ninth term*: $9^3 - 1 = 729 - 1 = 728$
- *Tenth term*: $10^3 - 1 = 1000 - 1 = 999$

Thus, the correct choices are **B (511) and C (215)**

Question

Find the number that can be inserted at the place of questions mark (?) in the series given below.

$$4, 10, 20, 34, 52, 74, ?$$

1. 98
2. 102
3. 97
4. 100

Explanation:
Answer. 4. 100
Step 1: Calculate the Differences
First, compute the differences between consecutive terms:

$$10 - 4 = 6$$
$$20 - 10 = 10$$
$$34 - 20 = 14$$
$$52 - 34 = 18$$
$$74 - 52 = 22$$

The differences are:

$$6, 10, 14, 18, 22$$

Step 2: Analyze the Differences
The differences themselves form a sequence:

$$6, 10, 14, 18, 22$$

- o   This sequence increases by **4** each time.
- o   The next difference will be:

$$22 + 4 = 26$$

Step 3: Compute the Next Term

Add the next difference to the last term in the series:

$$74 + 26 = 100 \dots Ans.$$

Question

What will be the value of P in the following number series?

$$0, 3, 26, 255, P, \dots ..$$

1. 624
2. 511
3. 1023
4. 3124

Explanation:

Answer. 4. 3124

1. $0 = 1^1 - 1$
2. $3 = 2^2 - 1$
3. $26 = 3^3 - 1$
4. $255 = 4^4 - 1$
5. $3125 = 5^5 - 1$

Question

Identify the numbers that occur in the given series: - 0,3, 10,21,36......

A. 55
B. 78
C. 99
D. 105
E. 136

1. A, B, C and D Only
2. B, C and E Only
3. C, D, E and A Only
4. A, B, D and E Only

Explanation:

Answer. 4. A, B, D and E Only

Let's compute the differences between consecutive terms:

1. $3 - 0 = 3$
2. $10 - 3 = 7$
3. $21 - 10 = 11$
4. $36 - 21 = 15$

The differences are:

$$3, 7, 11, 15, \dots$$

These differences themselves form a sequence that increases by 4 each time. The next difference will be:

$$15 + 4 = 19$$

Continuing this pattern:

$$36 + 19 = 55$$
$$55 + 23 = 78$$
$$78 + 27 = 105$$
$$105 + 31 = 136$$

From the given options:

- **A. 55**: Present in the series.
- **B. 78**: Present in the series.
- **C. 99**: Not present in the series.
- **D. 105**: Present in the series.
- **E. 136**: Present in the series.

Question

Find the next number in the number series:

$$48, 24, 72, 36, 108, ?$$

    (1) 115
    (2) 121
    (3) 110
    (4) 54

Explanation:

Answer. 4. 54

Let's examine the relationship between consecutive terms:

1. $48 \div 2 = 24$
2. $24 \times 3 = 72$
3. $72 \div 2 = 36$
4. $36 \times 3 = 108$

The pattern alternates between:
- Dividing by **2**,
- Multiplying by **3**.

$$108 \div 2 = 54 \dots Ans.$$

Question

Identify the numbers that occur in the series 1, 7, 17, 31, 49, ...

(A) 74
(B) 95
(C) 97
(D) 127
(E) 161

1. ABC
2. CDE
3. EBA
4. CDB

Explanation:
Answer. 2. CDE

$$For\ n = 1: 2(1^2) - 1 = 1$$
$$For\ n = 2: 2(2^2) - 1 = 7$$
$$For\ n = 3: 2(3^2) - 1 = 17$$
$$For\ n = 4: 2(4^2) - 1 = 31$$
$$For\ n = 5: 2(5^2) - 1 = 49$$
$$For\ n = 6: 2(6^2) - 1 = 71$$
$$\mathbf{For\ n = 7: 2(7^2) - 1 = 97.}$$
$$\mathbf{For\ n = 8: 2(8^2) - 1 = 127.}$$
$$\mathbf{For\ n = 9: 2(9^2) - 1 = 161.}$$

Letter Series and Codes:

Letter Series

The alphabets are arranged in a pattern or any particular rule in this question series. Here we have to find the pattern and the rules for arranging these letters. You may come across at least one question in the UGC NET exam. There are particular tips and tricks to solve them we will discuss in the later section of the book, but first, we need to know everything about the types of the question which can be asked in the exam. So let's see the types:

There are times when words or sentences are coded by changing the position of letters in English alphabetical order according to a definite pattern, so it is imperative to remember both the forward and backward positions of all the letters in English alphabetical order.

TABLE 1

A	B	C	D	E	F	G	H	I	J	K	L	M
1	2	3	4	5	6	7	8	9	10	11	12	13
N	O	P	Q	R	S	T	U	V	W	X	Y	Z
14	15	16	17	18	19	20	21	22	23	24	25	26

TABLE 2

Z	Y	X	W	V	U	T	S	R	Q	P	O	N
1	2	3	4	5	6	7	8	9	10	11	12	13
M	L	K	J	I	H	G	F	E	D	C	B	A
14	15	16	17	18	19	20	21	22	23	24	25	26

Tips to Solve Letter Series:

TIP 1

A	B	C	D	E
1	2	3	4	5
F	G	H	I	J
6	7	8	9	10
K	L	M	N	O
11	12	13	14	15
P	Q	R	S	T
16	17	18	19	20
U	V	W	X	Y

21	22	23	24	25
Z				
26				

TIP 2

Z	Y	X	W	V
1	2	3	4	5
U	T	S	R	Q
6	7	8	9	10
P	O	N	M	L
11	12	13	14	15
K	J	I	H	G
16	17	18	19	20
F	E	D	C	B
21	22	23	24	25
A				
26				

TIP 3

E	J	O	T	Y
5	10	15	20	25

TIP 3

V	Q	L	G	B
5	10	15	20	25

I. Alphabet Series:

In this type, letters of the English alphabet are arranged in a particular pattern like reverse order of letters, skipping of letters, the position of letters in alphabetical order etc.

Question: Find the next term in the series.

$$A, E, H, K, ?, Q$$

Solution: Every next term of the series is the next 3rd letter of the alphabet (according to position). Therefore, the missing term is N.

$$A + 3 = E$$
$$E + 3 = H$$
$$H + 3 = K$$
$$K + 3 = N$$
$$N + 3 = Q$$

Question: Find the missing term in the given series.

$$ABP, CDQ, EFR, ?$$

Solution: The given series is a combination of three series.

$$A, C, E, ?$$
$$B, D, F, ?$$
$$P, Q, R, ?$$

$$A + 2 = C + 2 = E + 2 = G$$
$$B + 2 = D + 2 = F + 2 = H$$
$$P + 1 = Q + 1 = R + 1 = S$$

Therefore, the missing letters are GHS.

II. Continuous Pattern Series:

It consists of small or capital letters that follow a specific pattern. There are, however, some letters missing from the series. There is a specific pattern to the series, and we must find the letters that should replace the blank spaces or question marks.

Question: a_ _b ab _b a_ _b

Solution: Here, the total places are 12, so we can form pairs of two and check if the pattern exists or not.

$$a\_\_b\ ab\ \_b\ a\_\_b$$
$$ab|ab|ab|ab|ab|ab$$

Question: abca_bcaab_ca_bbc_a

Solution: The pattern of the series is as shown below

$$abc \ / \ aabc \ / \ aabbc \ / \ aabbcc \ / \ a \ => \ abac$$

therefore, the missing letters are abac.

Question: _cb_ca_bacb_ca_bac_d

Solution:

acbd / cadb / acbd / cadb / acbd => addddb

The sequence alternately repeats two blocks, ' acbd' and 'cadb'. Therefore, the missing letters are addddb.

III. Mixed Series:

In this type, the series is based on the combination of both letters and numbers. Each term in the series follows a specific pattern based on either the alphabetical position of the letters or the numbers in different correlations.

Question: E10, J12, O15, T19, ___?

Solution: E+5|10+2, J+5|12+3, O+5|15+4, T+5|19+5, **Y24**

Therefore, the answer is Y24.

Question: C-3, E-5, G-7, I-9, ?, ?
Solution: C+2|3+2, E+2|5+2, G+2|7+2, I+2|9+2, **K11**
Therefore, the missing terms are K-11

Codes:

The purpose of coding is to hide the meaning of any message, whereas the purpose of decoding is to understand the actual meaning of the message. We should observe if the sequence is in ascending or descending order.
Types of coding - Decoding:

Type-1: Questions Based on Letter/Number coding:

The purpose of this coding is to replace the letters of a word with certain other letters or numbers according to a particular rule or pattern. In the exam, we must detect the coding pattern and answer the questions based on that coding pattern.

Letter Coding: A word's alphabet is replaced by other alphabets according to a specific rule to know its code. So, the common rule should be detected first. Some examples are given below:

Question: 'ZYXW' is coded as 'ABCD', then 'STUV' is coded as......
Solution:

ZYXW	Z-A	Y-B	X-C	W-D	**ABCD**
STUV	S-H	T-G	U-F	V-E	**HGFE**

HGFE Rule is front alphabet=back alphabet. Use the alphabet table.

Question: *'bcd'* is coded as *'def'* then *'True'* is coded as..........
Solution:

$b - d \ (+2)$	$c - e(+2)$	$d - f(+2)$

$+2$ *letters are the pattern.*
Therefore, True = ***Vtwg.***

Question: *'Hyderabad'* is coded as *'Ixedszcze'*, then *'Chennai'* is coded as.............
Solution:

$H - I(+1)$	$Y - X(-1)$	$D - E(+1)$	$E - D(-1)$	$R - S(+1)$
$A - Z(-1)$	$B - C(+1)$	$A - Z(-1)$	$D - E(+1)$	

Here if we observe alternatively, one letter increases and one letter decreases.

$$Therefore, Chennai = \boldsymbol{dgfmozj}.$$

Number coding: In this, each alphabet or word is assigned to the numeric values. We should observe the given letters and values and use the same rule to find the code's value.

Question: If CAB is written as 75, how will TAXI be written?

Solution: Reverse Order of the letters

C	A	B		75
24	26	25		24+26+25=75
T	A	X	I	
7	26	3	18	7+26+3+18=54

Therefore, the answer is 54.

Question: Apple is coded as 25563, and Rung is coded as 7148. Then purple is coded as

Solution:

- APPLE → 25563
- RUNG → 7148
- PURPLE → 517563

Each letter has a corresponding number.

- P = 5
- U = 1
- R = 7
- P = 5
- L = 6
- E = 3

PURPLE-517563; therefore, the answer is 517563.

Question: PUSH is coded as 1234, ROUGH is coded as 65274. Then SOUP is coded as

Solution: SOUP = 3521. Therefore, the answer is 3521.

Type-2: Question-Based on Direct Coding:

The code letters/numbers/symbols are arranged in the same sequence as the corresponding letters in words. The method is essentially a direct substitution.

Question: If CRAMP is written as SCVGT and CANNOT is written as SVAABD, then RAMPANT will be written as.
Solution:

$$CRAMP = SCVGT$$
$$CANNOT = SVAABD$$
$$RAMPANT = ?$$

The common words are C and A, and their corresponding letters are S and V.

$$Therefore, RAMPANT = CVGTVAD$$

Type-3: Question-Based on Deciphering or Fictitious language Coding:

You must identify the code for a particular word or message given in the form of a coded form of two or more sentences. The analysis of such codes is conducted by picking out two messages containing a common word or number. The common code will represent that particular word or number. The entire message can be decoded by picking up all possible combinations of two, and the codes for each word or number can be determined.

Sometimes, there is no common word or number in the message. When this is the case, the words or numbers are coded separately. The task is to identify the correct coding pattern and the code for the word or message.

Question: If bir le nac' means green and tasty in a certain code, pic nac hor' means tomato is green and "coc bir hor means food is tasty. Which of the following means tomato is tasty in that code?
Solution: The code for "tomato" is "oic". The code for "is" is "hor". The code for "tasty" is "bir" Hence, "tomato is tasty" can be coded as pic hor bir.

Type-4: Question-Based on Substitution Coding:

A particular word is coded with a substituted word, and the code of the given word is determined on the basis of the substituted word.

Question: If in a certain code, the earth is written as air, the air is written as water, water is written as the sky, the sky is written as light, and light is written as dust, then what would you drink?

Solution: In our everyday language, we drink water. But here, codes are given, and the code for water is the sky. So, the correct answer is 'sky'.

UGC NET PYQ Questions and Explanations on Letter Series

Question

What is the next letter in the following sequence?

$$B, D, G, K, P, V, C$$

1. K
2. L
3. M
4. N

Explanation:

Answer. 1. K

$$Alphabets: B, D, G, K, P, V, C \dots.$$
$$Place\ Value: 2, 4, 7, 11, 16, 22, 3$$
$$Difference: 2, 3, 4, 5, 6, 7 \dots.$$
$$We\ start\ recounting\ from\ 1, 2, 3, \dots\ after\ 26\ alphabet$$
$$(V = 22 \rightarrow 22 + 7 = 29 = 26 = 3)$$
$$Pattern: Difference\ is\ increasing\ with\ +1$$
$$Thus, next\ difference: 8$$
$$Next\ term = 3 + 8 = 11 \rightarrow K$$

Question

Find the next term of the letter series.

$$AaC, BbD, DdF, HhJ, -$$

1. L1N
2. MmO
3. PpR
4. NnP

Explanation:

Answer. 3 PpR because the pattern follows a specific sequence:

First letter: A → B → D → H → P (follows 1, 2, 4, 8, 16 pattern)
Second letter: a → b → d → h → p (same pattern as the first letter but in lowercase)
Third letter: C → D → F → J → R (follows 3, 4, 6, 10, 18 increasing with the difference 1, 2, 4, 8 pattern)

Question

Which of the given options will occupy the blank space in the series ?
$$B, DE, HIJ, \text{---}, VWXYZ$$

1. NOPQ
2. NOPQR
3. OPQRW
4. MNOPQ

Explanation:
Answer. 1. NOPQ
The pattern follows an increasing number of letters in each step:
- **B** (1 letter)
- **DE** (2 letters)
- **HIJ** (3 letters)
- **?** (4 letters)
- **VWXYZ** (5 letters)

The missing term should have **4 letters**, and the only option with 4 letters is: **NOPQ**.

Question

Choose the next term of the series A4C, E36G, I100K,

1. *L169M*
2. *N225O*
3. *M196O*
4. *M169O*

Explanation:
Answer. 3. *M196O*
Step 1: Identify the Alphabet Pattern
Observing the letters:
- A → E → I → ?

- o   A (1st), E (5th), I (9th) → The pattern increases by +4.
  - o   Next letter: **M (13th letter)**.
- o   C → G → K → ?
  - o   C (3rd), G (7th), K (11th) → The pattern increases by +4.
  - o   Next letter: **O (15th letter).**

Step 2: Identify the Number Pattern

Observing the numbers:

$$4, 36, 100, ?$$
$$2^2 = 4$$
$$6^2 = 36$$
$$10^2 = 100$$
$$Next\ number: 14^2 = 196$$

The next term should be M196O.

Question

Find the next term in the following letter series:
$$ALY, CJW, EHU, -$$

1. GFS
2. GES
3. FDT
4. GIS

Explanation:

Answer. 1. GFS

Step 1: Identify the Pattern in the First Letters

- o   *A → C → E → ?*
- o   *Positions: A (1), C (3), E (5)*
- o   *The pattern follows + 2.*
- o   *The next letter: G (7th letter).*

Step 2: Identify the Pattern in the Second Letters

- o   *L → J → H → ?*
- o   *Positions: L (12), J (10), H (8)*
- o   *The pattern follows − 2.*
- o   *The next letter: F (6th letter).*

Step 3: Identify the Pattern in the Third Letters
- *$Y \rightarrow W \rightarrow U \rightarrow$?*
- *Positions:* ***Y*** *(**25**),* ***W*** *(**23**),* ***U*** *(**21**)*
- *The pattern follows* $-$ **2***.*
- *The next letter:* ***S*** *(**19th letter**).*

The next term is **GFS**.

Question

What will be the tenth letter in the following sequence of letters?

$$B, B, C, D, F, N, V$$

1. D
2. G
3. W
4. Z

Explanation:

Answer. 1. D

$$Alphabets: B, B, C, D, F, I, N, V \rightarrow there\ are\ 8\ terms$$
$$Place\ values: 2, 2, 3, 4, 6, 9, 14, 22$$
$$Their\ difference: 0, 1, 1, 2, 3, 5, 8$$

Pattern: adding previous two difference to get next one.

$$0 + 1 = 1$$
$$1 + 1 = 2$$
$$2 + 1 = 3$$
$$3 + 2 = 5$$
$$5 + 3 = 8$$

Next difference $\rightarrow 8 + 5 = 13$

To find the next add difference 13 to place value of 22

Next term ($9th$) $\rightarrow 22 + 13 = 35$, As there's only 26 alphabets, then

$35 - 26 = 9$, which is place value of T

$$For\ 10th\ term,$$
$$Next\ difference \rightarrow 8 + 13 = 21$$
$$Next\ term\ (10th) \rightarrow 21 + 9 = 30$$
$$Again\ to\ find\ term = 30 - 26 = 4$$
$$and\ 4 \rightarrow D$$

Question

Find the next term in the following letter series.

$$BFD, ELG, HRJ, \_?$$

1. KUM
2. JXM
3. KTM
4. KXM

Explanation:

Answer. 4. KXM

Step 1: Identify the Pattern in the First Letters

- $B \rightarrow E \rightarrow H \rightarrow ?$
- *Positions*: B (2), E (5), H (8)
- *The pattern follows* $+3$.
- *Next letter*: K (**11th letter**).

Step 2: Identify the Pattern in the Second Letters

- $F \rightarrow L \rightarrow R \rightarrow ?$
- *Positions*: F (6), L (12), R (18)
- *The pattern follows* $+6$.
- *Next letter*: X (**24th letter**).

Step 3: Identify the Pattern in the Third Letters

- $D \rightarrow G \rightarrow J \rightarrow ?$
- *Positions*: D (4), G (7), J (10)
- *The pattern follows* $+3$.
- *Next letter*: M (**13th letter**).

The next term is **KXM**.

Question

Find the next term in the number series 2A11,4D13, 12G17,48J23,..._?

1. 245N32
2. 228L30
3. 240M31
4. 230M29

Explanation:

Answer. 3. 240M31

Step 1: Identify the Pattern in the First Numbers

The first numbers are: **2, 4, 12, 48, ?**
Checking the pattern:

$$2 \times 2 = 4$$
$$4 \times 3 = 12$$
$$12 \times 4 = 48$$
$$48 \times 5 = 240$$

So, the next term is **240**.

Step 2: Identify the Pattern in the Letters

The letters are: **A, D, G, J, ?**
Observing positions in the alphabet:

$$A\,(1) \rightarrow D\,(4) \rightarrow G\,(7) \rightarrow J\,(10)$$
The pattern follows $+3$ *each time.*
The next letter: **M** (**13th letter**).

Step 3: Identify the Pattern in the Last Numbers

The last numbers are: **11, 13, 17, 23, ?**
Checking the pattern:

$$11 \rightarrow 13 \rightarrow 17 \rightarrow 23$$
$$11 + 2 = 13$$
$$13 + 4 = 17$$
$$17 + 6 = 23$$

We are adding +2 in each sequence so the next increment should be

$$23 + 8 = 31$$

The missing term is **240M31**.

Question

Select the missing term of the series from the given options:
$$AYBZC, DWEXF.GUHVI, JSKTL, ?$$

1. MQORN
2. MQNRO
3. NQMOR
4. QMONR

Explanation:
Answer. 2. MQNRO
Step 1: Identify the Pattern in the First Letters

$$A \rightarrow D \rightarrow G \rightarrow J \rightarrow ?$$

Positions: A (1), D (4), G (7), J (10)
The pattern follows $+3$.
Next letter: M (**13th letter**).

Step 2: Identify the Pattern in the Second Letters

$$Y \rightarrow W \rightarrow U \rightarrow S \rightarrow ?$$

Positions: Y (25), W (23), U (21), S (19)
The pattern follows -2.
Next letter: Q (**17th letter**).

Step 3: Identify the Pattern in the Third Letters

$$B \rightarrow E \rightarrow H \rightarrow K \rightarrow ?$$

Positions: B (2), E (5), H (8), K (11)
The pattern follows $+3$.
Next letter: N (**14th letter**).

Step 4: Identify the Pattern in the Fourth Letters

$$Z \rightarrow X \rightarrow V \rightarrow T \rightarrow ?$$

Positions: Z (26), X (24), V (22), T (20)
The pattern follows -2.
Next letter: R (**18th letter**).

Step 5: Identify the Pattern in the Fifth Letters

$$C \rightarrow F \rightarrow I \rightarrow L \rightarrow ?$$

Positions: C (3), F (6), I (9), L (12)
The pattern follows $+3$.
Next letter: O (**15th letter**).

The missing term is **MQNRO**.

Question

Find the missing term in the following letter series

$$AMZ, BLY, CNX, DKW, EOV, \ldots\ldots ?$$

1. FPU
2. FJU
3. FQX
4. FRU

Explanation:

Answer. 2. FJU

Step 1: Identify the Pattern in the First Letters

$$A \to B \to C \to D \to E \to ?$$

The pattern follows $+1$.

The next letter: F.

Step 2: Identify the Pattern in the Second Letters

$$M \to L \to N \to K \to O \to ?$$

Positions: M (13), L (12), N (14), K (11), O (15)

The pattern alternates: $-1, +2, -3, +4$.

The next change should be -5:

$$O\ (15) - 5 = J.$$

Step 3: Identify the Pattern in the Third Letters

$$Z \to Y \to X \to W \to V \to ?$$

The pattern follows -1 each time.

The next letter: U.

The missing term is **FJU**.

Question

Find the next term (?) in the following letters series:

$$AM, GJ, MG, SD, ?,.$$

1. XZ
2. YC
3. XA
4. YA

Explanation:

Answer. 4. YA

Step 1: Identify the Pattern in the First Letters

$A \to G \to M \to S \to ?$

Positions: A (1), G (7), M (13), S (19)

The pattern follows $+6$ each time.

*The next letter: Y (**25th letter**).*

Step 2: Identify the Pattern in the Second Letters

$$M \to J \to G \to D \to ?$$

Positions: M (13), J (10), G (7), D (4)

The pattern follows -3 each time.

The next letter: **A** (**1st letter**).

The missing term is **YA**.

UGC NET PYQ Questions and Explanations on Coding and Decoding

TABLE 1

A	B	C	D	E	F	G	H	I	J	K	L	M
1	2	3	4	5	6	7	8	9	10	11	12	13
N	O	P	Q	R	S	T	U	V	W	X	Y	Z
14	15	16	17	18	19	20	21	22	23	24	25	26

TABLE 2

Z	Y	X	W	V	U	T	S	R	Q	P	O	N
1	2	3	4	5	6	7	8	9	10	11	12	13
M	L	K	J	I	H	G	F	E	D	C	B	A
14	15	16	17	18	19	20	21	22	23	24	25	26

Tips to Solve Letter Series:

TIP 1

A	B	C	D	E
1	2	3	4	5
F	G	H	I	J
6	7	8	9	10
K	L	M	N	O
11	12	13	14	15
P	Q	R	S	T
16	17	18	19	20
U	V	W	X	Y
21	22	23	24	25
Z				
26				

TIP 2

Z	Y	X	W	V
1	2	3	4	5
U	T	S	R	Q
6	7	8	9	10
P	O	N	M	L
11	12	13	14	15
K	J	I	H	G

16	17	18	19	20
F	E	D	C	B
21	22	23	24	25
A				
26				

TIP 3

E	J	O	T	Y
5	10	15	20	25

TIP 3

V	Q	L	G	B
5	10	15	20	25

Question

If a certain coding scheme, "DELHI" is coded as 5613910, then how is "MUMBAI" coded in

1. 1422143210
2. 132113219
3. 122012108
4. 1523154311

Explanation:
Answer. 1. 1422143210
Step 1: Identify the Letter-to-Number Mapping
Observing the position of each letter in the alphabet:

$$D\ (4) \rightarrow 5$$
$$E\ (5) \rightarrow 6$$
$$L\ (12) \rightarrow 13$$
$$H\ (8) \rightarrow 9$$
$$I\ (9) \rightarrow 10$$

It follows the pattern:
Position in the alphabet + 1.
Now, applying the same rule to **"MUMBAI"**:
Step 2: Apply the Rule to "MUMBAI"

$$M\ (13) \rightarrow 14$$
$$U\ (21) \rightarrow 22$$
$$M\ (13) \rightarrow 14$$
$$B\ (2) \rightarrow 3$$

$$A\,(1) \rightarrow 2$$
$$I\,(9) \rightarrow 10$$

Thus, "MUMBAI" is coded as **1422143210**.

Question

*If 'PEAK' is coded as 'KVZP' and 'FOUR' is coded as 'ULFI, the code of 'THIS'
will be:*

1. GRSH
2. GSRH
3. SHGR
4. HGRS

Explanation:
Answer. 2. GSRH
The pattern follows: Reverse Alphabet Positioning
(A ↔ Z, B ↔ Y, C ↔ X, ..., Z ↔ A)
Apply the Same Pattern to 'THIS'

$$T\,(20) \rightarrow G\,(7)$$
$$H\,(8) \rightarrow S\,(19)$$
$$I\,(9) \rightarrow R\,(18)$$
$$S\,(19) \rightarrow H\,(8)$$

Thus, THIS → GSRH.

Question

If in a certain coded language:
*"KASHMIR" is coded as "JZRGLHQ". then how "LUCKNOW? shall be coded in
that language?*

1. KTBJMNV
2. MVDLOPX
3. WONKCUL
4. KCULWON

Explanation:
Answer. 1. KTBJMNV
Comparing the original and coded letters:

$$K \rightarrow J\,(-1)$$
$$A \rightarrow Z\,(-1)$$

$$S \rightarrow R \ (-1)$$
$$H \rightarrow G \ (-1)$$
$$M \rightarrow L \ (-1)$$
$$I \rightarrow H \ (-1)$$
$$R \rightarrow Q \ (-1)$$

The pattern follows **shifting each letter backward by 1 position** in the alphabet.

Step 2: Apply the Same Pattern to "LUCKNOW"

$$L \rightarrow K$$
$$U \rightarrow T$$
$$C \rightarrow B$$
$$K \rightarrow J$$
$$N \rightarrow M$$
$$O \rightarrow N$$
$$W \rightarrow V$$

Thus, **LUCKNOW → KTBJMNV**.

Question

In a certain code language:

'617' means "Sweet and hot",
'735' means "Coffee is sweet",
'263' means "Tea is hot",

What is the code for "Coffee is hot" in that language?

1. 675
2. 537
3. 536
4. 573

Explanation:
Answer. 3. 536
Step 1: Identify the Common Words and Their Codes

"Sweet" appears in (617) and (735) → Common code: 7
"Hot" appears in (617) and (263) → Common code: 6
"Is" appears in (735) and (263) → Common code: 3

Thus, we can decode:

$$Sweet = 7$$
$$Hot = 6$$

$$Is = 3$$

Step 2: Identify the Code for "Coffee"

From **735 → "Coffee is sweet"**, we already identified:

$$Sweet = 7$$
$$Is = 3 \ Thus, Coffee = 5.$$

Step 3: Find the Code for "Coffee is hot"

$$Coffee = 5$$
$$Is = 3$$
$$Hot = 6$$

Thus, the correct code for **"Coffee is hot"** is **536**.

Question

In a certain coded language:

"CHAIR" is coded as: 61621836
"TABLE" is coded as: 40242410
"STOOL" is coded as: 3840303024

How "SOFASET" shall be coded in that language?

(1) 362810236840
(2) 3830123281400
(3) 3830122381040
(4) 362810328640

Explanation:
Answer. (3). 3830122381040
Step 1: Identify the Pattern
We will check how each letter is converted into numbers.
Observing "CHAIR" → 61621836

$$C\ (3) \rightarrow 6$$
$$H\ (8) \rightarrow 16$$
$$A\ (1) \rightarrow 2$$
$$I\ (9) \rightarrow 18$$
$$R\ (18) \rightarrow 36$$

Each letter seems to be **multiplied by 2**.
Observing "TABLE" → 40242410

$$T\ (20) \rightarrow 40$$

$$A\ (1) \rightarrow 2$$
$$B\ (2) \rightarrow 4$$
$$L\ (12) \rightarrow 24$$
$$E\ (5) \rightarrow 10$$

Each letter is **multiplied by 2**.

Observing "STOOL" → 3840303024

$$S\ (19) \rightarrow 38$$
$$T\ (20) \rightarrow 40$$
$$O\ (15) \rightarrow 30$$
$$O\ (15) \rightarrow 30$$
$$L\ (12) \rightarrow 24$$

Each letter is **multiplied by 2**.

Step 2: Apply the Pattern to "SOFASET"

Each letter is multiplied by 2:

$$S\ (19) \rightarrow 38$$
$$O\ (15) \rightarrow 30$$
$$F\ (6) \rightarrow 12$$
$$A\ (1) \rightarrow 2$$
$$S\ (19) \rightarrow 38$$
$$E\ (5) \rightarrow 10$$
$$T\ (20) \rightarrow 40$$

Thus, **"SOFASET"** → **3830122381040**.

Question

In a certain code, following sentences have been coded as mentioned below:
'Arjun is walking to school' is coded as:

$$'NA.,'ST','AG','DR','VI'$$

'Krishna is speaking to Arjun' is coded as:

$$'KA','TK','DR','ST','NA'$$

'School is within walking distance of Krishna' is coded as:

$$'VI','SI','NI','AG','LE','KA','OP'.$$

What is the code for 'walking'?

1. TK
2. VI
3. AG
4. SI

Explanation:
Answer. 3. AG
Step 1: Identify Common Words and Their Codes
- o   *"Arjun" appears in Sentence 1 and Sentence 2 → Common codes: 'NA'*
- o   *"Krishna" appears in Sentence 2 and Sentence 3 →*
  Common codes: 'KA'
- o   *"School" appears in Sentence 1 and Sentence 3 → Common codes: 'VI'*
- o   *"Is" appears in all three sentences → Common codes: 'ST'*
- o   *"To" appears in Sentences 1 and 2 → Common codes: 'DR'*

Step 2: Identify the Code for "Walking"
- o   "Walking" appears in Sentence 1 and Sentence 3.
- o   The common codes between ('NA', 'ST', 'AG', 'DR', 'VI') and ('VI', 'SI', 'NI', 'AG', 'LE', 'KA', 'OP') are:
  - ▪ 'AG'
  - ▪ 'VI'
- o   Now, checking the words:

"School" is already identified as 'VI'.
"Walking" should be 'AG'.

Question

In a certain code language, "INDORE" is coded as, "KPFQTG". How "CHENNAI" shall be coded in that language?

1.   EIGOPBK
2.   DIFOOBJ
3.   EJGPPCK
4.   KCPPGJE

Explanation:
Answer. 3. EJGPPCK
Step 1: Identify the Pattern
Comparing each letter of **INDORE** with **KPFQTG**:

$$I \rightarrow K\ (+2)$$
$$N \rightarrow P\ (+2)$$
$$D \rightarrow F\ (+2)$$
$$O \rightarrow Q\ (+2)$$
$$R \rightarrow T\ (+2)$$
$$E \rightarrow G\ (+2)$$

Each letter is shifted **+2 positions forward** in the alphabet.

Step 2: Apply the Same Pattern to "CHENNAI"

$$C \rightarrow E$$
$$H \rightarrow J$$
$$E \rightarrow G$$
$$N \rightarrow P$$
$$N \rightarrow P$$
$$A \rightarrow C$$
$$I \rightarrow K$$

Thus, **CHENNAI → EJGPPCK.**

Question

In a certain coding scheme, 'AC' is coded as 8 and 'PQ' as 33. What is the code of 'XZ"?

1. 100
2. 51
3. 71
4. 87

Explanation:
Answer. 1. 100

$$AC \rightarrow 8$$
$$A = 1, C = 3$$
$$Sum: 1 + 3 = 4$$
$$Multiply\ by\ 2: 4 \times 2 = 8$$

$$PQ \rightarrow 33$$
$$P = 16, Q = 17$$
$$Sum: 16 + 17 = 33$$
$$No\ multiplication\ needed.$$

$$XZ \rightarrow ?$$
$$X = 24, Z = 26$$
$$Sum: 24 + 26 = 50$$
$$Multiply\ by\ 2: 50 \times 2 = 100$$

Question

Match the column:

List I (Word)	List II (Unique Code)
A. QUAKE	(I) KTFUL
B. OFTEN	(II) VHQDU
C. PEACH	(III) IEYOU
D. DRIVE	(IV) JUYWR

1.   A-I B-III C-II D-IV
2.   A-II B-IV C-III D-I
3.   A-III B-I C-IV D-II
4.   A-IV B-II C-1 D-III

Explanation:

Answer. 3. A-III B-I C-IV D-II

If the pattern involves shifting letters or reversing positions, we can observe:
1.   QUAKE → IEYOU (A-III)
2.   OFTEN → KTFUL (B-I)
3.   PEACH → JUYWR (C-IV)
4.   DRIVE → VHQDU (D-II)

Question

In a certain coding language, the word 'FLOUT' is coded as 'IRRW', then the word 'CLING' will be coded as 'CLING'.

1.   ENKPI
2.   EHLJK
3.   FLILK
4.   FILKJ

Explanation:

Answer. 4. FILKJ

$$For\ 'C'\!: Shift\ +3\ \rightarrow\ 'F'$$
$$For\ 'L'\!: shift\ +6\ \rightarrow\ 'R'$$
$$For\ 'I'\!: Shift\ +3\ \rightarrow\ 'L'$$
$$For\ 'N'\!: Shift\ +2\ \rightarrow\ 'K'$$
$$For\ 'G'\!: No\ shift\ (0)\ \rightarrow\ 'J'$$

So, CLING becomes FILKJ

Question

In a certain code language:

"Bitter patience sweet fruit" is coded as : "Bo Po So To"
"Art is sweet happiness" is coded as : "Ao lo So Ho"
"Hoping is concealing bitter" is coded as : "Hp lo Co Bo"
"Patience is art of hoping" is coded as : "Po lo Ao Fo Hp"

How "Patience is happiness" will be coded in this language?
1.   Ho loPo
2.   Hp Ao Po
3.   Po Ao Hp
4.   Po lo Ho

Explanation:
Answer. 4. Po lo Ho
From the second and fourth statements:
- o   **"Art" appears in** (2) & (4) → Common code: **"Ao"**
- o   **"Is" appears in** (2), (3), (4) → Common code: **"lo"**
- o   **"Sweet" appears in** (1) & (2) → Common code: **"So"**
- o   **"Happiness" appears in** (2) only → Code: **"Ho"**
- o   **"Patience" appears in** (1) & (4) → Common code: **"Po"**

Find the Code for "Patience is Happiness"
- o   *"Patience"* → *"Po"*
- o   *"Is"* → *"lo"*
- o   *"Happiness"* → *"Ho"*

Thus, **"Patience is Happiness"** is coded as **"Po lo Ho"**.

Question

In some code language:

"Indian cuisines are good" is coded as "MI CI FI GI".
"They like Indian cuisines" is written as "AI LI MI Cl" in the encrypted code.
"People like Indian Chinese" is written as "PI LI MI HI" in the encoding code.
In the code for "They and people are best" it is written as "AI DI PI FI BI".

How will the words 'good', 'Chinese' and 'cuisines' be coded in this language?

1. GI, HI and CI
2. AI, LI and FI
3. MI, DI and BI
4. HI, CI and LI

Explanation:

Answer. 1. GI, HI and CI

Step 1: Identify the Code for "Good"

From sentence (1): *"Indian cuisines are good"* → *"MI CI FI GI"*

From sentence (2): *"They like Indian cuisines"* → *"AI LI MI CI"*

Common words in (1) *and* (2): *"Indian cuisines"* = *"MI CI"*

Remaining words in (1): *"Are good"* = *"FI GI"*

From sentence (4): *"They and people are best"* → *"AI DI PI FI BI"*

Common word "Are" in (1) *and* (4) → *"Are"* = *"FI"*

The only remaining word in (1) *"Good"* = *"GI"*

"Good" = GI

Step 2: Identify the Code for "Chinese"

From sentence (3): *"People like Indian Chinese"* → *"PI LI MI HI"*

We already identified "People" = *"PI" (from sentence* 4)

"Like Indian" is common in (2) *and* (3) → *"LI MI"*

The only remaining word is "Chinese" = *"HI"*

"Chinese" = HI

Step 3: Identify the Code for "Cuisines"

From sentence (1): *"Indian cuisines are good"* → *"MI CI FI GI"*

From sentence (2): *"They like Indian cuisines"* → *"AI LI MI CI"*

Common words "Indian cuisines" = *"MI CI"*

We already identified "Indian" = *"MI", so "Cuisines"* = *"CI"*

"Cuisines" = CI

Final Answer

- "Good" = GI
- "Chinese" = HI

"Cuisines" = CI

Blood Relationship:

Blood relation forms an essential part of the reasoning section in most UGC NET exams. The blood relationship describes the relationships among the members of a family. Based on the information provided, we must determine the relationship between various family members. This topic tests our analytical skills and demonstrates how we can solve logical problems using diagrams instead of calculations. The charts play an important role to solve this type of question.

Family Tree

In order to solve the problems in blood relations, it is necessary to be able to draw a family tree.

- o   A **circle** represents all the male members of the family. Write the name inside the circle. It can also be represented as (+)

- o   A **square** represents all the female members of the family. Write the name inside the square. It can also be represented as (-)

- o   The generation above should represent the up arrow. Draw two or three arrows if there are two or three generations above.

- o   **One arrow up:** Father or Mother, Uncle or Aunt, Maternal uncle/aunt.

- o **Two arrows up:** Grandfather or grandmother, maternal grandfather/grandmother

- o **Three arrows up:** Great grandfather/grandmother, Maternal great grandfather/grandmother, and great-grandfather/grandmother-in-law.

Similarly, the generation below should be represented as a down arrow. Draw two or three down arrows if there are two or three generations below.

- o **One arrow down:** son, daughter and nephew.

- o **Two arrows down:** Grandson or granddaughter and grandson/granddaughter-in-law,

- o **Three arrows down:** Great-grandson/daughter and great-grandson/granddaughter-in-law.

- o The relation between two family members is shown by connecting a **double-headed arrow** like brother/sister, cousin, husband/wife and brother/sister-in-law.

The spouse relation is symbolized by **the two ends of a double-headed arrow**.

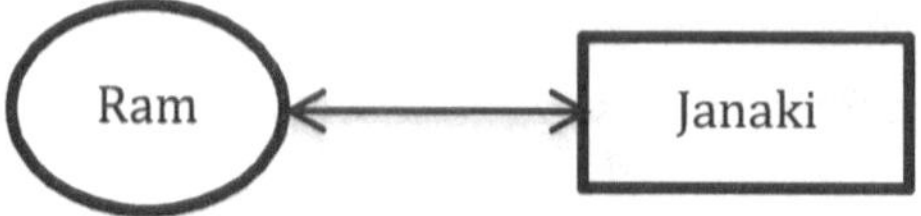

Shortcuts:

- **Circle** (+) → Male
- **Square** (-) → Female
- **Up arrow** (↑) → Older generation (Father, Mother, Uncle, Aunt, Grandparents, etc.)
- **Down arrow** (↓) → Younger generation (Children, Grandchildren, Great-grandchildren, etc.)
- **Double-headed arrow** (↔) → Sibling, Cousin, Spouse relations

Topic 1: Question-based on the jumbled descriptions or conversations:

Question 1: Pointing to a photograph of a boy Mr. Sekhar said, "He is the son of the only son of my mother." How is Mr Sekhar related to that boy?
Solution:
Step 1: There is a photograph and Mr. Sekhar. The photograph is of a man, and thus two circles are represented. But the relationship of Mr. Sekhar with the person in the photograph is not known yet.

Family Tree of Mr. Sekhar

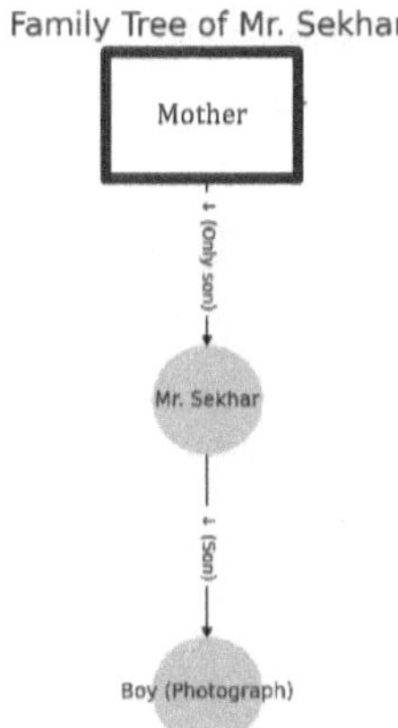

Step 2: The second line says Mr Sekhar has a mother. Mr Sekhar is the only son of his mother, and Sekhar has a son, and that photograph belongs to Mr Sekhar's son.

Only son of my mother so basically, he is talking about his own mother.

Therefore, Sekhar is the father of the boy.

Question: Pointing to a man, Surekha said, 'He is the brother of the mother of my father's son. How is the man related to Surekha?
Solution: The given relation is 'He is the brother of the mother of my father's son. It can be rewritten as: 'Man is the brother of the mother of Surekha's father's son.
Now, to simplify, take relations one by one.
Surekhas's father's son -> Surekhas's brother
Mother of Surekhas's brother -> Surekha's mother
Brother of Surekhas's mother -> Surekha's maternal uncle

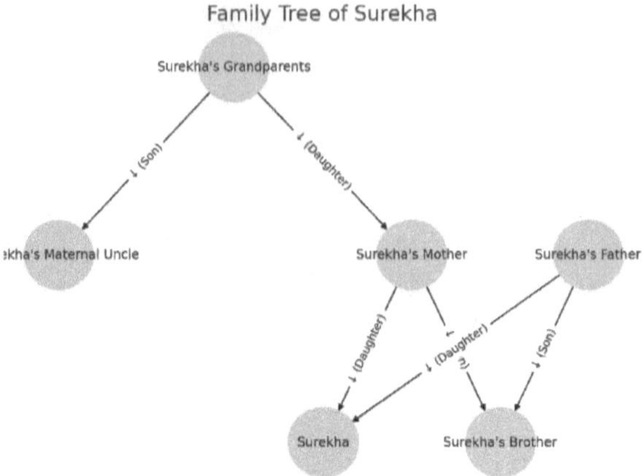

Topic 2: Question-based on Relational puzzle:

This section will provide all of the information about the family members in a straightforward and simple manner, as opposed to the previous section.

Question: Ravi is the son of Aman's father's sister. Sahil is the son of Divya, who is the mother of Gaurav and grandmother of Aman. Ashok is the father of Tanya and the grandfather of Ravi. Divya is the wife of Ashok. How is Ravi related to Divya?

Solution: There is no requirement for drawing a family tree to solve this question. Since Divya is the grandmother of Aman and Aman and Ravi are cousins (from the first statement). Ravi should be a grandson to Divya.

Picture

Question: A is the son of B and is not the father of A. C is the daughter of D. B and D are a married couple. How is A related to C?

Solution: **Picture**

Therefore A is the brother of C.

Topic 3: Question-based on Coded Relations:

In this section, the relationships among the members of the family are represented by certain specific codes or symbols such as +._ $,*,&,#,@,! Etc. The answers are obtained by decoding the relationships hidden in the symbols. The only tedious process here is to solve all the options to arrive at the final correct answer.

Question: Read the following instructions:

A + B indicates A is the brother of B;
A – B indicates A is the sister of B and
A x B indicates A is the father of B

Which of the following means that C is the son of M?

1. M – N x C + F
2. F – C + N x M
3. N + M – F x C
4. M x N – C + F

Solution:

Option A: According to this option, NxC indicates N is the father of c. Hence it is wrong.

Option B: According to this, option C is the brother of N, who is the father of M. Hence it is wrong.

Option C: According to this option, Fx C indicates F is the father of C. Hence it is wrong.

Option D: According to this option, M is the father of N, who is the sister of C; hence C and N are siblings, and C is the brother of F, so C is male.

Therefore, C is the son of M. Option D is the correct answer.

UGC NET PYQ Questions and Explanations on Blood Relations:

Question

K introduces N to his friend saying, 'He is the husband of the grand daughter of the father of my father". **How is N related to K?**

1. Brother
2. Son-in-law
3. Nephew
4. Brother-in-law

Explanation:

Answer. Brother-in-law

- ○ "Father of my father" → This means K's grandfather (↑↑).
- ○ "Granddaughter of the father of my father" → This means K's sister or K's cousin (↓↓).

- "Husband of the granddaughter of the father of my father" → This means N is the husband of K's sister (or cousin).
- **N is K's Brother-in-law (Husband of K's sister)**

Question

Consider the following statements.

He is the son of P, and M is the son of S. S is the mother of N who is the sister of P.

Which of the following is correct based on the above?

A. S is the maternal grandmother of P.
B. P is the sister of M.
C. M is the maternal uncle of H.
D. He is the grandson/granddaughter of S.

1. AB
2. BC
3. BCD
4. BD

Explanation:
Answer. 4. BD
Given Statements:
1. "He is the son of P"
    - This means P is the parent of "He."
2. "M is the son of S."
    - This means S is the mother of M (↑).
3. "S is the mother of N, who is the sister of P."
    - S is the mother of both N and P (↑).
    - N is the sister of P (↔).

Step-by-Step Breakdown of Relations:
- S (Mother) has two children: P and N.
- P has a child ("He").
- M is also a child of S, meaning M is a sibling of P and N.
- So, M is P's brother (↔).

Now, Check the Given Options:

A. "S is the maternal grandmother of P."
- o   Incorrect.
- o   S is the mother of P, not the grandmother.

B. "P is the sister of M."
- o   Correct if P is female.
- o   Since P and M are siblings, P is M's sister ($\leftrightarrow$).

C. "M is the maternal uncle of H."
- o   We don't know who H is.
- o   No mention of H in the given information.

D. "He is the grandson/granddaughter of S."
- o   Correct.
- o   "He" is the child of P.
- o   P is the child of S.
- o   So, "He" is the grandson/granddaughter of S ($\downarrow\downarrow$).

Question

A woman, while introducing a man, says "*His wife is the only daughter of my father*". **How is that man related to the woman?**

1.   Father-in-law
2.   Brother-in-law
3.   Husband
4.   Brother

Explanation:

Answer. 3. Husband

Given Statement:

> "*His wife is the only daughter of my father.*"

Step 1: Identify "Only Daughter of My Father"
- o   The only daughter of the woman's father is the woman herself.
- o   This means: "His wife = the woman herself."

Step 2: Identify the Man's Relationship to the Woman
- o   The man's wife is the woman.
- o   That means the man is her husband.

Question

A, B. C and D are all distinct individuals. The details of their relationships are given as:

i. *A is the daughter of B*
ii. *B is the son of C*
iii. *C is the Father of D*

Which of the following statements is true?

1. C is the Uncle of A
2. D and B are cousins
3. A is the daughter of D
4. If P is the daughter of B, then A and P are sisters.

Explanation:

Answer. 4. If P is the daughter of B, then A and P are sisters.

Given Statements:

1. *"A is the daughter of B"* → B is A's father (↑).
2. *"B is the son of C"* → C is B's father (↑).
3. *"C is the father of D"* → C is D's father (↑).

Step-by-Step Breakdown of Relations:

- C is the father of both B and D.
  - B is C's son.
  - D is also C's child.
  - So, B and D are siblings (↔).
- A is the daughter of B.
  - Since B and D are siblings, A is D's niece.

Now, Check the Given Options:

1. "C is the Uncle of A."
   - Incorrect.
   - C is A's grandfather, not uncle.
2. "D and B are cousins."
   - Incorrect.
   - B and D are siblings, not cousins.
3. "A is the daughter of D."
   - Incorrect.
   - A is the daughter of B, not D.
4. "If P is the daughter of B, then A and P are sisters."
   - Correct.

- o   If P is also the daughter of B, that means A and P share the same father (B).
- o   Thus, A and P are sisters (↔).

Correct option: (4) "If P is the daughter of B, then A and P are sisters."

Question

Raman said to Aman, "That boy playing football there is the younger of the two brothers of the daughter of my father's wife". How is the boy playing football related to Raman?

1.   Cousin
2.   Brother-in-law
3.   Son
4.   Brother

Explanation:
Answer. 4. Brother
Given Statement:
"That boy playing football there is the younger of the two brothers of the daughter of my father's wife."

Step 1: Identify "My Father's Wife"
- o   "My father's wife" refers to Raman's mother (assuming no remarriage).

Step 2: Identify "The Daughter of My Father's Wife"
- o   "The daughter of my father's wife" means Raman's sister.

Step 3: Identify "The Two Brothers of the Daughter"
- o   Raman's sister has two brothers.

Since Raman is also a child of his father and mother, he is one of these brothers.

*The boy playing football is described as "the younger of the two brothers" →
This means the boy is Raman's younger brother.*

Question

A man looks at the photograph of a person X and says "She is the daughter of the husband of only daughter of father of my brother-in-law (Wife's brother)". How is the person X related to the man?

1. Daughter
2. Sister
3. Wife
4. Mother

Explanation:
Answer. 1. Daughter
Given Statement:
"She is the daughter of the husband of only daughter of father of my brother-in-law (Wife's brother)."

Step 1: Identify "My Brother-in-Law"
- o   "My brother-in-law" refers to the wife's brother.

Step 2: Identify "Father of My Brother-in-Law"
- o   The father of my wife's brother is my wife's father.

Step 3: Identify "Only Daughter of Wife's Father"
- o   The only daughter of my wife's father means my wife.

Step 4: Identify "Husband of the Only Daughter of My Wife's Father"
- o   The husband of my wife is me (the man speaking).

Step 5: Identify "Daughter of Me"
- o   The statement now simplifies to:
  "She is the daughter of me (the man)."

This means X is the man's daughter.

Direction:

Direction type question is the common type of verbal reasoning which has been coming in the UGC exam. We must have sensical knowledge about the direction. Direction refers to the relative position of one point in relation to another without considering distance. There are four directions which are:

1. North
2. East
3. South
4. West

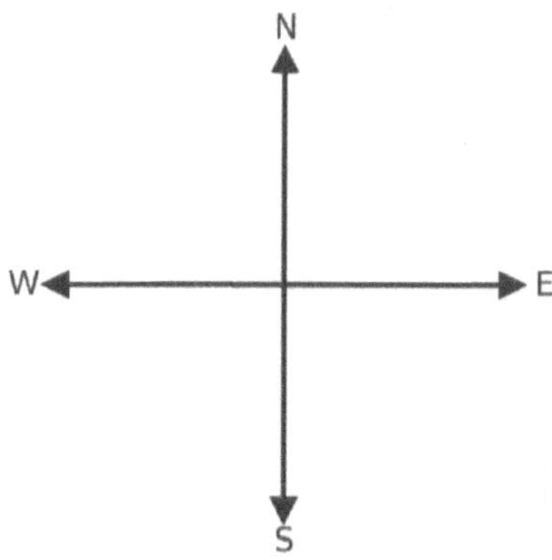

The cardinal directions are:

1. Northeast (NE),
2. Southeast (SE),
3. Southwest (SW),
4. Northwest (NW).

Whenever there are intercardinal and cardinal directions, the intermediate direction is called a secondary intercardinal direction. Below are the eight shortest points in the compass rose:

1. **North-Northeast (NNE)** (Between N and NE)
2. **East-Northeast (ENE)** (Between NE and E)
3. **East-Southeast (ESE)** (Between E and SE)

4. **South-Southeast (SSE)** (Between SE and S)
5. **South-Southwest (SSW)** (Between S and SW)
6. **West-Southwest (WSW)** (Between SW and W)
7. **West-Northwest (WNW)** (Between W and NW)
8. **North-Northwest (NNW)** (Between NW and N)

Pythagoras Theorem:

According to Pythagoras' theorem, the square of the hypotenuse in a right-angled triangle equals the sum of the squares of the other two sides. This theorem can be expressed as h2 = b2 + p2, where 'h' is the hypotenuse, and 'b' and 'p' are the triangle's two legs.

Formula

$$h^2 = b^2 + p^2$$

Where:

- h = *Hypotenuse (longest side, opposite the right angle)*,
- b = *Base (one leg of the right − angled triangle)*,
- p = *Perpendicular (the other leg of the right − angled triangle)*.

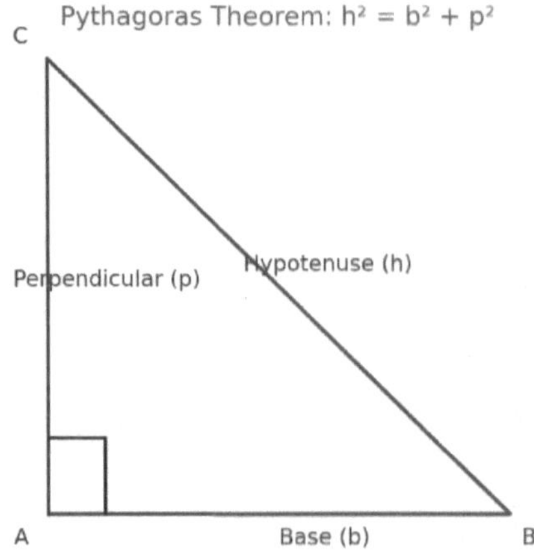

Types of Questions asked in the exam are:

I. Question-based on the right and left Directional movement:

Question: *Mr Sharma walks 5 km towards the South and then turns to the right. After walking 3 km, he turns to the left and walks 5 km.*

What direction is he facing right now?

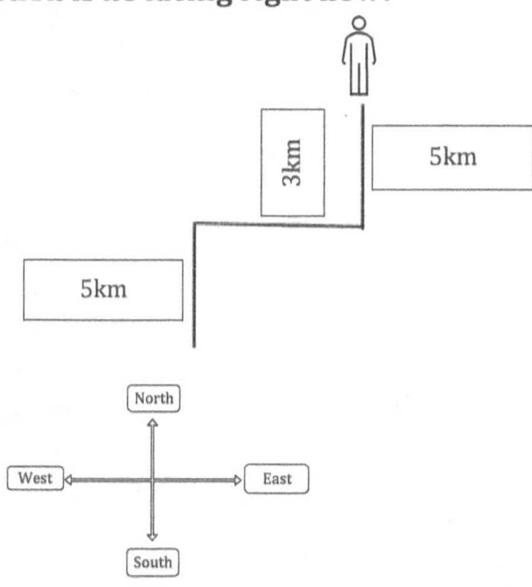

The right and left movements concern Mr Sharma. After walking 5 km towards the South, he takes a right turn and now will be facing West. After walking 3 more km, he turns left and walks five more km. Now he is facing South.

II. Question-based on the directional reference point:

Question: Aryan started walking towards the North. After 15 km, he took a left turn and walked for 10 km. Then again took a left turn and walked for 10 km. Then he again turned left and walked for 15 km.

(a) Find the total distance covered by him.
(b) How far is he from the starting point?
(c) In which direction is he travelling now?
(d) What is his direction concerning the starting point?

Solution: Aryan's journey can be drawn as:

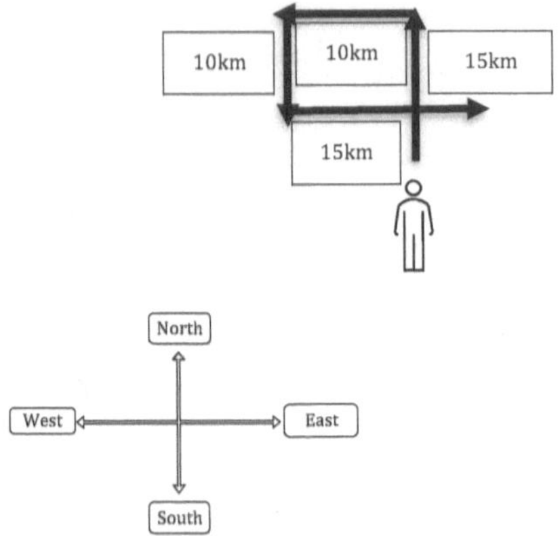

A. The total distance covered by Aryan will be the sum of all distances.
   Total distance = 15+10+10+15=50 km

B. Now, we can use the Pythagorean theorem to calculate the straight-line distance from the starting point:

$$Distance = \sqrt{(Horizontal\ distance)^2 + (Vertical\ distance)^2}$$
$$Distance = \sqrt{(5)^2 + (5)^2}$$
$$Distance = \sqrt{50}$$
$$Distance = 7.07km \ldots Ans.$$

C. After completing all his turns, Aryan is facing east.

D. Since Aryan ended up at (5, 5) and the starting point is (0, 0), he is in the **northeast** direction concerning his starting point.

III. Question-based on the directions of sun rays and shadow:

In this question, we are asked about the shadow and the degree, like Sunrise/sunset and the shadow.

Question: *One morning after sunrise, Nandita and Ravi sat on a lawn with their backs to each other. Nandita's shadow fell exactly towards her left-hand side. Which direction was Ravi facing?*

Solution: Since it was morning and Nandita's shadow fell exactly to her left-hand side, Nandita was facing North. Hence Ravi should be facing South.

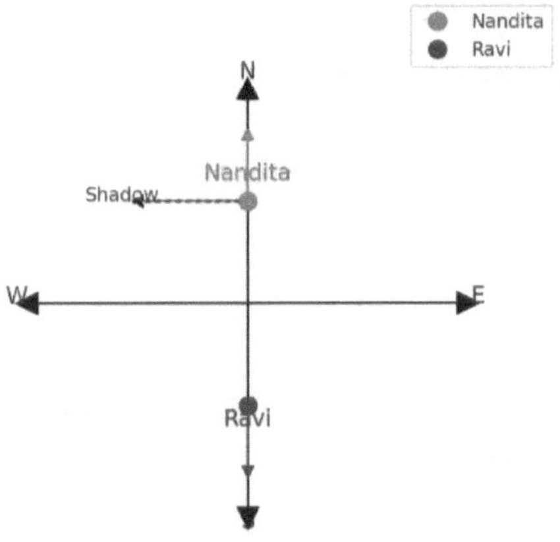

IV. Question-based on the correct map v/s wrong map:

This section involves the comparison of two maps which one is wrong. One has to find the correct direction on the wrong map by applying logical analysis.

Question: *At a crossing, there was a direction pole showing all four correct directions. But due to the wind, it turns so that now the West pointer is showing South. Harish went in the wrong direction, thinking that he was travelling East. In what direction was he travelling?*

Solution: He is travelling to the North.

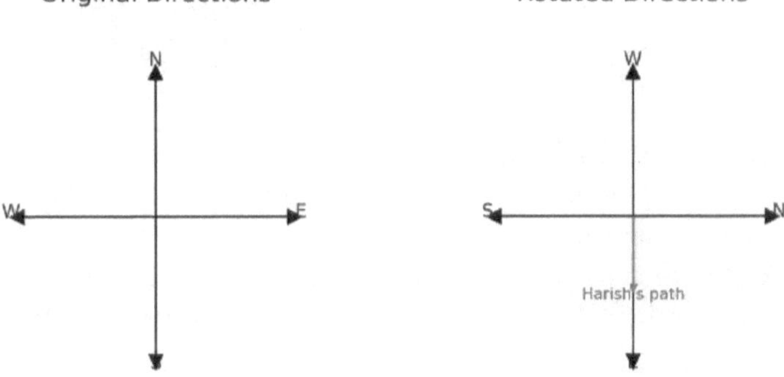

V. Question-based on the Directions in Clocks:

These types of questions are being asked in the UGC NET exam. We should know how to solve these types of questions. Here are a few examples which can help us to understand the solution.

Question: *A clock is so placed that at 2:00 p.m., the minute hand points towards North-west. In which direction does the hour hand point at 6:00 p.m.?*

Solution: We are given that at 2:00 PM, the minute hand (which normally points at 12) is pointing towards North-West. This means the entire clock is rotated.

Step 1: Understanding the Rotation
- o   Normally, at 2:00 PM, the minute hand should point to 12 (North).
- o   But here, it is pointing to North-West instead of North.
- o   This means the entire clock has been rotated 45° counterclockwise.

Step 2: Finding the Hour Hand's Direction at 6:00 PM
- o   Normally, at 6:00 PM, the hour hand points at 6 (South).
- o   Since the clock is rotated 45° counterclockwise, the South direction also shifts 45° counterclockwise, which now points to South-East.

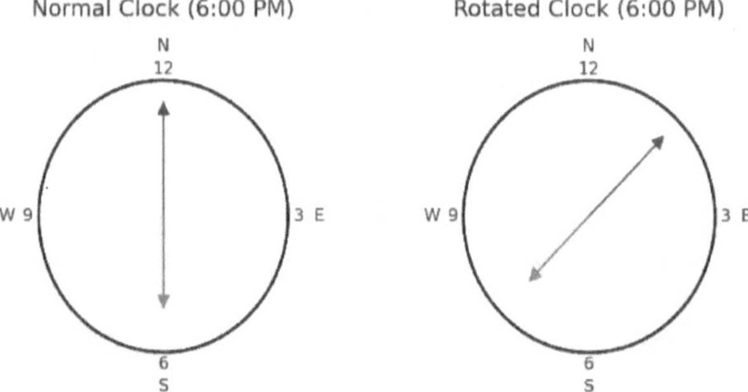

The diagram shows two clocks:
1. **Left Clock** - A normal clock where 6:00 PM has the hour hand pointing **South**.
2. **Right Clock** - The rotated clock where the entire face is shifted **45° counterclockwise**. This causes the **hour hand at 6:00 PM to point South-East.**

VI. Question based on the Directions in the Seating arrangement:

This section applies directional concepts to popular board games like Chess and Carrom board or Snake and ladder to solve the questions.

Question: *A chess piece undergoes the following motion during the game. It starts from D-8 and reaches H-5. From there, it reaches A-3. Finally, it moves to position H-8 and dies. In what direction was the piece when it died if the chess board is assumed to be placed in front of you?*

Solution: The H-8 is the position where the chess piece died. If the chessboard is assumed to be placed in front of us, then the position H-8 will lie between North and east. Hence, the answer is North-East.

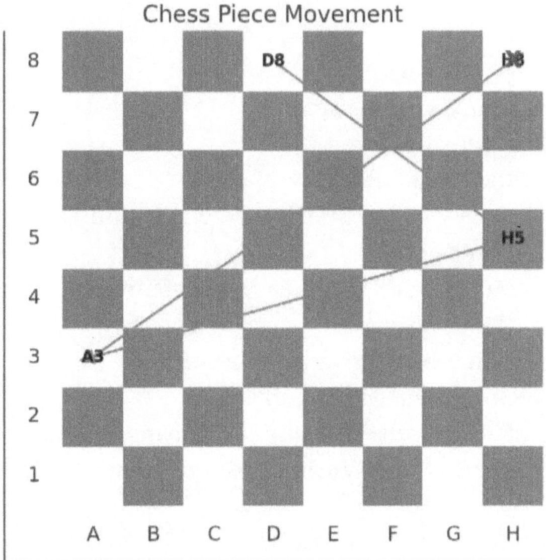

The diagram illustrates the chess piece's movement across the board:
1. **Starts at D8** (top-left area).
2. **Moves to H5** (diagonal right-down).
3. **Moves to A3** (diagonal left-down).
4. **Moves to H8** (diagonal right-up), where it dies.

UGC NET PYQ Questions and Explanations on Directions

Question

Aman walks 12 km towards south and then 7 km towards north. From here he walks 5 km towards his left. How far and in which direction is the man with reference to his starting point?

1. $5km, North - west$
2. $5km, south - west$
3. $5\sqrt{2}, south - west$
4. $5\sqrt{2}, south - east$

Explanation:

Answer. 4. $5\sqrt{2}, south - west$

Understanding Aman's Movement

1. **Walks 12 km South**
   - Initial position: (0,0)
   - Moves **12 km South** → New position: (0, -12)
2. **Walks 7 km North**
   - Moves **7 km North** → New position: (0, -5)
     (Since he was already at -12 on the y-axis, moving up reduces the distance southward)
3. **Walks 5 km towards his Left**
   - Facing **South**, turning **Left** means moving **West**
   - Moves **5 km West** → New position: (-5, -5)

Step 2: Distance from Starting Point

The displacement is the direct distance from (0,0) to (-5,-5).
Using the distance formula:

$$Distance = \sqrt{(x_2 - x_1)^2 + (y_2 - y_1)^2}$$
$$= \sqrt{(-5 - 0)^2 + (-5 - 0)^2}$$
$$= \sqrt{25 + 25} = \sqrt{50} = 5\sqrt{2} \dots Ans.$$

Question

A man is facing North direction. He turns 90 degrees in the anticlockwise direction and then 135 degrees in the same direction. He then turns 270 degrees in the clockwise direction.

Which direction is the man facing now?

1. North - East
2. North - West
3. South - East
4. South – West

Explanation:

Answer. 1. North – East

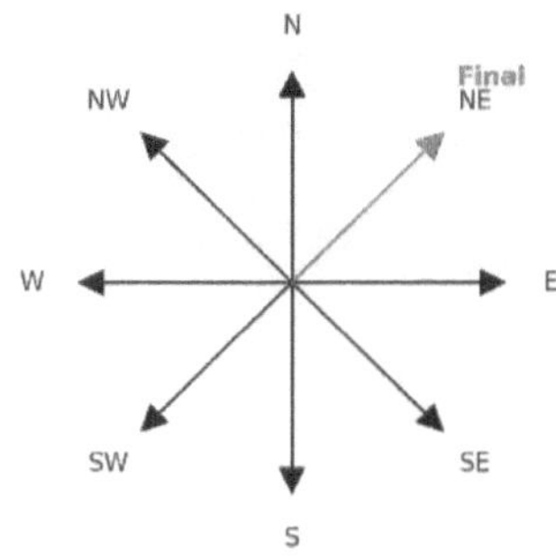

Step 1: Initial Position: The man is **facing North**.

Step 2: First Turn (90° Anticlockwise): Turning 90° left (anticlockwise) from North:

- **North → West**

Step 3: Second Turn (135° Anticlockwise) Turning 135° left (anticlockwise) from **West**:

- **90° from West → South**
- **Another 45° from South → South-East**

Now, he is **facing South-East**.

Step 4: Third Turn (270° Clockwise): Turning 270° right (clockwise) from **South-East**:

- 90° right → **South**
- 180° right → **West**
- 270° right → **North-East**

Question

A woman walks 100 metres towards north. Then she turns to her left and walks 50 metres. Again, turns left and walks 120 metres. Finally, she turns to her right at an angle of 45 degrees and starts walking. In which direction is the woman walking now?

1. North
2. South-West
3. West
4. North-West

Explanation:

Answer. 2. South-West

Step 1: Initial Position: The woman starts facing **North**.

Step 2: Movement Breakdown

1. **Walks 100 metres North**
   - Position: (0, 100)
   - Still facing **North**
2. **Turns Left (Now Facing West) and Walks 50 metres**
   - Moves **50 metres West**
   - Position: (-50, 100)
   - Now facing **West**
3. **Turns Left (Now Facing South) and Walks 120 metres**
   - Moves **120 metres South**
   - Position: (-50, -20)
   - Now facing **South**
4. **Turns Right at 45° and Starts Walking**
   - Turning **right** by **45°** from **South** means she is now facing **South-West**.
   - She is walking **diagonally** in the **South-West** direction.

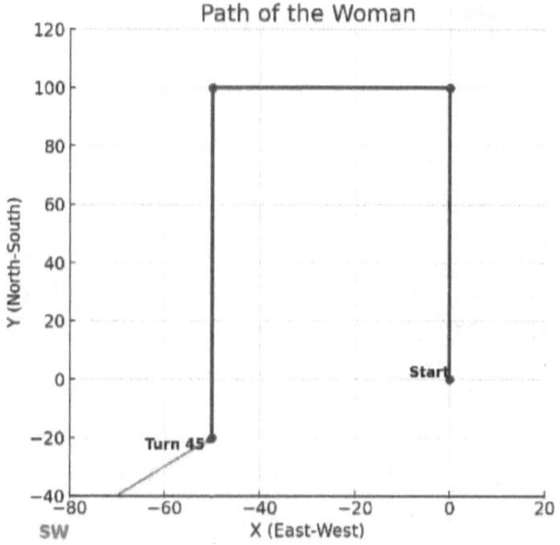

Question

A woman walks 70 meters to the south of her house. She then turns left and walks 30 meters and then again turning to north she walks 40 meters. Now she walks towards her house. In which direction is she walking now?

1. East
2. North-East
3. South-East
4. North-West

Explanation:

Answer. North-West

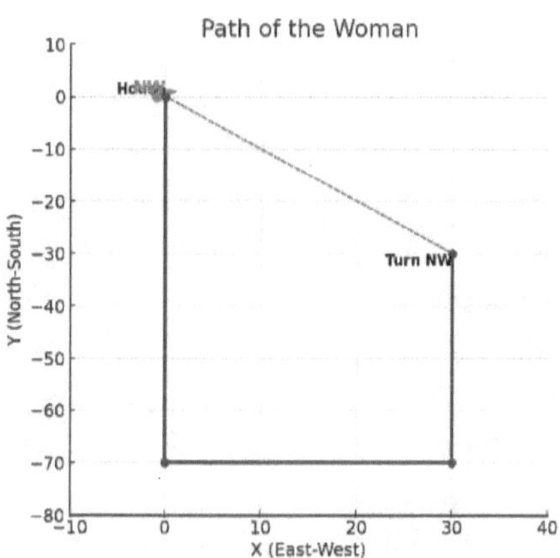

Step 1: Initial Position

- The **house** is at the **origin (0,0)**.

o   The woman **starts from her house**.

Step 2: Movement Breakdown
1. **Walks 70 meters South**
   - o   Position: **(0, -70)**
   - o   Still facing **South**
2. **Turns Left (Now Facing East) and Walks 30 meters**
   - o   Moves **30 meters East**
   - o   Position: **(30, -70)**
   - o   Now facing **East**
3. **Turns Left (Now Facing North) and Walks 40 meters**
   - o   Moves **40 meters North**
   - o   Position: **(30, -30)**
   - o   Now facing **North**
4. **Walks Towards Her House (0,0)**
   - o   She needs to move from **(30, -30)** to **(0,0)**.
   - o   This movement is **diagonal towards the North-West direction**.

Question

A policeman goes 20 meters towards South and then tums to his right and walks 40 meters. He again turns to his left and walks 10 meters. How far is he now from his starting point?

1. 375 meters
2. 50 meters
3. 30/2 meters
4. 40 meters

Explanation:
Answer. 2. 50 meters
Step 1: Movement Breakdown
1. Walks 20 meters South
   - o   Position: (0, -20)
2. Turns Right (Now Facing West) and Walks 40 meters
   - o   Position: (-40, -20)
3. Turns Left (Now Facing South) and Walks 10 meters
   - o   Position: (-40, -30)

Step 2: Distance Calculation

- The displacement is the straight-line distance from (0,0) to (40,-30).
- Using the distance formula:

$$Distance = \sqrt{(40-0)^2 + (-30-0)^2}$$
$$= \sqrt{1600 + 900} = \sqrt{2500} = 50$$

Question

A girl walks straight in the opposite direction of the front door of her house. The front door of the houses facing towards south After walking for 50 meters, the girl turns to her left and walks 100 meters, thereafter the girl turns right and stops after walking for 100 meters.

Which direction the girl is facing now?

1. North
2. South
3. North-west
4. North-east

Explanation:
Answer. 1. North

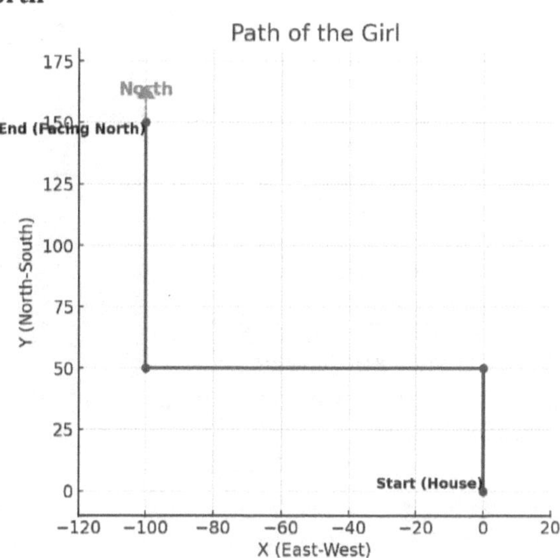

Step 1: Understanding the Initial Direction

- The **house's front door is facing South**.

- o The girl walks in the **opposite direction** of the front door, meaning she moves **North**.

Step 2: Movement Breakdown
1. **Walks 50 meters North**
   - o Position: **(0, 50)**
   - o Now facing **North**
2. **Turns Left (Now Facing West) and Walks 100 meters**
   - o Moves **100 meters West**
   - o Position: **(-100, 50)**
   - o Now facing **West**
3. **Turns Right (Now Facing North) and Walks 100 meters**
   - o Moves **100 meters North**
   - o Position: **(-100, 150)**
   - o Now facing **North**

Question

The house of a man is facing towards the south. From the front door of the house. the man starts walking and after walking for 20 meters straight. he turns to his left and walks for 50 meters. After this, the man turns to his right and walks for 80 meters and stops there. Find the distance from the point where the man stops to the front door of his house.

1. $25\sqrt{5}\,m$
2. $50\sqrt{5}\,m$
3. $50\,m$
4. $100\,m$

Explanation:
Answer. $2.\ 50\sqrt{5}\,m$
Step 1: Understanding the Initial Direction
   - o The **house's front door is facing South**.
   - o The man walks in the **same direction as the front door**, meaning he moves **South** first.

Step 2: Movement Breakdown
1. **Walks 20 meters South**
   - o Position: **(0, -20)**
   - o Now facing **South**

2. **Turns Left (Now Facing East) and Walks 50 meters**
   - o Moves **50 meters East**
   - o Position: **(50, -20)**
   - o Now facing **East**
3. **Turns Right (Now Facing South) and Walks 80 meters**
   - o Moves **80 meters South**
   - o Position: **(50, -100)**
   - o Now facing **South**

Step 3: Distance Calculation
   - o The displacement is the **straight-line distance** from the starting point **(0,0)** to **(50,-100)**.
   - o Using the distance formula:

$$Distance = \sqrt{(50 - 0)^2 + (-100 - 0)^2}$$
$$= \sqrt{2500 + 10000} = \sqrt{12500} = \sqrt{5 \times 25 \times 100}$$
$$= 50\sqrt{5}\, m \dots Ans.$$

Question

If South-east becomes east and North-west becomes West and all other directions are changed in the same manner. then what will be the direction for north?

1. South-west
2. North-west
3. South-east
4. North-east

Explanation:

Answer. 2. North-west

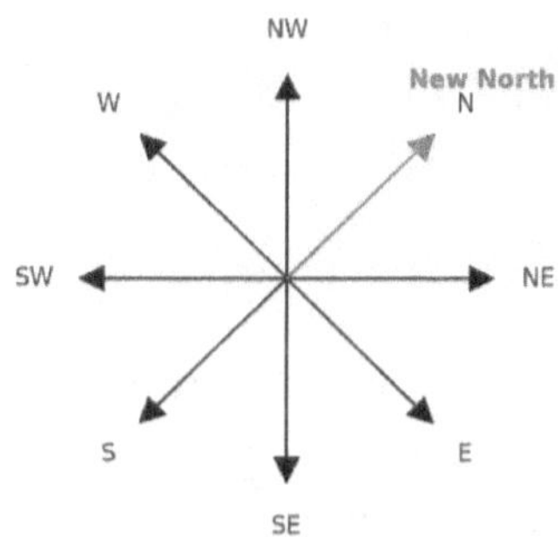

Question

A person starts from point A and walks 30 meters in the North direction and then 20 meters towards West and reaches a point B. Thereafter, he takes a southward turn and walks 10 meters to point C. After that, he turns eastward and covers 15 meters to reach point D. Finally, turning to his right he walks 20 meters, Find the distance from his starting point to the end point.

1. 4 meters
2. 5 meters
3. 8 meters
4. 10 meters

Explanation:

Answer. 2. 5 meters

Step 1: Movement Breakdown

1. **Walks 30 meters North**
    - Position: **(0, 30)**
2. **Walks 20 meters West**
    - Position: **(-20, 30)**
3. **Walks 10 meters South**
    - Position: **(-20, 20)**
4. **Walks 15 meters East**
    - Position: **(-5, 20)**
5. **Walks 20 meters South**
    - Position: **(-5, 0)**

Step 2: Distance Calculation

- The displacement is the **straight-line distance** from the starting point **(0,0) to (-5,0)**.
- Using the distance formula:

$$Distance = \sqrt{= (-5 - 0)^2 + (0 - 0)^2}$$
$$= \sqrt{25} = 5 \; meters \; ... Ans.$$

Question

A girl is standing outside her house facing north direction. Turing to her right she walks 50 metres. Then she turns to her left and walks 60 metres. She again turns to her right and walks 50 metres. Again, she turns to her right and walks 80 metres. Finally, she turns to her right again and walks 80 metres. In which direction is the girl now from the starting point.

1. North - West
2. South - East
3. North - East
4. South – West

Explanation:

Answer. 2. South - East

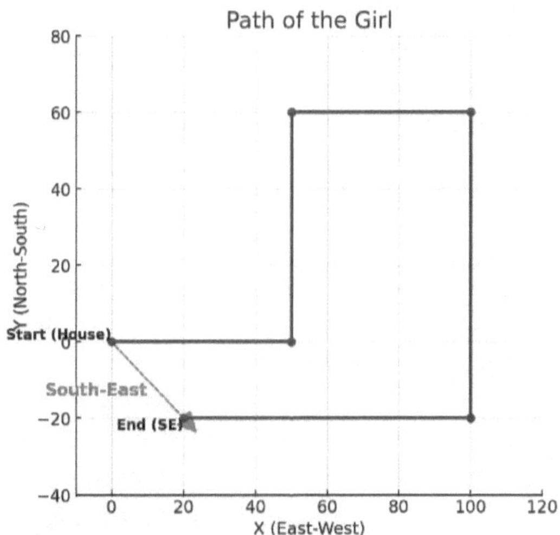

The diagram illustrates the girl's movement:

1. Starts at (0,0) - Her House
2. Moves 50m East
3. Turns Left (North) and Moves 60m
4. Turns Right (East) and Moves 50m
5. Turns Right (South) and Moves 80m
6. Turns Right (West) and Moves 80m
7. Final position is (20, -20), which is in the South-East direction from the starting point.

CHAPTER 6

DATA INTERPRETATION

Unit VI: Data Interpretations

Data interpretation is the process of analysing and making sense of data to extract useful information and draw conclusions. It involves interpreting and understanding data presented in various forms such as tables, graphs, charts, and figures. In data interpretations, you analyse the given data, identify patterns, relationships, and trends, and use this information to answer questions or solve problems.

Data interpretation often involves working with numerical data, percentages, ratios, averages, and other statistical measures. It requires critical thinking, mathematical skills, and the ability to analyse and draw logical conclusions from the data provided.

In various exams and real-life situations, data interpretation skills are essential to make informed decisions, solve problems, and understand complex information presented in a concise and meaningful way. It is commonly used in fields such as business, finance, economics, market research, and scientific research to analyse data and make data-driven decisions.

In data interpretation from table data, you can expect various types of questions that require you to analyse and interpret the information presented in the table. Here are some common question types that often appear in exams:

Comparison Questions

These questions ask you to compare values or characteristics between different categories or variables in the table. For example:

- o   Which category has the highest/lowest value?
- o   What is the difference between the values of two variables?

Question: In the table below, which city has the highest population?

City	Population
A	500,000
B	750,000
C	650,000
D	400,000

Answer: City B has the highest population (750,000). This can be determined by comparing the population values for each city and identifying the city with the highest value.

Calculation Questions:

Calculation Questions: These questions require you to perform calculations based on the data provided in the table. This may involve finding averages, percentages, ratios, or other mathematical operations. For example:

- o   Calculate the average value of a certain variable.
- o   Find the percentage change in a variable over a specific time period.

Question: What is the average rainfall in the given months based on the table below?

Month	Rainfall (mm)
January	50
February	40
March	60
April	70

Answer: The average rainfall can be calculated by summing up the rainfall values for all the months and dividing by the total number of months. In this case, the sum of the rainfall values is 50 + 40 + 60 + 70 = 220. Since there are 4 months, the average rainfall is 220/4 = 55 mm.

Trend Analysis Questions

Trend Analysis Questions: These questions focus on identifying trends or patterns in the data over time or across different categories. For example:

- o   Is there an increasing or decreasing trend in a particular variable?
- o   Which category shows the most significant change over time?

Question: Based on the table below, is there a decreasing trend in sales over the years?

Year	Sales (in thousands)
2018	500
2019	450
2020	400
2021	350

Answer: Yes, there has been a decreasing trend in sales over the years. This can be observed by looking at the sales values for each year, which decrease from 500 in 2018 to 350 in 2021.

Inference Questions

Inference Questions: These questions require you to make logical inferences or deductions based on the information in the table. You may need to combine data from different columns or draw conclusions based on given conditions. For example:

- o   Based on the data, what can be inferred about the relationship between the two variables?
- o   If certain conditions are met, what can be concluded about a particular category?

Question: Based on the table below, what can be inferred about the relationship between temperature and ice cream sales?

Temperature (°C)	Ice Cream Sales
30	100
35	120
40	140
45	160

Answer: It can be inferred that there is a positive relationship between temperature and ice cream sales. As the temperature increases, the sales of ice cream also increase. This can be seen by comparing the temperature values and the corresponding ice cream sales.

Application Questions:

Application Questions: These questions assess your ability to apply the information from the table to solve a problem or answer a specific question. You may need to analyze the data in combination with additional information or external knowledge. For example:

- o   Based on the data, recommend the best course of action or solution to a problem.
- o   Use the data to predict or estimate a future outcome.

Question: Based on the table below, recommend the best month for a hiking trip.

Month	Average Temperature (°C)	Rainfall (mm)
January	15	20
February	18	25
March	20	15
April	25	10

Answer: The best month for a hiking trip can be determined by considering both the average temperature and rainfall. In this case, March would be the recommended month as it has a relatively higher average temperature (20°C) and lower rainfall (15 mm) than the other months.

Percentage Calculation Questions

Percentage calculation questions in data interpretations require you to calculate percentages based on the information provided in the data.

Question: The table below shows the distribution of students in a school based on their favourite subjects. Calculate the percentage of students who prefer Mathematics.

Subject	Number of Students
Mathematics	120
Science	180
English	90
History	60
Total	450

Solution: To calculate the percentage of students who prefer Mathematics, you need to divide the number of students who prefer Mathematics by the total number of students and then multiply by 100.

Step 1: Calculate the percentage:

$$Percentage = \frac{Number\ of\ Students\ preferring\ Mathematics}{Total\ Number\ of\ Students} \times 100$$

Step 2: Substitute the values into the formula:

$$Percentage = \left(\frac{120}{450}\right) \times 100$$

Step 3: Simplify the calculation:
Percentage = 26.67%

Therefore, the percentage of students who prefer Mathematics is approximately 26.67%.

In this example, we used the given data from the table to calculate the percentage of students who prefer Mathematics. This type of question assesses your ability to analyse the data and perform basic percentage calculations. Remember to carefully read the question and use the appropriate formula to arrive at the correct answer.

Key Points or Words or Questions in Data Interpretations

Key words often found in data interpretation questions include:

- o **Total**: Indicates the sum or overall value of a certain category or variable.
- o **Increase/Decrease**: Indicates a change in value from one data point to another.

- o **Ratio:** Indicates the relationship or comparison between two quantities or variables.
- o **Average:** Indicates the mean or central value calculated from a set of data.
- o **Percentage**: Indicates the proportion or relative value of a quantity in relation to a whole, expressed as a percentage.
- o **Comparison**: Indicates the analysis or evaluation of different data points or categories.
- o **Difference:** Indicates the variance or contrast between two values or sets of data.
- o **Distribution:** Indicates the spread or allocation of data across different categories or variables.
- o **Trend:** Indicates the pattern or direction of change in data over a period of time.
- o **Calculation:** Indicates the need to perform mathematical operations such as addition, subtraction, multiplication, or division on data values.

GCD stands for Greatest Common Divisor, and it is a mathematical concept used to find the largest number that divides two or more integers without leaving a remainder. When it comes to data interpretation, the keyword "GCD" might appear in questions that involve finding common factors or ratios between different values or quantities.

Ratio: Ratio is a way to express the **relationship or comparison between two or more quantities or values.** It represents how many times one value is contained within another value. Ratios are typically written in the form of a **fraction or as a colon (:).**

In data interpretation, ratios can be found by comparing different quantities or values mentioned in the given data. To find a ratio in data interpretation, follow these steps:

1. Identify the quantities or values that need to be compared. These could be numbers, measurements, percentages, or any other relevant data.
2. Determine which quantities are being compared and which one is the reference or base value.
3. Express the comparison between the quantities by writing them in the form of a ratio. This can be done using a fraction or a colon (:).

4. Simplify the ratio, if possible, by dividing both sides by their greatest common divisor **(GCD) to** obtain the simplest form.
5. If required, interpret the ratio in the context of the given problem or question.

It's important to carefully read the data and understand the context to correctly identify the quantities to be compared and express the ratio accurately.

Let's look at an example to understand ratio better: Suppose you have a bag of coloured balls with 5 red balls, 3 blue balls, and 2 green balls. To find the ratio of red to blue balls, you would write it as:

$$Red : Blue$$

1. To simplify the ratio, you can divide both numbers by their greatest common divisor (GCD), which in this case is 1. So, the simplified ratio would be:

$$5 : 3$$

2. This means that for every 5 red balls, there are 3 blue balls.
3. **Ratios can also be expressed as fractions or decimals. In this case, the ratio 5:3 can be written as the fraction 5/3** or the decimal approximation 1.67.

It's important to note that ratios are a way to compare quantities, so they do not have units. They represent a relative relationship rather than an absolute value.

In data interpretation, ratios are often used to analyse and compare different data points or values, such as expenses, percentages, or proportions. By understanding how to interpret and calculate ratios, you can gain insights into the relationships between different variables or categories in the data.

Simple Ratio: This is the most basic type of ratio and compares two quantities directly. It is expressed as a ratio of two numbers, usually separated by a colon (:). For example, a simple ratio could be 3:5, which means for every 3 units of one quantity, there are 5 units of another quantity.

Compound Ratio: A compound ratio compares more than two quantities. It is formed by multiplying or dividing the individual ratios. For example, if you have a ratio of 2:3 and another ratio of 4:5, the compound ratio would be:

$$\left(\frac{2}{3}\right) \times \left(\frac{4}{5}\right) = \frac{8}{15}.$$

Rate Ratio: A rate ratio compares two quantities with different units of measurement, such as speed or price. It is expressed as a ratio of two rates. For example, if a car travels 60 miles in 2 hours, the rate ratio would be 60 miles/2 hours, or 30 miles per hour.

Proportion: A proportion is an equality of two ratios. It states that two ratios are equivalent. For example, if you have the ratios 2:3 and 4:6, you can set up a proportion as $\frac{2}{3} = \frac{4}{6}$. To solve the proportion, you cross-multiply and solve for the missing value.

Percentage: A percentage is a ratio that compares a part to a whole, expressed as a fraction out of 100. To find a percentage, you divide the part by the whole and multiply by 100. For example, if you scored 80 out of 100 in a test, the percentage would be:

$$\left(\frac{80}{100}\right) \times 100 = 80\%.$$

GCD: The quickest way to find the Greatest Common Divisor (GCD) of two numbers is by using the Euclidean algorithm. Here's a step-by-step process:

- Take the two numbers for which you want to find the GCD.
- Divide the larger number by the smaller number.
- Take the remainder from the division.
- Replace the larger number with the smaller number and the smaller number with the remainder.
- Repeat steps 2-4 until the remainder becomes zero.
- The last non-zero remainder you obtained is the GCD of the two numbers.

Here's an example to illustrate the process: Let's find the GCD of 54 and 24.

- Step 1: Divide 54 by 24. The remainder is 6.

- o   Step 2: Replace 54 with 24 and 24 with 6.
- o   Step 3: Divide 24 by 6. The remainder is 0.

Since the remainder is now zero, the GCD of 54 and 24 is 6.

Using the Euclidean algorithm allows you to quickly find the GCD without having to factorize the numbers completely. This method is efficient and commonly used to find the GCD of any two given numbers.

BASIC EXAMPLES OF DATA INTERPRETATIONS

These examples illustrate the different types of questions you may encounter in data interpretation from table data. Remember to carefully analyse the given information and apply appropriate calculations or reasoning to arrive at the correct answer.

TABLE 1

City	Population
A	500,000
B	750,000
C	650,000
D	400,000

Answer: City B has the highest population (750,000). This can be determined by comparing the population values for each city and identifying the city with the highest value.

Comparison Question:
Question: Which city has the highest population?
Answer: City B has the highest population, with 750,000 residents.

Calculation Question:
Question: What is the total population of all the cities?
Answer: The total population of all the cities can be calculated by adding up the population values:

$$500,000 + 750,000 + 650,000 + 400,000 = 2,300,000.$$

Trend Analysis Question:
Question: Is there a decreasing trend in population from city A to city D?

Answer: Yes, there is a decreasing trend in population from city A to city D. City B has a higher population than city C, which has a higher population than city D.

Inference Question:
Question: Can we infer that city B has a larger population than city A?
Answer: Yes, we can infer that city B has a larger population than city A based on the given data.

Application Questions: These questions assess your ability to apply the information from the table to solve a problem or answer a specific question. You may need to analyze the data in combination with additional information or external knowledge. For example:

- Based on the data, recommend the best course of action or solution to a problem.
- Use the data to predict or estimate a future outcome.

It's important to carefully read and understand the table, pay attention to the units and labels, and use logical reasoning to answer the questions accurately. Practising with various table data sets and different question types will help you improve your data interpretation skills.

TABLE 2

Month	Rainfall (mm)
January	50
February	40
March	60
April	70

Comparison Question:
Question: Which month had the highest rainfall?
Answer: April had the highest rainfall with 70 mm.

Calculation Question:
Question: What is the total rainfall for the four months?
Answer: The total rainfall for the four months is 50 + 40 + 60 + 70 = 220 mm.

Trend Analysis Question:
Question: Is there an increasing trend in rainfall over the months?
Answer: No, there is no clear increasing trend in rainfall over the months. The rainfall values vary, with March having the highest rainfall (60 mm).

Inference Question:
Question: Can we infer that the rainfall in February was less than in January?
Answer: Yes, we can infer that the rainfall in February (40 mm) was less than in January (50 mm).

Application Question:
Question: Based on the table, which month would be the best for outdoor activities?
Answer: The best month for outdoor activities would depend on personal preferences. However, if lower rainfall is preferred, April (70 mm) would be a better choice compared to March (60 mm).

These examples demonstrate different questions that can be generated based on the table. It's important to carefully analyze the data provided and draw logical conclusions to answer each question accurately.

Concept Check 22: Data Interpretations

TABLE 3

Year	Sales (in thousands)
2018	500
2019	450
2020	400
2021	350

Comparison Question:
Question 1: Which year had the highest sales?

Calculation Question:
Question 2: What is the total sales for the years 2018 to 2021?

Trend Analysis Question:
Question 3: Is there a decreasing trend in sales over the years?

Application Question:
Question 4: If the trend continues, what are the projected sales for the year 2022?

Percentage Calculation Question:
Question 5: Calculate the percentage decrease in sales from 2018 to 2021.

TABLE 4

Temperature (°C)	Ice Cream Sales
30	100
35	120
40	140
45	160

Comparison Question:
Question 6: Which temperature has the highest ice cream sales?

Calculation Question:
Question 7: What is the average ice cream sales for the given temperatures?

Trend Analysis Question:
Question 8: Is there a trend of increasing ice cream sales with higher temperatures?

Application Question:
Question 9: If the temperature is 38°C, what can we predict about the ice cream sales?

Percentage Calculation Question:
Question 10: By what percentage does the ice cream sales increase when the temperature increases from 35°C to 45°C?

TABLE 5

Month	Average Temperature (°C)	Rainfall (mm)
January	15	20
February	18	25
March	20	15

April	25	10

Comparison Question:
Question 11: Which month had the highest average temperature?

Calculation Question:
Question 12: What is the total rainfall for the months of January, February, and March?

Trend Analysis Question:
Question 13: Is there a trend of increasing average temperature over the months?

Application Question:
Question 14: Based on the average temperature and rainfall, which month is most suitable for outdoor activities?

Percentage Calculation Question:
Question 15: What is the percentage increase in average temperature from January to April?

TABLE 6

Subject	Number of Students
Mathematics	120
Science	180
English	90
History	60
Total	450

Question 16: What is the percentage of students studying each subject?
Question 17: Which subject has the highest number of students?
Question 18: Which subject has the lowest percentage of students?
Question 19: What is the total number of students studying Mathematics and English?
Question 20: What is the percentage of students studying either Mathematics or Science?
Question 21: If 20% of the students studying Science also study Mathematics, how many students study both subjects?

UGC NET PYQ Questions and Explanations on Data Interpretations

Data Interpretation 1

Consider the following table that shows the expenditures of a company (in lakh rupees) per annum over the given years. Answer the questions based on the data contained in the table:

Year	Salary	Transport	Bonus	Interest on Loans	Taxes
2008	150	90	2.00	20.0	80
2009	180	100	2.50	30.5	95
2010	200	110	2.75	35.5	105
2011	240	115	3.00	40.0	85
2012	250	125	3.25	42.5	100

Question 1

*The approximate **ratio** between the **total expenditure on taxes** for all the years and the **total expenditure on transport** for all the years is*

1. 31:40
2. 25:36
3. 27:30
4. 31:36

Explanations
Answer: 4. 31:36

To find the total expenditure on taxes and transport for all the years, we sum up the values for each category.

$$Total\ expenditure\ on\ taxes = 80 + 95 + 105 + 85 + 100 = 465$$
$$Total\ expenditure\ on\ transport = 90 + 100 + 110 + 115 + 125 = 540$$

$$Ratio = \frac{Total\ expenditure\ on\ taxes}{Total\ expenditure\ on\ transport} = \frac{465}{540}$$
$$= \frac{31}{36}\ (approximately)$$

Therefore, the approximate ratio between the total expenditure on taxes for all the years and the total expenditure on transport for all the years is 31:36.

Question 2

*The total **amount of bonus** paid by the company during the given period is approximately what per cent of the **total amount of salary** paid during this period?*

1. 0.9%
2. 1.3%
3. 1.6%
4. 2.0%

Explanations
Answer: 2. 1.3%

To find the total amount of bonus paid by the company during the given period as a percentage of the total amount of salary paid, we need to calculate these two values and then determine the percentage.

Total amount of bonus paid:

Year	Bonus Amount
2008	2.00 lakh rupees
2009	2.50 lakh rupees
2010	2.75 lakh rupees
2011	3.00 lakh rupees
2012	3.25 lakh rupees
Total	**13.50**

$$\text{Total amount of bonus} = 2.00 + 2.50 + 2.75 + 3.00 + 3.25$$
$$= \mathbf{13.50\ lakh\ rupees}$$

Total amount of salary paid:

Year	Salary Amount (lakh rupees)
2008	150
2009	180
2010	200
2011	240

2012	250
Total	**1020 Lakh rupees**

$$Total\ amount\ of\ salary = 150 + 180 + 200 + 240 + 250$$
$$= 1020\ lakh\ rupees$$

Now, let's calculate the percentage:

$$Percentage = \frac{Total\ amount\ of\ bonus}{Total\ amount\ of\ salary} \times 100$$
$$= \frac{13.50}{1020} \times 100$$

Simplifying this calculation, we get approximately 1.32%.

Therefore, the total amount of bonus paid by the company during the given period is approximately 1.3% of the total amount of salary paid.

Question 3

Total expenditure of all the items in 2008 was approximately what per cent of the total expenditure in 2012?

1. 66%
2. 69%
3. 72%
4. 75%

Explanations:

Answer: 1. 66%

We need to determine the total expenditure in **2008** as a percentage of the total expenditure in **2012**.

$$Total\ Expenditure\ in\ 2008 = Salary + Transport + Bonus + Interest\ on\ Loans + Taxes$$

$$Total\ Expenditure\ in\ 2008 = 150 + 90 + 2.00 + 20.0 + 80 = \mathbf{342}$$
$$Total\ Expenditure\ in\ 2012 = 250 + 125 + 3.25 + 42.5 + 100 = \mathbf{520.75}$$

Calculate Percentage:

$$Percentage = \left(\frac{Total\ Expenditure\ in\ 2008}{Total\ Expenditure\ in\ 2012}\right) \times 100$$

$$= \frac{342}{520.75} \times 100$$
$$= 65.67$$

Question 4

*The approximate **ratio** between the total expenditure of the company in the year **2008,** and the total expenditure of the company in the year **2009** is.*

1. 57:75
2. 52:68
3. 57:68
4. 68:57

Explanations:
Answer: 3. 57:68

To find the approximate ratio between the total expenditure of the company in the year 2008 and the total expenditure in the year 2009, we can use the values provided in the table.

Total expenditure in 2008: Salary + Transport + Bonus + Interest on Loans + Taxes
Total expenditure in 2009: Salary + Transport + Bonus + Interest on Loans + Taxes

The approximate ratio can be calculated as:
Total expenditure in 2008: Total expenditure in 2009
Substituting the values from the table:
(150 + 90 + 2.00 + 20.0 + 80): (180 + 100 + 2.50 + 30.5 + 95)
342.00: 408.00
57: 68

Therefore, the approximate ratio between the total expenditure of the company in the year 2008 and the total expenditure in the year 2009 is 57:68.

Question 5

*What is the average amount of **interest per year** that the company had to pay (in Rupees) during this period?*

1. 30.5 Lakh
2. 32.7 Lakh
3. 33.7 Lakh

4. 35.5 Lakh

Explanations:
Answer: 3. 33.7 Lakh

To find the average amount of interest per year, we need to calculate the total interest paid over the given period and then divide it by the number of years.

$$Total\ interest\ paid = Sum\ of\ interest\ for\ each\ year$$
$$Total\ interest\ paid = 20.0 + 30.5 + 35.5 + 40.0 + 42.5$$
$$Total\ interest\ paid = 168.5\ lakh\ rupees$$

$$Number\ of\ years = 5$$
$$Average\ amount\ of\ interest\ per\ year = \frac{Total\ interest\ paid}{Number\ of\ years}$$
$$Average\ amount\ of\ interest\ per\ year = \frac{168.5\ lakh}{5}$$
$$Average\ amount\ of\ interest\ per\ year = 33.7\ lakh$$

*Therefore, the average amount of interest per year that the company had to pay during this period is **33.7 lakh rupees.***

Data Interpretation 2

The following table shows the percentage of marks obtained by 6 students in 4 different subjects in an examination. Study the table and answer the questions that follow:

Students	Subject (Max Marks)			
	Physics (100)	Chemistry (100)	Maths (100)	English (100)
Radhika	90	85	95	98
Karan	92	90	90	93
Neeraj	86	82	75	77
Priyanka	63	48	55	75
Sujata	77	62	80	85
Preeti	50	52	40	59

Question 1

What are the average marks obtained by the students with four highest scores in Physics?

1. 86.5
2. 88.5
3. 78
4. 86.25

Explanations
Answer: 4. 86.25
Step 1: Identify the Four Highest Scores in Physics
The top four students in **Physics** are:

1. **Karan (92)**
2. **Radhika (90)**
3. **Neeraj (86)**
4. **Sujata (77)**

Total marks obtained by these four students:

$$92 + 90 + 86 + 77 = 345$$
$$Number\ of\ Students\ = 4$$
$$Average\ Marks = \frac{345}{4} = 86.25$$

Question 2

Which of the following received highest aggregate marks in all the four subjects?

1. Radhika
2. Karan
3. Neeraj
4. Sujata

Explanations
Answer: 1. Radhika

Student with Highest Aggregate Marks
Step 1: Calculate Total Marks for Each Student
Summing up the marks across **all four subjects**:

Student	Physics (100)	Chemistry (100)	Maths (100)	English (100)	Total Marks
Radhika	90	85	95	98	**368**
Karan	92	90	90	93	**365**
Neeraj	86	82	75	77	**320**
Sujata	77	62	80	85	**304**
Priyanka	63	48	55	75	241
Preeti	50	52	40	59	201

Step 2: Identify the Student with the Highest Aggregate Marks
Radhika has the highest total marks: **368**.

Question 3

Which of the following pair of students has the smallest ratio between Physics marks scored by them?

1. Radhika: Karan
2. Neeraj: Karan
3. Sujata: Neeraj
4. Priyanka: Sujata

Explanations
Answer: 4. Priyanka: Sujata

$$We\ compute\ the\ \mathbf{ratio}\ \frac{smaller\ value}{larger\ value}\ for\ each\ pair:$$

$$Radhika{:}Karan = \frac{90}{92} = 0.978$$

$$Neeraj{:}Karan = \frac{86}{92} = 0.932$$

$$Sujata{:}Neeraj = \frac{77}{86} = 0.895$$

$$Priyanka{:}Sujata = \frac{63}{77} = 0.818\ ...\ Ans.$$

Question 4

According to the marks obtained. what is the percentage of Neeraj in best three subjects?

1. 80%
2. 81.66%
3. 81.33%
4. 80.66%

Explanations
Answer: 2. 81.66%

Percentage of Neeraj in Best Three Subjects
Step 1: Extract Neeraj's Marks

From the table, Neeraj's marks in four subjects:

Subject	Marks
Physics	86
Chemistry	82
Maths	75
English	77

Step 2: Select the Best Three Subjects
Neeraj's top three highest marks are:
1. **Physics** → 86
2. **Chemistry** → 82
3. **English** → 77

Total marks in the best three subjects:

$$86 + 82 + 77 = 245$$

Step 3: Calculate the Percentage

Since each subject is out of **100**, the total possible marks for the best three subjects are:

$$3 \times 100 = 300$$

$$Percentage = \left(\frac{245}{300}\right) \times 100 = 81.66\% \ldots Ans.$$

Question 5

What is the overall percentage of Karan?

1. 92.25%
2. 90.75%
3. 91.5%
4. 91.25%

Explanations

Answer: 4. 91.25%

Overall Percentage of Karan

Step 1: Extract Karan's Marks

From the table, Karan's marks in four subjects:

Subject	Marks
Physics	92
Chemistry	90
Maths	90
English	93

Step 2: Calculate Total Marks

$$92 + 90 + 90 + 93 = 365$$

Total possible marks:

$$4 \times 100 = 400$$

$$Percentage = \left(\frac{365}{400}\right) \times 100 = 91.25\% \ldots Ans.$$

Data Interpretation 3

The following table shows the percent (%) profit earned by two companies A and B over the six years from 2018 to 2023. Based on the data in the table, answer the questions that follow.

Year-wise Profit details of Two Companies		
Year	Percent (%) Profit Earned by Company	
	A	B
2018	40%	25%
2019	25%	30%
2020	30%	50%
2021	60%	45%
2022	45%	30%
2023	50%	40%

Note:

$$Profit\% = \frac{Income - Expenditure}{Expenditure} \times 100$$

Question 1

For Company B, if the income in the year 2018 was equal to the expenditure in the year 2020, then what was the ratio of income of B in 2018 to that in 2020

1. 2:3
2. 3:2
3. 2:5
4. 5:2

Explanations
Answer: 1. 2:3
For Company B in 2018:
- Profit% = **25%**
- Profit fraction $= \frac{1}{4}$
- If **Expenditure = 4 units**, then
  $Income = 4 + 1 = 5 (Income : Expenditure = 5:4)$

For Company B in 2020:
- Profit% = **50%**
- Profit fraction $= \frac{1}{2}$
- If **Expenditure = 2 units**, then:
  $Income = 2 + 1 = 3 (Income : Expenditure = 3:2)$

Question 2

In the year 2022, if the income of Company B was Rs 52 Crore and the expenditures of both the Companies A and B were same, then what was the average of income of both the companies A and B?

1. 22 Crore
2. 33 Crore
3. 55 Crore
4. 44 Crore

Explanations

Answer: 3. 55 Crore

From the table, the **profit percentage of Company B in 2022** is **30%**.
Let the **common expenditure** of both companies be **E**.

$$30 = \frac{52 - E}{E} \times 100$$

$$\frac{52 - E}{E} = 0.30$$

$$52 - E = 0.30E$$

$$52 = 1.30E$$

$$E = \frac{52}{1.30} = 40 \; Crore$$

From the table, the **profit percentage of Company A in 2022** is **45%**.

$$45 = \frac{Income \; of \; A - 40}{40} \times 100$$

$$\frac{Income \; of \; A - 40}{40} = 0.45$$

$$Income \; of \; A - 40 = 0.45 \times 40$$

$$Income \; of \; A - 40 = 18$$

$$Income \; of \; A = 58 \; Crore$$

Step 3: Calculate the Average Income of Companies A and B

$$Average \; Income = \frac{(Income \; of \; A) + (Income \; of \; B)}{2}$$

$$= \frac{58 + 52}{2} = \frac{110}{2} = 55 \; ... Ans.$$

Question 3

If in the year 2021, the expenditure of Company A was equal to the expenditure of Company B. then what was the ratio of their respective incomes?

1. 3:2
2. 32:29
3. 2:5
4. 7:5

Explanations

Answer: 2. 32:29

Let the **common expenditure** of both companies in 2021 be **E**.

From the table, the **profit percentages** for 2021 are:
- Company A = 60%
- Company B = 45%

For **Company A**:

$$Income\ of\ A = E \times \left(1 + \left(\frac{60}{100}\right)\right) = E \times 1.6 = 1.6E$$

For **Company B**:

$$Income\ of\ B = E \times \left(1 + \frac{45}{100}\right) = E \times 1.45 = 1.45E$$

Step 3: Find the Ratio

$$Ratio\ of\ Income\ of\ A\ to\ B = \frac{1.6E}{1.45E} = \frac{1.6}{1.45}$$

Multiplying numerator and denominator by **100** to simplify:

$$\frac{160}{145} = \frac{32}{29} \dots Ans.$$

Question 4

In the year 2023, if the income of Company B was Rs 70 Crores, then what was the expenditure of the Company B in that year?

1. 20 Crore
2. 30 Crore
3. 40 Crore
4. 50 Crore

Explanations

Answer: 4. 50 Crore

We are given that in the year **2023**, the **income of Company B** was **Rs 70 Crore**, and we need to determine its **expenditure**.

Step 1: Use the Profit Percentage Formula
From the table, the **profit percentage of Company B in 2023** is **40%**.
We use the formula:

$$Profit\% = \frac{Income - Expenditure}{Expenditure} \times 100$$

Let **E** be the expenditure of **Company B**.

$$40 = \frac{70 - E}{E} \times 100$$

$$\frac{70 - E}{E} = 0.40$$

$$70 - E = 0.40E$$

$$E = \frac{70}{1.40} = 50 \; Crore \; ... Ans.$$

Question 5

If the ratio of expenditures of Company A in 2019 and 2023 is 4: 3, then the income of Company A in 2019 is how much % more than the income of Company A in 2023.

1. $\frac{70}{9}\%$

2. $\frac{80}{9}\%$

3. $\frac{40}{9}\%$

4. $\frac{100}{9}\%$

Explanations

Answer: 4. $\frac{100}{9}\%$

*We are given that the **ratio of expenditures of Company A in 2019 and 2023 is 4:3**, and we need to find **how much % more the income of Company A in 2019 is compared to its income in 2023**.*

Step 1: Define Variables

Let the **expenditure of Company A in 2019** be **4E**, and the **expenditure of Company A in 2023** be **3E**.

From the table, the **profit percentages** are:

- o Company A in 2019 = 25%
- o Company A in 2023 = 50%

Step 2: Calculate Incomes

For **2019**:

$$Income\ of\ A\ in\ 2019 = 4E \times \left(1 + \frac{25}{100}\right) = 4E \times 1.25 = 5E$$

For **2023**:

$$Income\ of\ A\ in\ 2023 = 3E \times \left(1 + \frac{50}{100}\right) = 3E \times 1.5 = 4.5E$$

Step 3: Find Percentage Increase

The percentage by which the **income of Company A in 2019** is more than the **income in 2023** is given by:

$$\left(\frac{Income\ in\ 2019 - Income\ in\ 2023}{Income\ in\ 2023}\right) \times 100$$

$$= \frac{5E - 4.5E}{4.5E} \times 100$$

$$= \frac{0.5E}{4.5E} \times 100$$

$$= \frac{0.5}{4.5} \times 100$$

$$= \frac{50}{450} \times 100$$

$$= \frac{100}{9}\ \% \dots Ans.$$

Data Interpretation 4

The following table shows the number of HB-Pencils sold by five different stores (A-E) along with the ratio of number of HB-Pencils to 6B-Pencils sold by these stores. Based on the data in the table, answer the questions that follow:

Store wise sale Details of Pencils		
Store	Number of HB-Pencil Sold	**Ratio**
		HB Pencils sold: 6B Pencils Sold
A	216	9:5
B	480	6:5
C	400	4:1
D	300	3:1
E	240	3:2

Question 1

What is the average number of 6B-Pencils sold by stores A and E together?

1. 140
2. 130
3. 160
4. 100

Explanations

Answer: 1. 140

Using the given ratio formula:

$$Number\ of\ 6B\ Pencils = \frac{HB\ Pencils\ Sold \times Second\ Part\ of\ the\ Ratio}{First\ Part\ of\ the\ Ratio}$$

For Store A:

- $HB Pencils\ Sold = 216$
- $Ratio\ (HB : 6B) = 9:5$

$$6B\ Pencils\ Sold = \frac{216 \times 5}{9} = \frac{1080}{9} = 120$$

For Store E:

- $HB\ Pencils\ Sold = 240$
- $Ratio\ (HB : 6B) = 3:2$

$$6B\ Pencils\ Sold = \frac{240 \times 2}{3} = \frac{480}{3} = 160$$

Find the Average

$$Average = \frac{6B\ Pencils\ Sold\ by\ A + 6B\ Pencils\ Sold\ by\ E}{2}$$

$$= \frac{120 + 160}{2} = \frac{280}{2} = 140 \ ...\ Ans.$$

Question 2

If the selling price of one HB-Pencil is Rs 5 and that of one 6B-Pencil is Rs 8, then what is the total revenue generated by store C?

1. Rs 3200
2. Rs 4000
3. Rs 2400
4. Rs 2800

Explanations

Answer: 4. Rs 2800

Step 1: Given Data
- HB-Pencils sold by Store C = 400
- Ratio of HB to 6B Pencils = 4:1
- Selling price of one HB-Pencil = Rs 5
- Selling price of one 6B-Pencil = Rs 8

Step 2: Calculate the Number of 6B-Pencils Sold

Using the ratio **4:1**, we calculate the number of 6B-Pencils:

$$6B\ Pencils\ Sold = \frac{400 \times 1}{4} = 100$$

Step 3: Calculate Revenue from HB-Pencils

$$Revenue\ from\ HB\ Pencils = 400 \times 5 = 2000$$

Step 4: Calculate Revenue from 6B-Pencils

$$Revenue\ from\ 6B\ Pencils = 100 \times 8 = 800$$

Step 5: Calculate Total Revenue

$$Total\ Revenue = 2000 + 800 = 2800$$

Question 3

The number of 6B pencils sold by store E is _ % less than the number of 6B pencils sold by store B.

1. 20
2. 40

3. 50
4. 60

Explanations

Answer: 4. 60

Using the given ratio formula:

$$Number\ of\ 6B\ Pencils = \frac{HB\ Pencils\ Sold \times Second\ Part\ of\ the\ Ratio}{First\ Part\ of\ the\ Ratio}$$

For Store B:

- o $HB\ Pencils\ Sold\ =\ 480$
- o $Ratio\ (HB:6B)\ =\ 6:5$

$$6B\ Pencils\ Sold = \frac{480 \times 5}{6} = \frac{2400}{6} = 400$$

For Store E:

$$HB - Pencils\ Sold\ =\ 240$$
$$Ratio\ (HB:6B)\ =\ 3:2$$
$$6B\ Pencils\ Sold = \frac{240 \times 2}{3} = \frac{480}{3} = 160$$

Calculate Percentage Decrease

$$Percentage\ Decrease = \frac{Difference}{Original\ Value} \times 100$$
$$= \frac{400 - 160}{400} \times 100$$
$$= \frac{240}{400} \times 100 = 60\% \ldots Ans.$$

Question 4

If out of the number of 6B pencils sold by B and C each, 40% and 20% defective 6B pencils are returned by the customers respectively, then what is the total number of original pencils sold by both stores B and C?

1. 800
2. 1080
3. 1200
4. 1280

Explanations

Answer: *3.* 1200

We need to find the **total number of original (non-defective) pencils sold** by both **Store B and Store C**, considering the **defective returns**.

Step 1: Calculate the Number of 6B-Pencils Sold by Each Store

Using the given ratio formula:

$$Number\ of\ 6B\ Pencils = \frac{HB\ Pencils\ Sold \times Second\ Part\ of\ the\ Ratio}{First\ Part\ of\ the\ Ratio}$$

For Store B:
- $HB - Pencils\ Sold = 480$
- $Ratio\ (HB : 6B) = 6:5$

$$6B\ Pencils\ Sold = \frac{480 \times 5}{6} = \frac{2400}{6} = 400$$

For Store C:
- $HB\ Pencils\ Sold = 400$
- $Ratio\ (HB : 6B) = 4:1$

$$6B\ Pencils\ Sold = \frac{400 \times 1}{4} = \frac{400}{4} = 100$$

Step 2: Find the Number of Defective 6B-Pencils Returned
- **Store B: 40%** of **400** are defective.

$$Defective\ 6B\ Pencils = \frac{40}{100} \times 400 = 160$$

Non-defective 6B-Pencils from Store B = 400 - 160 = 240
- **Store C: 20%** of **100** are defective.

$$Defective\ 6B\ Pencils = \frac{20}{100} \times 100 = 20$$

$$Non - defective\ 6B\ Pencils\ from\ Store\ C = 100 - 20 = 80$$

Step 3: Find the Total Number of Original (Non-Defective) Pencils Sold

$Total\ Original\ Pencils$
$$= HB\ Pencils\ Sold\ by\ B + Non\ defective\ 6B\ Pencils\ from\ B$$
$$+ HB\ Pencils\ Sold\ by\ C + Non\ defective\ 6B\ Pencils\ from\ C$$

$$= 480 + 240 + 400 + 80 = \mathbf{1200} \dots \boldsymbol{Ans.}$$

Question 5

What is the ratio between the total number of 6B pencils sold by both stores C and D and the number of 6B pencils sold by store A?

1. 3:5
2. 5:3
3. 5:4
4. 3:2

Explanations
Answer: 2. 5:3
For Store C:
- $HB\ Pencils\ Sold\ =\ 400$
- $Ratio\ (HB\ :\ 6B)\ =\ 4:1$

$$6B\ Pencils\ Sold = \frac{400 \times 1}{4} = 100$$

For Store D:

- $HB\ Pencils\ Sold\ =\ 300$
- $Ratio\ (HB\ :\ 6B) =\ 3:1$

$$6B - Pencils\ Sold = \frac{300 \times 1}{3} = 100$$

For Store A:
- $HB\ Pencils\ Sold\ =\ 216$
- $Ratio\ (HB\ :\ 6B) =\ 9:5$

$$6B\ Pencils\ Sold = \frac{216 \times 5}{9} = \frac{1080}{9} = 120$$

Calculate the Ratio
- $Total\ 6B\ Pencils\ Sold\ by\ C\ and\ D\ =\ 100\ +\ 100\ =\ 200$
- $6B\ Pencils\ Sold\ by\ A\ =\ 120$

$$Required\ Ratio = 200:120$$
$$= \frac{200}{40} : \frac{120}{40} = 5:3 \ldots Ans.$$

Data Interpretation 5

The following table shows the percentage distribution of employees working in six different departments of a company, namely. IT, Accounts, HR, Marketing, Production, and Sales in a given year. Number of employees working in Marketing department is 560. Based on the data in the table, answer the questions that follow:

Department-wise details of Employees in a Company	
Department	**Percentage Distribution of Employees**
IT	8%
Accounts	18%
HR	12%
Marketing	14%
Production	32%
Sales	16%

Understanding the Table:

- o The table gives the **percentage distribution** of employees across six departments.
- o The **number of employees in the Marketing department is given as 560**.
- o Using this, we can calculate the **total number of employees in the company**:

$$Total\ Employees = \frac{Employees\ in\ Marketing \times 100}{Percentage\ of\ Marketing\ Department}$$

$$= \frac{560 \times 100}{14} = \frac{56000}{14} = 4000$$

So, the **total number of employees in the company is 4000**.

Question 1

If the ratio of the number of male and female employees in Accounts department is 5: 4 and 60% of the employees in HR department are females, then what is the total number of male employees in Accounts and HR departments together?

1. 592
2. 594
3. 596
4. 598

Explanations
Answer: 1. 592

From our previous calculation, the **total number of employees in the company** is **4000**.

Using the percentage distribution:
For Accounts Department:

$$Employees\ in\ Accounts = \frac{18}{100} \times 4000 = 720$$

Given the **male-to-female ratio** is **5:4**, the total parts = **5 + 4 = 9**.

Male employees in Accounts:

$$\frac{5}{9} \times 720 = \frac{3600}{9} = 400$$

For HR Department:

$$Employees\ in\ HR = \frac{12}{100} \times 4000 = 480$$

It is given that **60% of HR employees are females**, so:

Female employees in HR:

$$\frac{60}{100} \times 480 = 288$$

Male employees in HR:

$$480 - 288 = 192$$

Find the Total Number of Male Employees in Accounts & HR

$$Total\ Male\ Employees = Male\ in\ Accounts + Male\ in\ HR$$
$$= 400 + 192 = 592 \dots Ans.$$

Question 2

What is the average of the total number of employees in Accounts, HR, marketing, and Production departments together?

1. 760
2. 780
3. 800

4. 820

Explanations
Answer: 1. 760
For Accounts Department:

$$Employees\ in\ Accounts = \frac{18}{100} \times 4000 = 720$$

For HR Department:

$$Employees\ in\ HR = \frac{12}{100} \times 4000 = 480$$

For Marketing Department:

$$Employees\ in\ Marketing = \frac{14}{100} \times 4000 = 560$$

For Production Department:

$$Employees\ in\ Production = \frac{32}{100} \times 4000 = 1280$$

Calculate the Average

$$Total\ Employees\ in\ these\ Departments = 720 + 480 + 560 + 1280$$
$$= 3040$$

$$Average = \frac{3040}{4} = 760 \ldots Ans.$$

Question 3

If the number of employees in IT and marketing department increases by 60%
and 20%, respectively in the next year, then what will be the ratio of number
of employees in IT and Marketing departments in the next year?

1. 13:19
2. 3:4
3. 16:21
4. 2:3

Explanations
Answer: 3. 16:21

We know the **total number of employees in the company** is **4000**.
For IT Department:

$$Employees\ in\ IT = \frac{8}{100} \times 4000 = 320$$

For Marketing Department:

$$Employees\ in\ Marketing = \frac{14}{100} \times 4000 = 560$$

Apply the Percentage Increase

IT Department Increase: **60%**

$$New\ IT\ Employees = 320 + \left(\frac{60}{100} \times 320\right) = 320 + 192 = 512$$

Marketing Department Increase: **20%**

$$New\ Marketing\ Employees = 560 + \left(\frac{20}{100} \times 560\right) = 560 + 112 = 672$$

Find the Ratio

$$Required\ Ratio = 512 : 672$$

Simplifying by dividing both terms by **16**:

$$= \frac{512}{16} : \frac{672}{16} = 32 : 42$$

Further simplifying by dividing by **2**:

$$= \mathbf{16 : 21} \dots Ans.$$

Question 4

The number of employees in HR department is ___% less than the number of employees in Production department.

1. 64.5
2. 61.5
3. 63.5
4. 62.5

Explanations

Answer: 4. 62.5

We know the **total number of employees in the company is 4000.**

- **HR Department Employees**:

$$\frac{12}{100} \times 4000 = 480$$

- **Production Department Employees**:

$$\frac{32}{100} \times 4000 = 1280$$

Step 2: Calculate the Percentage Difference

To find how much **less** the HR department is compared to the Production department:

$$Percentage\ Less = \frac{Difference}{Production\ Employees} \times 100$$

$$= \frac{1280 - 480}{1280} \times 100$$

$$= \frac{800}{1280} \times 100 = 62.5\% \ ... Ans.$$

Question 5

If the number of employees in Sales department increases by 25% in the next year, then what will be the number of employees in that department in the next year?

1. 700
2. 800
3. 900
4. 920

Explanations
Answer: 2. 800

Find the Current Number of Employees in Sales
We know the **total number of employees in the company** is **4000**.
From the table, the **percentage of employees in Sales** is **16%**.

$$Employees\ in\ Sales = \frac{16}{100} \times 4000 = \textbf{640}$$

Step 2: Apply the 25% Increase
The **new number of employees** after a **25% increase**:

$$Increased\ Employees = 640 + \left(\frac{25}{100} \times 640\right)$$

$$= 640 + \frac{160}{1}$$

$$The\ number\ of\ employees\ in\ the\ next\ year\ = 640 + 160 = \textbf{800} \ ... \textbf{\textit{Ans.}}$$

Data Interpretation 6

The following table shows the percentage (%) of population below poverty line in six Indian States A-F for the financial year 2023-24, along with the ratio of males (M) to females (F) below poverty line and above poverty line. Based on the data in the table, answer the questions that follow.

State	Percentage of Population below Poverty Line	Ratio of male and female	
		Below Poverty Line (M:F)	Above Poverty Line (M:F)
A	16%	5:3	4:3
B	10%	3:7	5:4
C	22%	6:5	7:6
D	28%	3:4	5:7
E	12%	1:3	6:5
F	20%	2:3	3:5

(Table title: State-wise Poverty Details of Populations)

Question 1

If the population of males above poverty line in State D is 27 lakh, then what is the total population of State D?

1. 60 lakh
2. 70 lakh
3. 80 lakh
4. 90 lakh

Explanations
Answer: 4. 90 lakh

From the table:
- o   Percentage of population below poverty line in State D = 28%
- o   Ratio of males to females above poverty line (M:F) in State D = 5:7
- o   Number of males above poverty line = 27 lakh

Let the total **population above the poverty line** be **X**.
Since the ratio of **males to females above the poverty line** is **5:7**, the total above-poverty population is divided into **5 + 7 = 12 parts**.

Calculate Total Population Above Poverty Line

$$\frac{5}{12} \times X = 27 \; lakh$$

$$X = \frac{27 \times 12}{5}$$

$$X = \frac{324}{5} = 64.8 \; lakh$$

So, the **total number of people above the poverty line = 64.8 lakh**.

Calculate Total Population of State D
- o   Since **28% of the population is below the poverty line**, this means **72% of the population is above the poverty line**.
- o   Let the total population of State D be **P**.

$$72\% \; of \; P = 64.8 \; lakh$$

$$\frac{72}{100} \times P = 64.8$$

$$P = \frac{64.8 \times 100}{72}$$

$$P = \frac{6480}{72} = 90 \; lakh \; ... Ans.$$

Question 2

If the total population of the State A is 70 lakhs, then what is the difference between the population of males below poverty line and females above poverty line in the same state?

1. 18.2 lakh
2. 16.4 lakh
3. 20.6 lakh
4. 19.8 lakh

Explanations
Answer: 1. 18.2 lakh

Step 1: Find the Population Below and Above the Poverty Line
From the table:
- o   Percentage of population below the poverty line in State A = 16%
- o   Percentage of population above the poverty line in State A = 100% - 16% = 84%

Population Below Poverty Line:

$$Population \; Below \; Poverty \; Line = \frac{16}{100} \times 70 = 11.2 \; lakh$$

Population Above Poverty Line:

$$Population\ Above\ Poverty\ Line = \frac{84}{100} \times 70 = 58.8\ lakh$$

Step 2: Find the Number of Males Below Poverty Line
- o The **male-to-female ratio below the poverty line** in State A is **5:3**.
- o Total parts = **5 + 3 = 8**.
- o **Males below poverty line**:

$$Males\ Below\ Poverty\ Line = \frac{5 \times 11.2}{8} = \frac{56}{8} = 7\ lakh$$

Step 3: Find the Number of Females Above Poverty Line
- o The **male-to-female ratio above the poverty line** in State A is **4:3**.
- o Total parts = **4 + 3 = 7**.
- o **Females above poverty line**:

$$Females\ Above\ Poverty\ Line = \frac{3}{7} \times 58.8$$

$$= \frac{3 \times 58.8}{7} = \frac{176.4}{7} = 25.2\ lakh$$

Find the Difference

$$Difference = 25.2 - 7 = 18.2\ lakh \ldots Ans.$$

Question 3

If the population of the State C is 90 lakh, then what is the population of males above poverty line in the same state?

1. 42.6 lakh
2. 35.9 lakh
3. 37.8 lakh
4. 34.5 lakh

Explanations
Answer: 3. 37.8 lakh

Step 1: Find the Population Below and Above the Poverty Line
From the table:
- o Percentage of population below the poverty line in State C = 22%

- o Percentage of population above the poverty line = 100% - 22% = 78%

Population Below Poverty Line:

$$Population\ Below\ Poverty\ Line = \frac{22}{100} \times 90 = 19.8\ lakh$$

Population Above Poverty Line:

$$Population\ Above\ Poverty\ Line = \frac{78}{100} \times 90 = 70.2\ lakh$$

Step 2: Find the Number of Males Above Poverty Line
- o The **male-to-female ratio above the poverty line** in State C is **7:6.**
- o Total parts = **7 + 6 = 13.**
- o **Males above the poverty line:**

$$Males\ Above\ Poverty\ Line = \frac{7}{13} \times 70.2$$

$$= \frac{7 \times 70.2}{13} = \frac{491.4}{13} = 37.8\ lakh\ ...\ Ans.$$

Question 4

What is the ratio of population of females below poverty line and males above poverty line in State F?

1. 2:5
2. 5:2
3. 2:3
4. 3:2

Explanations
Answer: 1. 2:5

We need to find the **ratio of the population of females below the poverty line to males above the poverty line** in State F.

Step 1: Find the Total Population Below and Above the Poverty Line
From the given table:
- o Total population of State F is Not directly given, so we assume it as P.
- o Percentage of population below the poverty line in State F = 20%

- o Percentage of population above the poverty line = 100% - 20% = 80%

Population Below Poverty Line:

$$Population\ Below\ Poverty\ Line = \frac{20}{100} \times P = 0.2P$$

Population Above Poverty Line:

$$Population\ Above\ Poverty\ Line = \frac{80}{100} \times P = 0.8P$$

Step 2: Find the Number of Females Below Poverty Line

- o The male-to-female ratio below the poverty line in State F is 2:3.
- o Total parts = 2 + 3 = 5.
- o Females below poverty line:

$$Females\ Below\ Poverty\ Line = \frac{3}{5} \times 0.2P$$
$$= \frac{0.6P}{5} = 0.12P$$

Step 3: Find the Number of Males Above Poverty Line

- o The **male-to-female ratio above the poverty line** in State F is **3:5**.
- o Total parts = **3 + 5 = 8**.
- o **Males above the poverty line:**

$$Males\ Above\ Poverty\ Line = \frac{3}{8} \times 0.8P$$
$$= \frac{2.4P}{8} = 0.3P$$

Step 4: Find the Ratio

$$Required\ Ratio = \frac{Females\ Below\ Poverty\ Line}{Males\ Above\ Poverty\ Line}$$
$$= \frac{0.12P}{0.3P}$$

Cancel **P** from both numerator and denominator:

$$= \frac{12}{30} = \frac{2}{5} \dots Ans.$$
$$Ratio = 2:5 \dots Ans.$$

Question 5

If the ratio of the total populations of State C and D is 7:4, then what is the ratio of populations of males below poverty line in State C and females above poverty line in State D?

1. 1:2
2. 2:1
3. 2:7
4. 7:2

Explanations

Answer: 1. 1:2

Step 1: Define Variables and Use Given Ratio

Let the **total population of State C = 7X**

Let the **total population of State D = 4X**

From the table:

- o Percentage of population below the poverty line in State C = 22%
- o Percentage of population below the poverty line in State D = 28%
- o Male-to-female ratio below the poverty line in State C = 6:5
- o Male-to-female ratio above the poverty line in State D = 5:7

Step 2: Find the Number of Males Below Poverty Line in State C

Total **population below poverty line in State C**:

$$Population\ Below\ Poverty\ Line\ in\ C = \frac{22}{100} \times 7X = 1.54X$$

Since the **male-to-female ratio below poverty line in C is 6:5**, total parts = **6 + 5 = 11**.

$$Males\ Below\ Poverty\ Line\ in\ C = \frac{6}{11} \times 1.54X$$

$$= \frac{9.24X}{11} = 0.84X$$

Step 3: Find the Number of Females Above Poverty Line in State D

Total **population above poverty line in State D**:

$$Percentage\ of\ population\ above\ poverty\ Line\ in\ D = 100 - 28 = 72\%$$

$$Population\ Above\ Poverty\ Line\ in\ D = \frac{72}{100} \times 4X = 2.88X$$

Since the **male-to-female ratio above the poverty line in D is 5:7**, total parts = **5 + 7 = 12**.

$$Females\ Above\ Poverty\ Line\ in\ D = \frac{7}{12} \times 2.88X$$

$$= \frac{20.16X}{12} = 1.68X$$

Step 4: Find the Ratio

$$Required\ Ratio = \frac{Males\ Below\ Poverty\ Line\ in\ C}{Females\ Above\ Poverty\ Line\ in\ D}$$

Cancel **X** from both numerator and denominator:

$$= \frac{0.84}{1.68} = \frac{1}{2} \dots Ans.$$

Data Interpretation 7

The following table shows the 40% of the number of cameras sold and half of the number of Printers sold by four different shops, namely. A, B, C and D, along with the ratio of the number of Cameras to Speakers sold. Based on the data in the table, answer the questions that follow.

Shop-wise Sale Details of Cameras, Printers and Speakers			
Shop	40% of the number of Cameras sold	Half of the number of Printers sold	Ratio of number of Cameras to Speakers sold
A	200	(Unknown)	5:3
B	320	220	(Unknown)
C	(Unknown)	300	(Unknown)
D	240	190	6:7

Note:

1. Total number of Cameras, Printers and Speakers sold by shop A is 1160.
2. Ratio of number of Cameras to Speakers sold by B is 10:7
3. For shop C, the number of Cameras sold is four times the number of Speakers sold.
4. Some Values are missing in the table that you are expected to compute, if needed.

Solutions to the Notes:

Compute the Missing Values:

- ○ **For Shop A:**

$$Total\ Cameras\ Sold = \frac{200 \times 100}{40} = 500$$

- ○ **For Shop B:**

$$Total\ Cameras\ Sold = \frac{320 \times 100}{40} = 800$$

- ○ **For Shop D:**

$$Total\ Cameras\ Sold = \frac{240 \times 100}{40} = 600$$

Find the Total Number of Printers Sold by Each Shop

We know that **half of the number of Printers sold** is given:

$$Total\ Printers\ Sold = 2 \times (Half\ of\ Printers\ Sold)$$

- ○ **For Shop B:**

$$Total\ Printers\ Sold = 2 \times 220 = 440$$

- ○ **For Shop C:**

$$Total\ Printers\ Sold = 2 \times 300 = 600$$

- o **For Shop D:**

$$Total\ Printers\ Sold = 2 \times 190 = 380$$

Find the Total Number of Speakers Sold by Each Shop

We use the given ratios:

- o **For Shop A (Cameras:Speakers = 5:3)**
  - o **Cameras Sold = 500**, so

$$Speakers\ Sold = \frac{3}{5} \times 500 = 300$$

- o **For Shop B (Cameras:Speakers = 10:7)**
  - o **Cameras Sold = 800**, so

$$Speakers\ Sold = \frac{7}{10} \times 800 = 560$$

- o **For Shop C (Cameras = 4 × Speakers)**
  - o Let **Speakers Sold = x**, so **Cameras Sold = 4x**
  - o Since **40% of Cameras Sold** is unknown, we solve for **x** using the other total sales data when needed.
- o **For Shop D (Cameras:Speakers = 6:7)**
  - o **Cameras Sold = 600**, so

$$Speakers\ Sold = \frac{7}{6} \times 600 = 700$$

Question 1

The total number of Cameras and Printers sold by shop A is more than the number of printers sold by shop D.

1. 480
2. 380
3. 640
4. 300

Explanations

Answer: 1. 480

$$In\ A, 40\%\ camera\ sold\ number\ is\ 200$$
$$Then, 100\%\ is\ =\ 500$$
$$Camera: speaker\ 5:3$$
$$Then, speaker\ is\ =\ 300$$
$$Total\ Things\ sold\ in\ A\ is\ 1160$$
$$Then, Printer\ sold\ in\ A\ is\ 360$$

$$In\ D, half\ of\ printer\ sold\ is\ 190$$
$$Then\ total\ is\ 380$$
$$The\ total\ number\ of\ Cameras\ and\ Printers\ sold\ by\ shop\ A = 500 + 360$$

The total number of Cameras and Printers sold by shop A is (500+360)-380 = 480 more than the number of printers sold by shop D

Question 2

In shop A if the number of Pen Drives sold is 120% of the average number of Speakers and Cameras sold, then what is the difference between the number of Pen Drives and Printers sold?

1. 120
2. 180
3. 140
4. 160

Explanations
Answer: 1. 120

We need to find the **difference between the number of Pen Drives and Printers sold** in **Shop A**, given that:
- **Number of Pen Drives sold = 120% of the average number of Speakers and Cameras sold**
- We have already calculated the **number of Cameras and Speakers sold** in Shop A.

Step 1: Find the Average Number of Speakers and Cameras Sold in Shop A
From previous calculations:
- **Cameras Sold by Shop A = 500**
- **Speakers Sold by Shop A = 300**

$$Average = \frac{Cameras\ Sold + Speakers\ Sold}{2}$$
$$= \frac{500 + 300}{2} = \frac{800}{2} = 400$$

Step 2: Find the Number of Pen Drives Sold
$$Pen\ Drives\ Sold = 120\% \times Average$$

$$= \frac{120}{100} \times 400 =$$
$$= 1.2 \times 400 = 480$$

Step 3: Find the Difference Between Pen Drives and Printers Sold

From previous calculations:

- o **Printers Sold by Shop A = 360**
- o **Pen Drives Sold by Shop A = 480**

$$Difference = 480 - 360 = 120$$

Question 3

What is the ratio of the number of speakers sold by shop B to the number of speakers sold by shop D?

1. 9:2
2. 7:8
3. 4:5
4. 3:2

Explanations

Answer: 3. 4:5

Speakers Sold by Shop B

- o The **ratio of Cameras to Speakers sold by Shop B is 10:7.**
- o **Total Cameras Sold by Shop B = 800.**
- o Using the ratio:

$$Speakers\ Sold\ by\ Shop\ B = \frac{7}{10} \times 800$$
$$= \frac{5600}{10} = 560$$

Speakers Sold by Shop D

- o The **ratio of Cameras to Speakers sold by Shop D is 6:7.**
- o **Total Cameras Sold by Shop D = 600.**
- o Using the ratio:

$$Speakers\ Sold\ by\ Shop\ D = 7.6 \times 600$$
$$= \frac{4200}{6} = 700$$

Step 2: Find the Ratio

$$Required\ Ratio = Speakers\ Sold\ by\ Shop\ B : Speakers\ Sold\ by\ Shop\ D$$
$$= 560 : 700$$

Simplify by dividing both terms by **140**:

$$= \frac{560}{140} : \frac{700}{140} = 4 : 5 \ ... Ans$$

Question 4

For shop B, the number of Printers and Speakers sold is __ % more than the number of cameras sold.

1. 40
2. 25
3. 10
4. 35

Explanations

Answer: 2. 25

We need to determine by **what percentage the total number of Printers and Speakers sold in Shop B is more than the number of Cameras sold**.

$$Cameras\ Sold\ by\ Shop\ B = 800$$
$$Printers\ Sold\ by\ Shop\ B = 440$$
$$Speakers\ Sold\ by\ Shop\ B = 560$$
$$Total\ Printers\ and\ Speakers = 440 + 560 = 1000$$

Calculate the Percentage Increase

The formula for **percentage increase**:

$$Percentage\ Increase = \frac{Increase\ in\ Value}{Original\ Value} \times 100$$

$$= \frac{(Total\ Printers\ and\ Speakers) - (Cameras\ Sold)}{Cameras\ Sold} \times 100$$

$$= \frac{1000 - 800}{800} \times 100$$

$$= \frac{200}{800} \times 100 = 25\% \ ... Ans.$$

Question 5

If the average number of Printers and Speakers sold by shop C is 350, then what is the average number of Cameras and Printers sold by shop C?

1. 480
2. 540

3. 420

4. 500

Explanations

Answer: 4. 500

We need to find the **average number of Cameras and Printers sold by Shop C**, given that the **average number of Printers and Speakers sold is 350**.

$$Total\ Printers\ and\ Speakers = 350 \times 2 = 700$$
$$Printers\ Sold\ by\ Shop\ C = 600$$
$$Speakers\ Sold = 700 - 600 = 100$$

The **number of Cameras sold by Shop C is four times the number of Speakers sold**.

$$Cameras\ Sold\ by\ Shop\ C = 4 \times 100 = 400$$

Find the Average Number of Cameras and Printers Sold [Using Given Formula]

$$Average = \frac{Cameras\ Sold + Printers\ Sold}{2}$$
$$= \frac{400 + 600}{2} = \frac{1000}{2} = 500 \ ... Ans.$$

Practice Data Interpretations

Data Interpretations 8

The following table shows the percentage (%) increase in income and expenditure of various types of Banks, namely PSU Banks, Old Private Banks, New Private Banks and Foreign Banks over the previous year during the year 2021-2022 and 2022-2023. Based on the data in the table, answer the questions that follow:

Income and expenditure details of Banks

Banki Type	Percentage Increase in			
	Income over previous year		Expenditure over previous year	
	2021-2022	**2022-2023**	**2021-2022**	**2022-2023**
PSU Banks	15%	17%	13%	22%
Old Private Banks	20%	14%	15%	17%
New Private Banks	44%	37%	42%	44%
Foreign Banks	9%	12%	4%	11%

Note:

In the above table, the meaning of any figure x% is as follows:

(I) x% in 2021-2022 means income or expenditure in 2021-2022 is x% more than that in 2020-2021.

(II) x% in 2022-2023 means income as expenditure in 2022-2023 is x% more than that is 2021-2022

Question 1

If the expenditure of foreign Banks in 2020-2021 is equal to their income in that year and is equal to 60,000 crores, then in 2022-2023, what is the difference in income and expenditure of Foreign Banks?

1. 3984 crores
2. 4000 crores
3. 5462 crores
4. 3460 crores

Question 2

In 2021-2022, if the income of PSU Banks is twice the expenditure of Foreign Banks, then in 2022 2023, what will be the ratio of income of PSU Banks to the expenditure of Foreign Banks?

1. 1:2
2. 78:37
3. 75:29
4. 2:1

Question 3

In 2021-2022, if the income of Foreign Banks is four times its expenditure, then what will be the approximate ratio of income to the expenditure of foreign Banks in 2022-2023?

1. 1:4
2. 4:1
3. 5:1
4. 1:5

Question 4

Consider the income of new Private Banks in 2021-2022 as 8000 Crore. If the expenditure of new Private Banks in 2021-2022 is same as their income, then the difference in income of new Private Banks in 2021-2022 and 2022-2023 will be approximately __% of the difference in expenditure of new private banks in 2021-2022 and 2022-2023.

1. 52
2. 76
3. 84
4. 118

Question 5

Consider the income of PSU Banks in 2020-2021 as 10,00,000 crores. If the expenditure of PSU Banks in 2022-2023 is equal to the income of PSU Banks in 2020-2021, then the income of PSU Banks in 2022-23 will be approximately -% more than the expenditure of PSU Banks in 2021-2022.

1. 62
2. 44
3. 56
4. 64

Data Interpretation 9

The following table shows the number of items sold by five persons A-E on five different days (Monday through Friday). Some data is missing in the table that you are expected to calculate, if required. Based on the data in the table, answer the questions that follow:

Day	Persons				
	A	**B**	**C**	**D**	**E**
Monday	840	880	480	-	560
Tuesday	720	-	1040	420	820
Wednesday	560	480	820	850	-
Thursday	1080	1020	-	1260	320
Friday	-	920	700	1020	800

Question 1

If the number of items sold by C on Thursday is the average of the number of items sold by C on 'Wednesday and Friday, then the total number of items sold by C on all the five days is:

1. 3500
2. 3800
3. 3400
4. 3700

Question 2

If the total numbers of items sold by A and B on all the five days is 4000, and 4400, respectively. then the number of items sold by B on Tuesday is __% more than the number of items sold by A on Friday.

1. 37.5
2. 23.5
3. 32.95
4. 425

Question 3

If the total number of items sold by A on all the five days is 3600, then the difference between the number of items sold by A on Monday and Friday is:

1. 640
2. 450
3. 420
4. 440

Question 4

If the ratio of the number of items sold by B and C together on Thursday to the number of items sold by C and E together on the same day is 2:1, then the number of items sold by C on Thursday is:

1. 300
2. 420
3. 380
4. 340

Question 5

If the average number of items sold by D on Monday and Tuesday is 490, then the number of items sold by E on Friday is % more than the number of items sold by D on Monday.

1. 39.76
2. 42.86
3. 48.23
4. 45

Data Interpretation 10

The following table shows the percentage (%) distribution of viewers of JO TV channel in five different towns (A, B, C, D and E) along with the number of viewers who subscribed the channel among them in the year 2023. Number of viewers in the town E is 1200. Based on the data in the table, answer the questions that follow.

Town-wise Details of Channel Viewers

Town	Percentage Distribution of Channel Viewers	Number of Viewers who subscribed for the channel
A	12%	440
B	15%	500
C	28%	880
D	25%	700
E	20%	360

Note: *For each town, number of channel viewers is the sum of number of viewers who subscribed for the channel and the number of viewers who did not subscribe for the channel.*

Question 1

If out of the number of viewers from Town-C, 325/7% are female and 7/13 of the number of female viewers are unsubscribed viewers, then the number of unsubscribed male viewers from Town-C is.

1. 340
2. 360
3. 380
4. 420

Question 2

*If P is the total number of unsubscribed viewers in Town-B and Town-C together, and Q is the number of subscribed viewers in Town-E. then Q is __%
less than P*

1. 65
2. 80
3. 60
4. 70

Question 3

If the number of male unsubscribed viewers in Town-D is 200/3 more than that of female unsubscribed viewers, then what is the ratio of number of male unsubscribed viewers in Town-D to the number of unsubscribed viewers in Town-A and Town-C together?

1. 25:53

2. 25:54

3. 7:9

4. 2:3

Question 4

What is the difference between the number of unsubscribed viewers and subscribed viewers, taking all the towns together?

1. 320

2. 240

3. 340

4. 300

Question 5

If P is the total number of unsubscribed viewers in Town- B and Town-C together, and Q is the number of unsubscribed viewers in town-E, then Q is _% of P.

1. 60

2. 70

3. 80

4. 75

Answer Keys

Concept Check 1: Identify the Type of Number

1. **5** → Integer, Rational Number, Real Number, Natural Number, Whole Number
2. **-8** → Integer, Rational Number, Real Number
3. **0.25** → Rational Number, Real Number
4. **$\sqrt{3}$** → Irrational Number, Real Number
5. **7 + 4i** → Complex Number
6. **12** → Integer, Rational Number, Real Number, Natural Number, Whole Number
7. **$\frac{1}{7}$** → Rational Number, Real Number
8. **13** → Integer, Rational Number, Real Number, Natural Number, Whole Number
9. **π (Pi)** → Irrational Number, Real Number

Concept Check 2: Exponents

1. 64
2. 81
3. 1
4. 64
5. $\frac{1}{125}$

Concept Check 3: Converting Fractions

1. *Proper, Improper, Mixed*
2. $2\frac{3}{5}$
3. $\frac{30}{7}$
4. $\frac{5}{9}$

Concept Check 4: Operation on Fractions

1. $\frac{2}{3}$
2. $\frac{11}{8}$
3. $\frac{12}{35}$
4. $\frac{7}{6}$
5. $\frac{3}{10}$

Concept Check 5: Advance Concepts of Fractions

1. $\frac{5}{36}$
2. 0.875
3. $\frac{3}{8}$
4. $\frac{5}{9}, \frac{7}{12}, \frac{2}{3}$
5. 80%
6. $\frac{7}{9}$

Concept Check 6: Word Problem

1. Rs. 200
2. 100 km
3. 3 liters
4. 64 minutes
5. 100 minutes

Concept Check 7: Problem Solving Techniques

1. $x = 10$
2. $x - 2$
3. $\frac{5}{8}$
4. $x = 4$
5. $\frac{5}{12}$

Concept Check 8: Equations

1. 9
2. 30, 15
3. 15 years
4. Apple = Rs. 15, Banana = Rs. 10
5. 2 hours 24 minutes

Concept Check 9: Ratio

1. 2:3
2. 3:4, 9:12
3. 45 pens
4. 3:5

Concept Check 10: Simplifying Ratio

1. 3:4
2. 14:18, 21:27
3. 5:8 < 3:4
4. Yes

5. 5:8

Concept Check 11: Ratio and Proportion
1. 9
2. Rs. 480
3. 3 hours 25 minutes
4. 20
5. 35

Concept Check 12: Applications of Ratio
1. 45 apples
2. 5:8
3. 4 hours 48 minutes
4. 16 liters
5. Rs. 20,000 and Rs. 28,000

Concept Check 13: Advanced Ratio
1. Rs. 20,000 and Rs. 30,000
2. 15 days
3. Rs. 40,000
4. 30 liters
5. 5:4

Concept Check 14: Percentage
1. 4% increase
2. 92,610
3. 300
4. ₹3,825
5. ₹15,000

Concept Check 15: Profit and Loss
1. 25%
2. ₹800
3. 5.26%
4. ₹800
5. ₹1500

Concept Check 16: Interest
1. Simple Interest on ₹5000 for 4 years at 6% interest rate: ₹1200
2. Final amount for ₹8000 at 10% CI per annum for 2 years: ₹9680

3. Population after 2 years if it increases by 5% annually (Initial: 120000): 132300
4. Final amount for ₹7000 invested for 3 years at varying rates (5%, 6%, 7%): ₹8336.37
5. Difference between CI and SI for ₹10000 at 12% per annum for 2 years: ₹144

Concept Check 17: Discounting

1. Selling Price after 30% Discount: ₹2800
2. Final Discount Percentage after three successive discounts (10%, 20%, 30%): 49.40%
3. Banker's Discount for ₹10,000 due in 2 years at 8% per annum: ₹1600
4. Percentage Discount on Cycle (Marked ₹5000, Sold ₹4250): 15%
5. Final Price after 15% Trade Discount and 5% Cash Discount on ₹8000: ₹6460

Concept Check 18: Speed, Time, & Distance

1. Average Speed for the round trip: 48 km/hr
2. Speed of the train crossing the platform: 54 km/hr
3. Speed of the second train: 30 km/hr

Concept Check 19: Boat and Stream

1. Time to travel 32 km downstream: 2 hours
2. Speed of the stream: 2 km/hr
3. Speed in still water: 12.5 km/hr

Concept Check 20: Time and Work

1. Days required if A and B work together: 7.2 days
2. Days required if A and B work together (A twice as efficient): 5.33 days
3. Men **required to complete the task in 6 days:** 20 men

Concept Check 21: Number Series

1. 36
2. 38
3. 42

4. 1
5. 13

Concept Check 22: Data Interpretations

Table 3: Sales Data (2018-2021)

1. Highest Sales Year: 2018
2. Total Sales from 2018 to 2021: 1700
3. Is Sales Trend Decreasing? Yes
4. Projected Sales for 2022: 300
5. Percentage Decrease in Sales from 2018 to 2021: 30%

Table 4: Ice Cream Sales Data

6. Temperature with Highest Ice Cream Sales: 45°C
7. Average Ice Cream Sales: 130
8. Is Ice Cream Sales Trend Increasing? Yes
9. Predicted Ice Cream Sales at 38°C: 130
10. Percentage Increase in Ice Cream Sales (35°C to 45°C): 33.33%

Table 5: Temperature & Rainfall Data

11. Month with Highest Average Temperature: April
12. Total Rainfall (Jan-March): 60 mm
13. Is Temperature Increasing Over Months? Yes
14. Most suitable month for outdoor activities? → March
    (Moderate temperature of 20°C with low rainfall of 15mm)
15. Percentage Increase in Temperature (Jan to April): 66.67%

Table 6: Subject & Student Data

16. **Percentage of Students in Each Subject:**
    o   Mathematics: **26.67%**
    o   Science: **40.00%**
    o   English: **20.00%**
    o   History: **13.33%**
17. **Subject with Highest Students:** Science
18. **Subject with Lowest Percentage of Students:** History
19. **Total Students in Mathematics & English:** 210
20. **Percentage of Students Studying Mathematics or Science:** 66.67%
21. **Students Studying Both Mathematics & Science:** 36

Practice Data Interpretations
Data Interpretations 8
1. Answer: 1. 4000 crores
2. Answer: 2. 78:37
3. Answer: 2. 4:1
4. Answer: 3. 84
5. Answer: 4. 64

Data Interpretation 9
1. Answer: 2. 3800
2. Answer: 1. 37.5
3. Answer: 4. 440
4. Answer: 3. 380
5. Answer: 2. 42.86

Data Interpretation 10
1. Answer: 3. 380
2. Answer: 4. 70
3. Answer: 2. 25:54
4. Answer: 2. 240
5. Answer: 2. 70

Usage Policy for NerdSchool Notes

Created by: Instructors from NerdSchool
Owned by: NERDSTABLE PVT LTD

The following notes are the intellectual property of **NERDSTABLE PVT LTD** and are made available exclusively to students who have paid for access. By using these notes, you agree to the terms and conditions outlined below:

Policy of Usage:

Personal Use Only: These notes are intended for your **personal study and exam preparation**. You are permitted to **read** and **print** them for your own reference.

No Unauthorized Distribution or Sale: You **may not sell**, **distribute**, or **replicate** these notes in any form, whether digitally or physically. This includes sharing copies with others, regardless of the medium (online platforms, printed materials, etc.).

No Plagiarism: You **may not claim** the contents of these notes as your own. Any form of direct publication or submission under your name, without proper citation, is strictly prohibited.

Non-Transferable Access: Access to these notes is restricted to the individual purchaser. **Sharing your login credentials** or any other means of access to these materials with others is a violation of this policy.

Additional Guidelines:

For Educational Use Only: These notes are designed to help students succeed in their academic exams and should be used responsibly. They are meant to supplement your learning, not to replace the guidance of instructors or textbooks.

No Commercial Use: The content in these notes cannot be used for **commercial purposes**. This includes using the material in any form of paid tutoring or educational courses that you offer without the explicit permission of NERDSTABLE PVT LTD.